James Heywood

Academic Reform and University Representation

James Heywood

Academic Reform and University Representation

ISBN/EAN: 9783337297404

Printed in Europe, USA, Canada, Australia, Japan

Cover: Foto ©Suzi / pixelio.de

More available books at **www.hansebooks.com**

ACADEMIC REFORM

AND

UNIVERSITY REPRESENTATION.

BY

JAMES HEYWOOD, F.R.S.,

B.A., TRINITY COLLEGE, CAMBRIDGE.

LONDON:
EDWARD T. WHITFIELD, 178, STRAND.
1860.

PRINTED BY
JOHN EDWARD TAYLOR, LITTLE QUEEN STREET,
LINCOLN'S INN FIELDS, LONDON.

PREFACE.

VARIOUS Examinations for public employment and academic reward are described in the following Work, so as to exhibit important requirements of the public service, as well as the subjects of examination for the degree of Bachelor of Arts, and for some other degrees.

Memorials relating to academic improvement are presented to the reader, as registers of the progress of amelioration, and, in several cases, as records of unsettled subjects still demanding public attention. Among the latter class of Memorials may be noticed the Petition against the continuance of compulsory celibacy for College Fellows at Cambridge, drawn up in the courteous form of requesting the University Commissioners to consider the restrictions upon marriage to which the tenure of Fellowships is subject. This Memorial received the signatures of 371 Graduates of the University of Cambridge, 107 of whom were either past or present Fellows of Colleges * in that University.

Living languages obtain, at present, a large share of public favour. The ancient English Universities, in their

* See *infra*, p. 76.

local Examinations of junior Candidates, allow a liberty of choice with respect to languages, which has resulted in a decided preference, on the part of the junior Candidates, for Latin and French subjects, with comparatively slight concern for Greek.* English now frequently forms a subject of Examination by national Educational Bodies,† as well as by the authorities of the Civil and Engineering Services.

Equal numbers of marks are assigned to proficiency in Greek, Latin, French, and German, by the Examiners of the Woolwich Royal Military Academy,‡ whilst the rules of the Indian Civil Service Competitive Examinations award double the number of marks to proficiency in Greek or Latin,§ which they permit to excellence in either French or German.

So large a proportion of the successful Candidates in the Indian Civil Service Examinations are monopolized by the three ancient Universities of Oxford, Cambridge, and Dublin, that the principal share of Indian Civil Service patronage seems to have been practically transferred to members of these academic Corporations. ||

Of twenty successful Candidates at the Indian Civil Service Examination in 1858, six came from Trinity College, Dublin, five of whom were holders of classical Scholarships; nine Candidates were elected at the same time from classical Oxford, and three from Cambridge.

---

* See *infra*, p. 313.

† See the Examinations of the University of London, p. 22, and of the Committee of Council, p. 34. See also pp. 11, 262, 264.

‡ See *infra*, p. 264. § See p. 11.

|| See *infra*, pp. 10 and 260, the places of education of successful candidates for the Indian Civil Service, in 1858 and 1859.

At the Indian Civil Service Examination of July, 1859, of forty successful Candidates, twelve came from Oxford, nine from Cambridge, and seven from Trinity College, Dublin.

Preparation for a severe public Competitive Examination somewhat resembles the training of a race-horse for Newmarket or Doncaster. A series of preliminary trials of speed and strength are requisite to fit the Candidate for the more serious course which lies before him, and the arrangements of good private tutors are admirably adapted, in the case of ambitious Students, to supply methodical and constant exercises in different branches of learning.

Considerable exertions were made by the Oxford University Commissioners to improve the elections to College Fellowships at Oxford, so that these rewards of learning may be determined, speaking generally, by the personal merits and fitness of the successful Candidate, and not by accidental social considerations, or by the Candidate having been born in some particular district or educated at a particular school.

Obstacles have, however, been interposed to some of the good intentions of the Oxford University Commissioners. St. John's College, Oxford, prefers to retain a majority of its Fellows elected exclusively from five ancient schools; and All Souls College finds means to elect Candidates to Fellowships in accordance with the somewhat aristocratic social considerations of the College.

Cambridge University Commissioners have obtained the consent of the Trinity College authorities to the omission of a declaration by newly-elected Fellows, that they would make Theology the end of their studies, and students of law, who obtain Fellowships, will, consequently, be no longer subject to such an exclusive test.

The scheme of College government arranged between the Cambridge Commissioners and the authorities of Trinity College and St. John's College, has not been well adapted to the modern state of these Colleges, which contain, in each case, resident Students of different religious denominations. Compulsory Ordination is insisted upon for the Master, and compulsory celibacy is directed for the eight senior Fellows of each institution, nearly all of whom are usually clergymen of the Church of England.

On the 14th February, 1860, these College arrangements were discussed in the House of Commons, when Mr. Walpole mentioned a recent instance of consideration on the part of the governing Board of Trinity College for the conscientious scruples of a Jewish Undergraduate, in whose favour attendance at the College Chapel has been dispensed with. During the same debate, Lord Stanley, one of the Cambridge University Commissioners, observed that the Cambridge University Act of 1856 had clearly stated, that no person should be required, on taking a Degree, or obtaining a Scholarship, Exhibition, or other College emolument, to make or subscribe any declaration of religious belief, and that, in his opinion, the enforcement of attendance at College Chapel, in cases where conscientious objections to the chapel service are felt, would be contrary to the spirit and intention, if not to the letter of the Cambridge Act.

At Haileybury College, short forms of prayer were usual, and at the principal Church of England Normal School, in the north of London, a short service, varying on different days of the week, is read to the assembled students.

Scholarships cannot be fully opened to the nation, in Cambridge Colleges, without some modification of the daily reading of Church of England services at the College Chapel.

Prayers for the Parliament are published in this Work, p. 99, as an example of a short general liturgical form adapted to a mixed assembly, including Members in the House of Commons belonging to different religious denominations.

Suitable forms of ordinary chapel service, for College Students at Oxford and Cambridge, may be prepared on a similar principle with the Prayers for the Parliament, so as not to weary the audience, and to be read to a congregation comprising individuals of various theological opinions.

In both the ancient English Universities, the majority of the registered Electors are in Holy Orders, nor can any plan of academical reform be complete which does not embrace the improvement of the Examinations of Clerical Candidates and the revision of the religious tests still required for Ordination. The Appendix to the present Work contains some Divinity Examination Papers, which have been prepared in a freer spirit than would be encouraged by the academical authorities on the Cam and the Isis, and were intended for Theological Students who do not subscribe either to Articles or Confessions of faith, and who therefore prepare themselves in Theology as an independent science.

Several questions set at recent Examinations for Holy Orders of Priests and Deacons are given in this volume, p. 225, relating to Old Testament History and Original Sin; questions on Original Sin are also quoted from the Cambridge University Theological Examination of October, 1858, and May, 1859.*

Preparation in the dogmatic views of the sixteenth century must be made by Candidates for the Church of England ministry, in order to answer these questions, and some revision appears desirable of the Thirty-nine Articles and the Liturgy, for an improved Theological training of the Church of England clergy.

In the University of Oxford, optional religious tests are still offered to the Student, on graduating as a Bachelor of Arts. For the degree of Master of Arts, which confers the elective suffrage, the Candidate is obliged, at Oxford, to subscribe the Thirty-nine Articles, together with the Three Articles of the Thirty-sixth Canon of the Church of England.

Cambridge University confers the degree of Bachelor of Arts without any religious test, and the degree of Master of Arts may be obtained without either attendance or test in that University; but the established privilege belonging to a Master of Arts, of becoming an Elector of the University, is only allowed, under the Cambridge University Act of 1856, in cases where the Master of Arts has subscribed himself a *bonâ fide* member of the Church of England.

* See *infra*, pp. 231, 232.

In both the ancient English Universities, the right of voting for representatives in Parliament is restricted to members of the Church of England, whilst the burgesses returned to Parliament for these academical Corporations possess the power of legislating for all denominations of the British people.

An extension of the University suffrage to Bachelors of Arts, of three years' standing, would diminish the expense of registration for individual voters in each of the ancient seats of academical learning, retaining at the same time all the examinations of intellectual proficiency which are now required for the elective franchise and opening the suffrage without religious tests.

The claims of the University of London, with its 1,200 Graduates, to be recognized by Parliament, as a constituency, are contained in the present Work (pp. 204-213); and as the suffrage of Bachelors of Arts of three years' standing has been already adopted for its academical convocation, the same franchise will form the basis of the electoral rights which may probably be conferred upon that University under a new Reform Bill.

Sir George Lewis, Bart., the Home Secretary, has recently introduced a bill into the House of Commons, for the consideration of the disputed case of St. John's College, Oxford, by a Committee of five Privy Councillors, to be named by order of the Queen in Council. This Committee will probably have before them the Report of the Oxford University Commission, which is referred to, pp. 126-132 in the present Work, and may either adopt or modify the ordinance suggested by the Commissioners. The Report of the Committee, when approved by her Majesty in Council, is proposed to become a statute of the College.

When, on future occasions, Academical reforms are again referred to any Committee or Commission, a national sanction can hardly be expected to their measures, unless some representation be allowed, in that body, of the large portion of the community who do not belong to the Church of England, and who are deeply interested in enlarging the great system of English public instruction.

Very recently, the claims of moral and natural sciences have been recognized at Cambridge, by the proposed admission of Candidates to the degree of Bachelor of Arts, who show that they have attained sufficient proficiency to deserve honours in the University Examinations connected with either the moral sciences or the natural sciences.

The extension of the privileges of the Cambridge Academical Senate to Bachelors of Arts of three years' standing, would form a valuable portion of a new measure of academic reform, and would confer dignity on successful Graduates in moral and natural sciences, as well as in classics, mathematics, mixed classical and mathematical subjects, law, medicine, and music.

CONTENTS.

	PAGE
EXAMINATIONS	1

Clerkships under Committee of Council on Education: Attachés to Embassies 1
Woolwich Royal Military Academy: Staff College: Indian Civil Service: Latin and Greek Prose and Verse Composition 2
B.A. Degree at the Universities of Oxford, Cambridge, and London 14
Teacherships under the Committee of Council on Education: Training Schools for Masters and Mistresses 32
MEMORIALS RELATING TO ACADEMICAL IMPROVEMENT . . 49
Inquiry into the Universities of Oxford and Cambridge . . 49
Removal of Religious Tests at the ancient English Universities 56
Changes, as to the Restriction on Marriage, in the Conditions of the tenure of Cambridge College Fellowships . . . 76
Dean Peacock on short Services in College Chapels . . . 98
Prayers for the Parliament 99
Questions on Dogmatical Divinity in Cambridge ordinary B.A. Examination 102
Degrees in Science in the University of London 106
Moral and Economic Science and Alternation of Subjects at Matriculation in the University of London 114
University of London Local Examinations for Matriculation and B.A. Degree 116

CONTENTS.

	PAGE
Report on St. John's College, Oxford, having declined to accept the Statutes of the Oxford Parliamentary Commissioners	126
Bill for Reforming the Book of Common Prayer	140
Cambridge Proctors, and the Power of Search by the University Proctors exercised in the Town of Cambridge	160
UNIVERSITY REPRESENTATION	165
Religious Tests for University Electors of Oxford and Cambridge	169
Summary of English Academical Electors	170
Scotch University Franchise	176
Overwork in Study	180
High Fees for the Registration of Electors in the Universities of Oxford and Cambridge	183
Moderate Fee for Life Composition, as an Elector, in the University of Dublin, directed by 5 & 6 Vict. c. 74	185
Fee for Life Membership at Trinity College, Cambridge	186
Religious Examination Tests presented to a Church of England Candidate for a B.A. Degree at Oxford	188
Act of Uniformity Tests for Heads and Fellows of Colleges	192
Earl Granville on the Parliamentary Representation of the University of London	198
Memorial of the Senate of the University of London, in favour of the Parliamentary Representation of that University	205
Examinations of the University of London, for the Degrees of Bachelor of Laws and Bachelor of Medicine	215
Scheme of Cambridge University Local Examination, for Senior Candidates, in 1858	218
Religious Tests for Clergymen of the Church of England	224
Ordination Questions on Old Testament History	225
Cambridge Questions, in the Theological Examinations of 1858–9, on Original Sin	231
German and American Views on the Paradisiacal Narrative in Genesis, and the Progressive Elevation of Human Nature	232

CONTENTS. xiii

PAGE

Recent Increase in the Expression of Denominational Differences in Trust-deeds, on account of the Committee of Council System 238
Modern Rules of the Court of Chancery as to Educational Charities 240
Mr. Dillwyn's Endowed Schools Bill 241
Extension of the University Franchise to Bachelors of Arts of three years' standing 247

OPENING AND IMPROVEMENT OF CAMBRIDGE COLLEGE HEADSHIPS, FELLOWSHIPS, AND SCHOLARSHIPS . . 248

Cambridge College Opposition to Proposals of the Cambridge Parliamentary Commissioners 249
Concessions of the Commissioners 249
Compulsory Ordination proposed for future Masters of Trinity and St. John's Colleges 250
Limited Tenure of Fellowships 251
Mr. Pollard-Urquhart's Address to the Crown against the compulsory Ordination of College Master, compulsory Celibacy of Senior Fellows, and the Board for regulating the Attendance of Students on Chapel Services 252
Clauses of compulsory Theological Study omitted in new Trinity College Statutes 253
Tests of Conformity to the Liturgy, injurious 255
Suggestions for short Chapel Service 256
Declaration of Faith required from Fellows of Trinity College, Cambridge 256
Examination for Trinity College Fellowships 258
Places of Education of Candidates for Indian Civil Service . 260
Subjects brought up, by three Members of Trinity College, Cambridge, in the Indian Civil Service Examination . . 262
Subjects in 1859, of the Woolwich Royal Military Academy Examination 263
Improvement of Trinity College Scholarship and Fellowship Examinations at Cambridge 265
Ignorance of many English Schoolboys on English Grammar and History, Physical Science, and Modern Languages . 267

CONTENTS.

	PAGE
College Endowments partially opened at Oxford to Merit in Mathematics and Physical Science	270
Balliol College Fellowships open at Oxford, to any Bachelor of Arts of any British or Irish University	272
New Church of England Test for Fellowships, in the revised Statutes of St. John's College, Cambridge	273
Proportionate Numbers of Members of the Church of England in the Nation	274
American Omission of the Athanasian Creed	275
College Fellowships not "Offices"	277
Trinity College stipends to the Master and to each of the Fellows and Scholars at Cambridge	280
College Tuition in Trinity College	281
Probable Annual Amount paid for Private Tuition	282
Entrance Examination for Trinity College	283
Examining Bodies for Entrance into the Medical Profession	285
Oxford University Local Examination for Junior Candidates	285
Trinity College Lectures at Cambridge	287
Scholarship Examination in Trinity College	289
Daily Lessons in Trinity College Chapel, read by Scholars	291
Bill proposed to enable the Crown to dispense with the Act of Uniformity by Letters Patent	293

INTENDED ENCOURAGEMENT OF MODERN STUDIES IN ALL SOULS COLLEGE, OXFORD 297

Professorship of International Law and Diplomacy, to be endowed from All Souls College Funds	297
Professorship proposed in Modern History	298
Estimated Value of an All Souls College Fellowship	299
Candidates for Fellowships to be examined in Jurisprudence and Modern History	300
Institution of Scholarships contemplated	300
Limited Tenure of Fellowships recommended	302
Termination suggested of compulsory Classical Studies in the second year of Academical Residence	303
Subjects of Public Examination in Law, of Candidates for the Profession of a Barrister	305

CONTENTS.

	PAGE
Scholarships in Modern Languages recommended for All Souls College, Oxford	307
Best Men in Examinations not always elected to Fellowships in All Souls College	308
Livings in the Gift of All Souls College	309
College Funds recommended not to be laid out in the Purchase of Advowsons	311
Board of Management at Oxford and Cambridge, of University Local Examinations	312
Results of Local University Examinations connected with Oxford and Cambridge, as to Proficiency in Languages	313
UNIVERSITY OF LONDON, DEGREES IN SCIENCE	315
Appendix: Manchester New College, London, Divinity Examination Papers	319
Introduction to the Old Testament	319
Hebrew	321
Evidences of Natural Religion	322
History of Doctrine	324
Ecclesiastical History of the Fourth and Fifth Centuries	328
INDEX	331

SUBJECTS REQUIRED AT MATRICULATION IN TRINIT[Y]
WITH THE COMPULSORY AND OPTIONAL SECULA[R]
LOCAL

Matriculation in Trinity College, Cambridge.	University of London Matriculation Examination.	Secular [ature]
Compulsory Subjects.	*Compulsory Subjects.*	*Compulsory Secula[r] Subjects.*
Latin :— Cicero, de Amicitiâ, and de Senectute. 1st Book of the Æneid. Greek :— 1st Book of Xenophon's Memorabilia. 1st Book of Homer's Iliad. Gospel of St. Luke. Arithmetic, including Fractions and Decimals. Algebra, as far as Simple Equations. Euclid, Books I. and II.	English Language. Orthography. Writing from Dictation. Grammatical Structure of the English Language. English Composition. Modern Geography. Outlines of English History to the end of Seventeenth Century. Latin. Greek. Mathematics. Natural Philosophy. Chemistry. *Optional Subjects.* French or German.	*Junior Candidate[s]* Reading aloud. Writing from Dicta[tion]. Analysis of English [sen]tences. Early Rules of Ar[ith]metic. Modern Geography. Outlines of Eng. Hi[story] Under the Ox[ford] scheme, a short Eng[lish] composition is also [re]quired. For Senior Ca[ndi]dates, under both Oxford and Cambr[idge] schemes, a knowledg[e of] English subjects, an[d] English Composition required.

E, CAMBRIDGE, AND IN THE UNIVERSITY OF LONDON,
S OF THE OXFORD AND CAMBRIDGE UNIVERSITY
TIONS.

OXFORD AND CAMBRIDGE UNIVERSITY LOCAL EXAMINATIONS.

Optional Secular Subjects.

Junior Candidates.		Senior Candidates.	
)RD PLAN.	CAMBRIDGE PLAN.	OXFORD PLAN.	CAMBRIDGE PLAN.
, at least, ed of the fol- ; eight sub- nd not more)ur:—	Two, at least, required of the fol- lowing nine sub- jects, and not more than five:—	Two required of the following sec- tions, or one with either Drawing or Music:—	Two required of the following sec- tions, or one with either Drawing or Music:—
	English.	1. English.	1. English.
.	Latin.	2. Latin, Greek, French, Ger- man, (one lan- guage sufficient for a pass).	2. Latin, Greek, French, or Ger- man.
1.	Greek.		
in.	French.		3. Mathematics, Elementary Na- tural Philoso- phy.
matics.	German.		
nics and hanism.	Pure Mathema- tics.	3. Pure and Mixed Mathematics:—	
stry. y and Zoo- ·.	Elementary Prin- ciples of Mecha- nics and Hydro- statics.	Algebra, to the end of Quadra- tic Equations, and the first four Books of Euclid, suffi- cient for a pass.	4. Chemistry, Op- tics, etc.
——— wing and may be	Chemistry.		5. Comparative Anatomy, Phy- siology, etc.
	Zoology and Bota- ny.		
	———	4. One subject in Physics.	
	Drawing and Music may be added.		

EXAMINATIONS.

For the Civil Service of the British Government at home, a nomination by either parliamentary or private influence is the first requisite: candidates thus obtain a place on the list for examination in the department to which they desire to belong; and the examinations vary according to the requirements of the different offices of State.

Under the Committee of Council for Education, the preliminary examination for clerkships includes writing from dictation, arithmetic, book-keeping, the précis and digest of forms into summaries, the making of fair copies from rough notes, and the calculation of percentages.

A competitive examination follows, which comprises English composition, geography, history, mathematics, and natural science.

Unpaid attachés to British Embassies are examined under the Foreign Office, in writing from dictation, précis, geography, modern history, especially of the country to which the candidate is to proceed, and French; and a translation is expected from either German, Latin, Spanish, or Italian, at the option of the candidate.

Paid attachés to Embassies are required to prove a speaking and writing knowledge of the languages of the countries in which they have resided since their first appointment to the service: they are examined in international law, and have to prepare reports upon the constitution and condition of the countries in which they have resided.

No examinations are required for the junior offices held by Members of Parliament, but the late Sir Robert Peel, when Prime Minister, selected a staff of distinguished Oxonians around him, most of whom had obtained high class honours in the University of Oxford, including Messrs. Gladstone, Cardwell, and Sidney Herbert, Lord Ashley, now Earl of Shaftesbury, and the Earl of Lincoln, now Duke of Newcastle.

War has been useful in modern times for the improvement of military education. The Polytechnic School of Paris was established after the experience of French wars under the great Napoleon, and the recent Russian campaigns may have assisted in the adoption of competitive examinations for admission into the British Royal Engineers and Royal Artillery at Woolwich, as well as into the staff of the army.

The organization of competitive examinations for the Royal Military Academy, Woolwich, was carried into effect with the aid of the Right Hon. W. Monsell, M.P., Sir Benjamin Hawes, and the Rev. H. Moseley. Age in the candidates is limited to between seventeen and twenty years; a certificate of good character is required from each candidate, and an inspection by military surgeons is ordered, to prove the bodily fitness of the candidates for the performance of military duties.

No nomination is requisite, but the examination is conducted on the basis of the general education of the country, and is intended to admit the competition of candidates educated in the public schools; so that candidates for the Royal Artillery and Royal Engineers may have secured the acknowledged advantages of the training of these schools, which are connected quite as much with the large open playgrounds and bold athletic games of the boys as with the scholastic system, in which the number of masters does not always suffice for the complete superintendence of daily instruction.

A preliminary examination of the candidates for the Woolwich Royal Military Academy takes place, in which their general knowledge is tried of translating French prose, and of copying an easy drawing.

Of 115 candidates who presented themselves at Burlington House, Piccadilly, London, on the 20th June, 1857, for admission into the Woolwich Academy, four were rejected by the Medical Board, five failed in the French examination, and four in drawing, so that only 102 remained of the total number to compete for the vacancies in the Royal Military Academy.

Nine subjects of examination were appointed, of which one, including pure and mixed mathematics, was obligatory on all the candidates, and each candidate was desired to select any four of the remaining subjects for his examination.

The number of candidates who thus entered themselves for examination in different subjects, in June, 1857, was as follows:—

	Candidates.
Mathematics, pure and mixed, obligatory on all the candidates	102
Drawing	94
English	92
French	78
Classics, *i. e.* Latin and Greek	55
Experimental Sciences	40
Moral Sciences	27
German	12
Natural Sciences	4
Total	504

Every examination-paper was divided into sections, and each section contained three questions, for the most part on the same subject, or in the same part or principal division of a subject. One of the three questions was easy; the next, not so easy; and the third, the least easy.

Practically, a similar division of examination-papers into sections has for the last ten years been made in questions proposed by the Committee of Council on Education, to teachers who are candidates for certificates, and the plan has been found to be a great help to the Examiners in looking over the answers, as well as an assistance to the young men under examination.

Two Examiners were appointed in every subject, except the natural and experimental sciences. Each Examiner proposed an independent set of questions to the candidates, and carrying home with him the answers, looked them over alone, and assigned to them the marks as though he had been the only Examiner. The lists of marks thus given by the different Examiners were then sent to Mr. Moseley, who took, in respect to every subject, the *mean* of the numbers of marks given to every candidate by the two Examiners in that subject.

Having tabulated these mean numbers, and taken the sum of the number of marks thus obtained by each candidate, Mr. Moseley formed a list of the candidates whose aggregates were the highest, and transmitted this list with the returns of the Examiners, from which it was collected, to the War Office, for verification.

Nine names were subsequently added to the thirty thus selected, in consequence of a large force of artillery having been suddenly placed under orders for India, which rendered it requisite to commission forty cadets at once for that corps. The nine names selected were those next in order on the list of candidates who had been examined for the Military Academy.

The University of Dublin has instituted a special class to prepare candidates for the examinations of the Royal Military Academy; it consists mainly of students, who have made considerable progress in College studies, particularly in the experimental sciences.

A recent order from the War Office has appointed the following subjects of examination for officers desirous of admission into the Staff College, with a view to appointments on the staff of the army.

Obligatory Subjects.

	Marks.
Mathematics	600
Fortification	600
Military Art, History, and Geography	600
Military Drawing and Surveying	300
French	300

Voluntary Subjects.

German	300
Hindustani	300
Chemistry	150
Geology	150

The attainment of one-third of the marks in each of the obligatory subjects is requisite for success in passing this examination.

EXAMINATIONS FOR THE INDIAN CIVIL SERVICE.

In November, 1854, a Report was presented to the Right Hon. Sir Charles Wood, Bart., M.P., President of the Board of Control, from a Committee, consisting of Lord Macaulay, Lord Ashburton, the Rev. H. Melville, the Rev. Professor Jowett, and Sir John George Shaw Lefevre, on the examination of candidates for the Civil Service of the East India Company, in which the Committee recommended, that a considerable number of the civil servants of the Company should be men who had taken the first degree in arts, either at Oxford or Cambridge. The Committee hoped, that among the successful competitors would frequently be young men who had obtained the highest honours of Oxford and Cambridge.

The Committee, among whom Lord Macaulay is understood to have taken the lead, observe, that at Trinity College, Cambridge, about four Fellowships are given annually by competition, and that the examinations for Trinity Fellowships have, directly and indirectly, done much to give a direction to the studies of Cambridge, and of all the numerous schools, which are the feeders of Cambridge.

A scheme of examination was submitted to Sir Charles Wood by the Committee of 1854, and was adopted, and acted on. The practical result of the Committee's experiment is thus described in a Report, dated Agra, 4th October, 1858, from C. Raikes, Esq., Commissioner of Lahore, and officiating judge in the Sudder Courts of the North-west Provinces, at Agra, addressed to H. Ricketts, Esq., Commissioner for the revision of civil salaries and establishment throughout India.*

"The distant threats of cutting down salaries have already, I observe, taken effect; and it is notorious in England, that a petty living of £200 or £300 per annum, already holds out

* Notes on the Revolt of the North-western Provinces of India, by Charles Raikes, Esq., Judge at Agra, p. 181.

greater inducements to men of learning and talent than the civil service of India. The candidates for examination this year are far too few, and only half in number of those of last year, although this year (1856) we have peace, and last year (1855) were plunged in war."

Judge Raikes estimates the population of the Northwestern Provinces of India at thirty millions. That portion of Hindustan is divided into thirty-one districts, and the appointments held in these Provinces by regularly appointed civil servants, for the administration of civil and criminal justice, and the collection of the public revenue, are as follows :—

	£.
6 Commissioners of Revenue and Police, at £3800 each per annum	22,800
19 Civil and Session Judges, at £3000 per annum	57,000
1 Additional Judge, at £2400 per annum	2,400
30 Magistrates and Collectors, at £2700 each per annum	81,000
22 Joint Magistrates (under the Magistrates and Collectors), with Salaries of £1200 each per annum	26,400
10 Joint Magistrates at £840 each per annum	8,400
40 Junior Assistants, with Average Salaries of £480 each per annum	19,200
Total	£217,200

In these offices, the powers of the judges are limited to the administration of civil justice, the trial of criminal cases at the Sessions, and the hearing of appeals from the orders passed by the magistrates in criminal trials. The magistrate is a more important personage in a district than a judge; he is to the people the direct and powerful representative of the Government, has large patronage, and a wide discretion and power, which the judge may fetter or restrain, but cannot exercise in his own person.*

Unfortunately the administration of justice is not popular in many parts of India: the worst side at times gains a victory, by resolute false swearing on the part of witnesses; and then fatigue, anxiety, risk, and uncertainty of prosecuting criminals, prevent many persons from bringing cases before the magistrates. Promotion in the Indian Civil Service, is usually determined by seniority alone, and it is therefore essential that the best possible selection should be made of candidates at their first entrance into that department.

Candidates for the Indian Civil Service are required to be between the ages of eighteen and twenty-three; and a medical certificate of the absence of any physical infirmity, with a satisfactory testimonial of good moral character, is the principal introduction requisite to admit a candidate to the examination for entrance. The business of regulating the examination has been entrusted to the Civil Service Commissioners, the Right Hon. Sir Edward Ryan and Sir John Shaw Lefevre, whose central office is at Dean's Yard, near Westminster Abbey. In the month of July in the present year, 1858, the candidates were examined in the large rooms of Burlington House, Piccadilly, London: sixty-five candidates were arranged in order of merit after this examination, of whom the first twenty were appointed to the Indian Civil Service. An Irish newspaper-writer, on looking over the list, noticed at once that a larger number of successful candidates had come from classical Oxford, nine out of the twenty having been Oxonians; six suc-

* Judge Raikes's Report, p. 185.

cessful candidates were members of the University of Dublin, and of these five were holders of classical scholarships in Trinity College. Altogether, of the twenty who succeeded, there were sixteen classical men elected to the Indian Civil Service.

Increased activity in the department of Classics has been naturally suggested by the Irish writer, both in the University of Dublin and in the public schools of Ireland, after considering the influence of classical scholarship and kindred acquirements in the recent examination for India. But a more important question remains, with reference to the people of India, whether the study of Oriental languages can be promoted by the devotion of so large a portion of the years of youth to Greek and Latin as would be required for high classical attainments.

With a view to the improvement of successful candidates for the Civil Service of India, the following special studies were recommended by the Committee of 1854 for a period of probation after the first Examination; the history, geography, statistics, and constitution of India; the general principles of jurisprudence, as well as of financial and commercial science, including an acquaintance with standard treatises on political economy; and, lastly, an elementary knowledge of at least one Indian language. If the age required for the candidates could be somewhat reduced, an increased aptitude would probably be found in the junior Civil Servants of the Indian Government for the attainment of familiarity with Hindoo dialects.

Ages and Places of Education of the first Twenty successful Candidates for the Royal Military Academy and the Indian Civil Service.

ROYAL MILITARY ACADEMY.

	Age.	Place of Education.
1.	17	University of Dublin.
2.	17	Kensington Proprietory School.
3.	18	University of Dublin.
4.	17	University of Dublin.
5.	17	University of Dublin.
6.	18	Privately.
7.	18	Cheltenham College.
8.	17	Privately.
9.	18	University of Dublin.
10.	17	Privately.
11.	18	Privately.
12.	18	Grammar School, Clapham.
13.	17	University of Dublin.
14.	19	Marlborough College.
15.	19	Privately.
16.	17	Privately.
17.	19	Merton College, Oxford.
18.	19	University of Dublin.
19.	17	Privately.
20.	18	Rugby School.

INDIAN CIVIL SERVICE.

1.	20	Trinity College, Dublin.
2.	20	Trinity College, Dublin.
3.	21	Trinity College, Dublin.
4.	22	Oriel College, Oxford.
5.	22	Edinburgh University.
6.	20	Trinity College, Dublin.
7.	22	University College, Oxford.
8.	21	Merton College, Oxford.
9.	22	Brazenose College, Oxford.
10.	22	Wadham College, Oxford.
11.	22	Magdalen College, Oxford.

	Age.	Place of Education.
12.	22	Trinity College, Dublin.
13.	22	Caius College, Cambridge.
14.	20	Queen's College, Oxford.
15.	20	Trinity College, Dublin.
16.	22	Corpus Christi College, Oxford.
17.	20	St. Peter's College, Cambridge.
18.	22	Trinity Hall, Cambridge.
19.	20	King's College, London.
20.	22	Christ Church, Oxford.

Number of Marks assigned for excellence in answering Questions in the following different branches of knowledge, in the competitive Examinations for the admission of Candidates into the

ROYAL MILITARY ACADEMY. June, 1857.		INDIAN CIVIL SERVICE. July, 1858.	
	Marks.		Marks.
Mathematics, pure	2000	Mathematics, pure and mixed	1000
" mixed	1500		
Latin	1000	Latin	750
Greek	750	Greek	750
French	1000	French	375
German	750	German	375
		Italian	375
English Literature	1250	English Literature, including the history of the laws and constitution	1000
		English composition	500
Natural Science	750	Natural Science	500
Moral Science	1000	Moral Science	500
Experimental Science	1000	Sanscrit	375
Drawing	1000	Arabic	375

Age of candidates directed to be from 17 to 20 years; successful candidates were 17, 18, and 19 years of age.

Age of candidates directed to be above 18 and under 23 years; successful candidates were 20 to 22 years of age.

If the number of marks given for the same branches of knowledge in the examination of candidates for the Military Academy and the Indian Civil Service be compared, it will be seen, that for India twice as many marks are given for Latin and Greek as for French and German; whilst for the Artillery and Engineers, French and Latin hold a similar position, and to Greek and German are allotted a smaller number of honorary rewards. For Woolwich, 5250 marks are assigned in all to different departments of mathematical and physical science. Experimental science, as a separate subject, does not find a place in the Indian Civil Service examination, whilst it counts for 1000 marks in the Military list. Greek composition is wisely omitted for the Artillery, but a special paper is given for the Indian Civil Service, in which are found a passage of English prose to be translated into Attic prose, and a portion of English verse to be translated into Greek tragic trimeters, the whole to be correctly accentuated.

Success in such an exercise depends, generally, on a long-continued technical preparation at school; and the Dean of Ely remarks on both Latin and Greek verse, that a young man of energy and ambition who has not been taught the art of making verses, feels discouraged or arrested in his labours by the necessity of making an enormous sacrifice of time for the very imperfect acquisition of a very useless accomplishment.

Dean Peacock is of opinion, that "a very general mistake prevails in the public mind, with respect to the extent to which the power of classical composition is communicated to the boys who are educated at our public schools; if it has once been imperfectly acquired, the suspension of the practice of it, during the one or two years which are interposed between school and the University will be found generally sufficient to obliterate all traces of its existence; for it may be safely asserted, that there is not one in ten of the entire number of those who enter the University of Cambridge, who is capable of writing Latin verse, and still fewer Latin prose, with tolerable correctness or elegance."*

In the revision, which is now in progress, both of military and civil arrangements for India, the benefit of the Hindoo people must naturally be regarded as of paramount importance, to be preferred even before the indulgence of mediæval tastes in exercising the mind by Greek and Latin composition. A large, intelligent, and strong-minded part of the British nation are just as much excluded from competitive examinations, in which sixteen successful candidates out of twenty are proficients in classics, as when the majority of these sixteen gentlemen were obliged, some years ago, to subscribe to an ecclesiastical test, and are now compelled to submit in their Colleges to the liturgical observances of the Act of Uniformity of 1662. The system of long-continued training at a public school, and frequent examinations in the Universities of Oxford, Cambridge, and Dublin, give an advantage to a persevering public schoolman, from his intimate acquaintance with a few departments of knowledge; but the number of first-rate candidates in the old University subjects is likely to continue small, as many persons at the present day decline to enter on an academical career in any of the ancient Universities, on account of conscientious scruples with respect to the religious tests imposed on entrance into Holy Orders in the Church of England, which lead numerous individuals

* Observations on the Statutes of the University of Cambridge, p. 161.

to prefer some other line of life, in which they may enjoy the happiness of mental independence and freedom.

UNIVERSITY OF OXFORD.

College rooms at Oxford are deemed essential for a student on his first residence in that University, and the number of applicants in the more popular Colleges frequently renders it expedient, that the name of a young man should be submitted to the Head of the College for approbation, and entered on the College books, several years before the undergraduate comes up to the University.

A slight College entrance examination in classics is usually required, which is more severe in some Colleges. Attendance at the ordinary daily Church of England services in the College chapel is expected, and the power of translating from English into Latin is almost essential.

Undergraduates are required to pass three public trials before they proceed to their B.A. degree; as follows:—

RESPONSIONS to be holden three times in each year, [*i. e.* 5th of Dec.; Monday after the fourth Sunday in Lent; Thursday after the first Sunday after Trinity;] and to be passed in the third to the seventh Term inclusive.

SUBJECTS.—One Latin, one Greek Author, or a portion of each; the chief object being to ascertain that the principles of these two languages are well understood. Arithmetic (which will be required of all), Euclid, or Algebra. [A smaller quantity of text than has been required under the old system,—two books of Euclid,—Algebra, to Simple Equations inclusively,—Arithmetic, to the Extraction of the Square Root inclusively, will suffice.] The same passage in English to be translated into Latin will be set to all the Candidates at once; and also a paper of Grammatical Questions, and a paper of Arithmetical or Mathematical Questions. Sixteen Candidates may be examined *vivâ voce* in one day.

FIRST PUBLIC EXAMINATIONS.

These examinations take place twice in the year, commencing *on the 20th November,* and the *Wednesday next after the first Sunday after Easter.*

SUBJECTS. *Minimum.*—The Four Gospels in Greek, except in the case of persons not members of the Church of England, when some one Greek Author is to be substituted. One Greek, one Latin Author; of which one must be a Poet, the other an Orator. The books brought up at Responsions cannot be tendered at this Examination, unless the Candidates shall bring up at least four books. A piece of English to be translated into Latin, a paper of Grammatical Questions, and a paper of Mathematical or Logical Questions, will be set to all the Candidates at once. Pass-men must bring up either Logic or three Books of Euclid and Algebra.

Honours will be awarded in this Examination. Candidates for Classical Honours are required especially to bring up Poets and Orators: Homer, Virgil, Demosthenes, and Cicero being recommended by name. The highest Honour cannot be obtained without Logic, and it is to have great weight in the distribution of both Honours. Those who do not tender Logic will be examined in Euclid and Algebra. Passages will be set with a view to elegance and accuracy of translation. Philological and Critical Questions will always be proposed, as well as Greek and Latin Translations, in Prose and Verse.

Honours will be also awarded for " Pure Mathematics."

The names of all who pass will be printed at the end of the Schedule of Honours.

3. The " PUBLIC EXAMINATION " (held twice in the year, commencing on the Thursday after the Second Sunday after Easter, and the 24th October, or day following, if either of those mentioned should fall on a Festival), in two Schools at

least, but not necessarily in the same Term, as early as the thirteenth, and, for Honours, as late as the eighteenth, Term of standing.

Candidates must present a Certificate from a Professor or Public Reader, showing that they have attended Two Courses of Public Lectures.

FIRST SCHOOL—to be passed first and by all—called the School of "LITERÆ HUMANIORES," or, Polite Literature.

Minimum.—The Four Gospels and the Acts of the Apostles in Greek; Sacred History; the subjects of the Books of the Old and New Testament; the Evidences and the Thirty-nine Articles, with Scripture proofs, except in the case of persons not members of the Church of England, when an equivalent in Greek or Latin, or some one Greek or Latin Author is required; the said books substituted not, however, to tell in the distribution of Honours. One Philosopher, one Historian, Greek or Latin, but not the same books which had been brought up at Responsions; those brought up before the Moderators, being a Poet and an Orator, cannot of course avail for this Examination. There will be no translations into Latin, but questions will be set, and passages from the books brought up will have to be translated into English.

For Honours.—Candidates for Honours may add to the Divinity above mentioned, one or more of the Apostolical Epistles and Ecclesiastical History. They will have to bring up the Greek and Latin Languages, Greek and Roman History, Chronology, Geography, Antiquities; Rhetoric and Poetics; Moral and Political Philosophy. These subjects may be illustrated by Modern Authors. Logic must be tendered by all who seek to obtain a first or second Class, and it is to have great weight in the distribution of Honours. Questions to be answered, passages to be translated, and subjects to be treated in Greek, Latin, or English, will be proposed by the Examiners.

SECOND SCHOOL.—MATHEMATICS.

Minimum.—The first six books of Euclid, or the first part of Algebra.

For Honours.—Mixed as well as Pure Mathematics.

THIRD SCHOOL.—NATURAL SCIENCE.

Minimum.—An acquaintance with the principles of two of these three branches of Natural Science,—Mechanical Philosophy, Chemistry, Physiology: and with some one branch of Science which falls under Mechanical Philosophy.

For Honours.—An acquaintance with the principles of the three branches of Natural Science named above, and of some one of the Physical Sciences which fall under the above-named branches of Natural Science.

FOURTH SCHOOL.—LAW AND MODERN HISTORY.

Minimum.—History of England from the Conquest to the accession of Henry VIII., with Blackstone on Real Property; or from the Accession of Henry VIII. to that of Queen Anne, with Blackstone on Personal Property and the Rights of Persons. Justinian's Institutes may be brought up in lieu of Blackstone.

For Honours.—Law, especially the Law of England. Candidates for the three superior Classes must bring up either Civil Law or International Law. Adam Smith on the Wealth of Nations may be offered. Modern History to the year 1789. But Candidates for Honours must necessarily include in their list the subjects required of those who seek merely to pass.

UNIVERSITY OF CAMBRIDGE.

The following method of study is directed in Arts:—

In order to take the degree of Bachelor of Arts at the regular time, the person must be admitted of some College before the end of the Easter Term of the year in which he purposes to come into residence. The mode of admission is, either by a personal examination before the Tutor and some of the College officers, or, which is more usual, by sending to the Tutor a recommendatory certificate, signed by some

Master of Arts of this University, stating the name, age, qualifications, etc. etc. of the candidate, and transmitting with it the caution-money. If this certificate be considered satisfactory, the admission takes place, and the person's name is immediately placed on the boards which are suspended in the butteries of the several Colleges. The person thus admitted usually comes into residence about the 20th of October following, and then commences his Academical Course.

The matriculation in the University, or enrolment of the Students' names in the University Books, is done on the day after the division of the Term. At this time also the fees to the University are paid to the Registrary; he presents to each Student a Book of Extracts from the Statutes, containing such directions as relate to his duty.

Undergraduates are examined in their respective Colleges yearly, in those subjects which have engaged their studies; and, according to the manner in which they acquit themselves in these examinations, their names are arranged in classes, and those who obtain the honour of the first places receive prizes of different value.

By this course the Students are prepared for those *public* Examinations which the University requires Candidates for the degree to pass. The first, viz. the Previous Examination, takes place in the Lent and October Terms, in the second year of academical residence, according to the following plan.

GENERAL PREVIOUS EXAMINATION.

The subjects of the Examination shall be one of the four Gospels in the original Greek, Paley's Evidences of Christianity, one of the Greek and one of the Latin Classics, the Elements of Euclid, Books I., II., and III., and Arithmetic.

The appointment of the particular Gospel, and in regard to the Classical subjects, the appointment both of the authors and of the portions of their works which it may be expedient to select, shall rest with the Vice-Chancellor for the time being, the three Regius Professors of Divinity, Civil Law, and Physic, the Regius Professor of Greek, and the Public Orator (provided that not more than two of them are members of the same College); upon this clear understanding, that in the exercise of the powers thus to be vested in them, they shall so limit the examination, that every one who is to be examined may be reasonably expected to show a competent knowledge of all the subjects.

ADDITIONAL EXAMINATION OF CANDIDATES FOR HONOURS.

There shall be Additional Subjects of Examination in Mathematics for those Students who intend to be Candidates for Honours in Mathematics, or Classics, or Law; and no Student shall be admitted to examination as a Candidate for such Honours, who has not passed an Examination in the said Additional Subjects to the satisfaction of the Examiners.

The said Additional Subjects shall be the Elements of Euclid, Books IV. and VI.; the following elementary parts of Algebra, viz. addition, subtraction, multiplication, and division of simple algebraical quantities, and simple algebraical fractions, the elementary rules of ratio and proportion, easy equations of a degree not higher than the second, involving one or two unknown quantities, and questions producing such equations; and Elementary Mechanics, treated so as not necessarily to require a knowledge of Trigonometry, viz. the composition and resolution of forces acting in one plane on a point, the mechanical powers, and the properties of the centre of gravity.

The Examination in the Additional Subjects shall be conducted by printed papers, containing questions in Algebra, propositions in Euclid and in Mechanics, and such questions and applications as arise directly out of the said propositions.

The examination in the Additional Subjects shall be held as follows: viz. in Euclid on the Monday before the commencement of the general Previous Examination from 9 till 12; in Algebra on the same day from 1 till 4, and in Mechanics on the following day from 9 till 12.

The names of those Students who have passed the general

Previous Examination, and have also passed the Examination in the Additional Subjects, to the satisfaction of the Examiners, shall be placed alphabetically in one class.

Examination of Candidates for the degree of Bachelor of Arts with Honours in Mathematics and Physical Science, at the end of three years and three months of academical residence.

Days.	Hours.	Subjects.
1st day	9 to 12	Euclid and Conic Sections.
	1½ to 4	Arithmetical Algebra and Plane Trigonom.
2nd day	9 to 12	Statics and Dynamics.
	1½ to 4	Hydrostatics and Optics.
3rd day	9 to 12	Newton and Astronomy.
	1 to 4	Problems in all the preceding subjects.
4th day	9 to 12	Natural Philosophy.
	1½ to 4	Pure Mathematics.
5th day	9 to 12	Easy Problems.
	1½ to 4	Natural Philosophy.
6th day	9 to 12	Problems.
	1½ to 4	Pure Mathematics.
7th day	9 to 12	Problems
	1½ to 4	Pure Mathematics and Natural Philosophy.
8th day	9 to 12	Pure Mathematics and Natural Philosophy.
	1½ to 4	Pure Mathematics and Natural Philosophy.

Examination of Persons who are Candidates for the B.A. Degree, with Honours in Classics, at the end of three years and three months of academical residence.

The minimum required for the Examination of Candidates for Honours in the Classical Tripos is the power of construing, at sight, Greek and Latin authors, of the best age, with general accuracy; and translation is deemed more important than composition. The papers include exercises for the translation of English prose into Greek prose, English prose into Latin prose, English verse into Latin verse; English verse into Greek Verse; as well as numerous passages from Greek and Latin prose and verse writers of the best age to be translated into English.

Examination for the B.A. Degree of Persons who are not Candidates for Honours. To be held at the end of two years and eight months of academical residence.

Days.		Hours.	Subjects.
1st	. . . . 1st Div.	9 to 12	Euclid.
	2nd Div.	$12\frac{1}{2}$ to $3\frac{1}{2}$	Algebra.
2nd	. . . . 1st Div.	9 to 12	Algebra.
	2nd Div.	$12\frac{1}{2}$ to $3\frac{1}{2}$	Euclid.
3rd	. . . . 1st Div.	9 to 12	Mechanics and Hydrostatics.
	2nd Div.	$12\frac{1}{2}$ to $3\frac{1}{2}$	Mechanics and Hydrostatics.
4th	. . . . 1st Div.	9 to 12	Latin Subject.
	2nd Div.	$12\frac{1}{2}$ to $3\frac{1}{2}$	Greek Subject.
5th	. . . . 1st Div.	9 to 12	History of the Reformation.
	2nd Div.	$12\frac{1}{2}$ to $3\frac{1}{2}$	Acts of the Apostles.
6th	. . . . 1st Div.	9 to 12	Acts of the Apostles.
	2nd Div.	$12\frac{1}{2}$ to $3\frac{1}{2}$	History of the Reformation.
7th	. . . . 1st Div.	9 to 12	Greek Subject.
	2nd Div.	$12\frac{1}{2}$ to $3\frac{1}{2}$	Latin Subject.

Students who are not Candidates for Honours, shall, in addition to what is now required of them, have attended, before they are admitted to Examination for their respective Degrees, the Lectures delivered during one Term at least, by one or more of the following Professors:—

Regius Professor of Laws,
Regius Professor of Physic,
Professor of Moral Philosophy,
Professor of Chemistry,
Professor of Anatomy,
Professor of Modern History,
Professor of Botany,
Woodwardian Professor of Geology.

Jacksonian Professor of Natural and Experimental Philosophy,
Downing Professor of the Laws of England,
Downing Professor of Medicine,
Professor of Mineralogy,
Professor of Political Economy;

and shall have obtained a Certificate of having passed an Examination satisfactory to one of the Professors whose Lectures they have chosen to attend.

Each Examination for a Professor's Certificate will require

the Candidate to answer a small number (say 10 to 15) of questions such as correspond to each article of the Syllabuses, authorized by the respective Professors.

UNIVERSITY OF LONDON.
Matriculation Examination.

Two examinations of a similar kind for Matriculation are to be held in each year, one in January and the other in July.

Each of these examinations is open to students who have completed their sixteenth year, and have paid a fee of two pounds. Every student may choose for himself whether he would prefer the examination of January or of July, in any year, for Matriculation.

Candidates shall not be approved by the Examiners unless they show a competent knowledge in

1. Classics;
2. The English Language, English History, and Modern Geography;
3. Mathematics and Natural Philosophy;
4. Chemistry;
5. Either the French or the German Language.

In the first week of examination the Examinations shall be conducted in the following order :—

Afternoon, 3 to 6.

Monday ....French, 2 to 4; German, 4 to 6.
Tuesday ....English History.
Wednesday .... Chemistry.
Thursday ....Natural Philosophy.
Friday, 2 to 5 ......The English Language.

Morning, 10 to 1.

Tuesday ....Mathematics.
Wednesday ....Greek Classic and History.
Thursday ....Mathematics.
Friday ....Roman Classic and History.

In each of the French and German Examination Papers, a translation into English is expected.

Under the head of Outlines of English History, the History of England to the end of the seventeenth century is included; a knowledge of Modern Geography is also expected.

Chemistry comprises the following subjects of Examination:—

Powers of Matter. Aggregation, crystallization, chemical affinity, definite equivalents.
Heat. Natural and artificial sources; its effects. Expansion; solids, liquids, gases. Thermometer; conduction; radiation; capacity; change of form; liquefaction; steam.
Combustion. Flame; nature of ordinary fuel; chief results of combustion, *i. e.*, the bodies produced.
The Atmosphere. Its general nature and condition; its component parts. Oxygen and Nitrogen; their properties. Water and Carbonic Acid. Proportions of these substances in the air.
Chlorine and Iodine, as compared with Oxygen.
Water. Its general relation to the atmosphere and earth; its natural states and relative purity. Sea-water, river-water, spring-water, rain-water. Pure water: effects of heat and cold on it; its compound nature; its elements.
Hydrogen. Its nature and proportion in water; its presence in most ordinary fuels; its product when burnt.
Sulphur, Phosphorus, and Carbon generally.
Nitric Acid, Sulphuric Acid, Carbonic Acid; their elements.
Hydrochloric or Muriatic Acid. Alkalies, Earths, Oxides generally. Salts. Their nature generally; Sulphates, Nitrates, Carbonates.
Metals generally. Iron, Copper, Lead, Tin, Zinc, Gold, Silver, Platinum, Mercury.
The chief elements of Vegetable bodies; of Animal bodies.

The knowledge required of the following subjects in Natural Philosophy will be such as may be attained by attending a course of Experimental Lectures:—

MECHANICS. Composition and Resolution of Statical Forces. Simple Machines (*Mechanical Powers*), and Ratio of the

Power to the Weight in each. Centre of Gravity. General Laws of Motion, and chief experiments by which they may be illustrated. Law of the Motion of Falling Bodies.

HYDROSTATICS, HYDRAULICS, AND PNEUMATICS. Pressure of the Liquids and Gases, its equal diffusion, and variation with the depth. Specific Gravity, and the mode in which the specific gravity of bodies may be ascertained. Barometer, Siphon, Common Pump, and Forcing-Pump, and Air-Pump.

ACOUSTICS. Nature of Sound.

OPTICS. Laws of Reflection and Refraction. Formation of Images by Simple Lenses.

Under the head of the English Language, are comprised, Orthography; Writing from Dictation; the Grammatical Structure of Language; and Composition.

Mathematics include the following subjects:—

ARITHMETIC AND ALGEBRA. The ordinary Rules of Arithmetic. Vulgar and Decimal Fractions. Extraction of the Square Root. Addition, Subtraction, Multiplication, and Division of Algebraical Quantities. Proportion. Arithmetical and Geometrical Progression. Simple Equations.

GEOMETRY. The First Four Books of Euclid:—or, The principal properties of Triangles, and of Squares and other Parallelograms, treated geometrically: The principal properties of the Circle, and of its inscribed and circumscribed figures, treated geometrically.

Greek and Roman Classics, and History, form the subjects of Examination Papers, which contain passages of the ancient authors to be translated into English, and simple and easy sentences of English to be translated into Latin, as well as questions in Greek and Latin Grammar, History, and Geography.

The Classical Matriculation subjects for 1859, are Homer, Iliad, Book V., and Cicero, De Amicitiâ, and Pro Lege Maniliâ. As a general rule, one Greek and one Latin subject are selected one year and a half previously by the Senate, from the works of the undermentioned authors:—

Homer, one book; *Xenophon*, one book; *Terence*, one play; *Virgil*, one book of the Georgics, and one book of the Æneid; *Horace*, two books of the Odes; *Sallust*, the Conspiracy of Catiline, or the War with Jugurtha; *Cæsar*, two books of the Gallic War; *Livy*, one book; *Cicero*, De Senectute or De Amicitiâ, with one of the following Orations:—Pro Lege Maniliâ, one of the four Catilinarian Orations, Pro Archiâ, Pro M. Marcello; *Ovid*, one book of the Metamorphoses, and one book of the Epistles or Heroides.

The names of all the Candidates who have passed the Matriculation Examination are to be arranged in three divisions, each in alphabetical order.

On the Tuesday week after each Matriculation Examination, any of the Candidates who have passed may be examined for honours in Mathematics and Natural Philosophy, and after the conclusion of this Examination, subsequent days are appointed for honour Examinations in Classics, Chemistry, and Natural History.

The Examiners publish, in the order of proficiency, a list of the Candidates for honours who acquit themselves to their satisfaction.

BACHELOR OF ARTS.

Candidates for the Degree of Bachelor of Arts shall be required to have passed the Matriculation Examination, and to pass Two subsequent Examinations.

FIRST B.A. EXAMINATION.

The First B.A. Examination shall take place once a year, and shall commence on the third Monday in October.

No Candidate shall be admitted to this Examination within One Academical Year of the time of his passing the Matriculation Examination; nor unless he have produced a satisfactory Certificate of Good Conduct. This Certificate shall be transmitted to the Registrar at least one calendar month before the commencement of the Examination.

The Fee for this Examination shall be Five Pounds.

Candidates shall not be approved by the Examiners unless they show a competent knowledge in

1. Latin, and Roman History;
2. English Language, Literature, and History;
3. Mathematics;
4. Either the French or the German Language.

In the first week of examination the Examinations shall be conducted in the following order:—

Morning, 10 *to* 1.
Monday ......Latin.
Tuesday ......Mathematics.
Wednesday...English History.
Thursday ....French.

Afternoon, 3 *to* 6.
Monday ......Latin, and Roman History.
Tuesday ......Mathematics.
Wednesday...English Language and Literature.
Thursday ....German.

Latin.

Two Latin subjects, one in prose, the other in verse; to be selected two years previously by the Senate from the works of the undermentioned authors:—*

Terence, one play; *Virgil*, the Eclogues; or two books of the Georgics; or two books of the Æneid; *Horace*, the Odes; or the Satires; or the Epistles; *Cicero*, one of the Orations; or one book from any of the Philosophical or Rhetorical Works; *Livy*, one book; *Tacitus*, one book of either the Annals or the Histories.

The papers in Latin shall contain passages of the ancient Authors to be translated into English, and short passages of English

* Subjects for 1859:—*Livy*, Book XXXI.; *Horace*, The Satires.

to be translated into Latin. The papers shall also contain questions in Latin Grammar, Roman History to the death of Augustus, and Geography.

Mathematics.

ARITHMETIC AND ALGEBRA. The ordinary Rules of Arithmetic. Vulgar and Decimal Fractions. Extraction of the Square Root. Addition, Subtraction, Multiplication, and Division of Algebraical Quantities. Algebraical Proportion and Variation. Permutations and Combinations. Arithmetical and Geometrical Progression. Simple and Compound Interest; Discount and Annuities for terms of years. Simple and Quadratic Equations, and Questions producing them. The nature and use of Logarithms.

GEOMETRY. The relations of similar figures. The Eleventh Book of Euclid to Prop. 21. The equation to the Straight Line and the equation to the Circle referred to rectangular co-ordinates. The equations to the Conic Sections referred to rectangular co-ordinates.

PLANE TRIGONOMETRY. Plane Trigonometry as far as to enable the Candidate to solve all the cases of Plane Triangles. The following propositions:—

$$\sin (A \pm B) = \sin A \cos B \pm \cos A \sin B$$
$$\cos (A \pm B) = \cos A \cos B \mp \sin A \sin B$$
$$\tan (A \pm B) = \frac{\tan A \pm \tan B}{1 \mp \tan A \tan B}$$

The expression for the Area of a Triangle in terms of its sides.

THE ENGLISH LANGUAGE, LITERATURE, AND HISTORY. Writing out the substance of a paragraph previously read by the Examiner; the Grammatical Structure of the Language; Composition; History of England to the end of the seventeenth century; other special subjects* to be defined from time to time.

THE FRENCH OR THE GERMAN LANGUAGE. Translation into English. Translation from English into French or German.

On Monday Morning at Nine o'clock, in the following week,

---

* Special English subjects for 1859 :—History of English Literature during the reigns of Elizabeth and James I.; Bacon's Essays; and King Lear.

the Examiners shall arrange in Two Divisions, each in alphabetical order, such of the Candidates as have passed.

Any Candidate who has passed the First B.A. Examination may be examined on subsequent days specially appointed, for Honours in Mathematics, in Latin, and in English, and for Prizes in the French and German Languages and Literature. The names of the successful candidates for honours are arranged in the order of proficiency.

SECOND B.A. EXAMINATION.

The Second B.A. Examination shall take place once a year, and shall commence on the fourth Monday in October.

No Candidate shall be admitted to this Examination within one academical year of the time of his passing the First B.A. Examination; nor unless he have produced a satisfactory certificate of good conduct. This certificate shall be transmitted to the Registrar at least one calendar month before the commencement of the Examination.

The Fee for this Examination shall be Five Pounds.

Candidates shall not be approved by the Examiners unless they show a competent knowledge in

1. Classics.
2. Grecian History.
3. Natural Philosophy.
4. Animal Physiology.
5. Logic and Moral Philosophy.

In the first week of examination the Examinations shall be conducted in the following order:—

Morning, 10 *to* 1.

Monday ..... Greek.
Tuesday ...... Grecian History.
Wednesday ... Natural Philosophy.
Thursday .... Logic and Moral Philosophy.

Afternoon, 3 *to* 6.

Monday ...... Greek and Latin.
Tuesday ...... Animal Physiology.
Wednesday ... Natural Philosophy.
Thursday .... Logic and Moral Philosophy.

Classics.

THE GREEK AND LATIN LANGUAGES. One Greek subject and one Latin Prose subject, to be selected two years previously by the Senate from the works of the undermentioned authors:—

Homer, six books; *Æschylus*, one play; *Sophocles*, one play; *Euripides*, one play; *Herodotus*, one book; *Thucydides*, one book; *Plato*, Apology of Socrates, and Crito; *Xenophon*, two books, from any of his larger works; *Demosthenes*, one of the longer or three of the shorter public Orations; or two of the private Orations; *Cicero*, one of the Orations; or one Book from any of the Philosophical or Rhetorical Works; *Livy*, one book; *Tacitus*, one book of either the Annals or the Histories.

The papers in Classics shall contain passages of the ancient Authors to be translated into English, and short passages of English to be translated into Latin. The papers shall also contain questions in Grammar, History, and Geography.

HISTORY. History of Greece to the death of Alexander.

Natural Philosophy.

MECHANICS. The Composition and Resolution of Forces. The Mechanical Powers. The Centre of Gravity. The general laws of Motion. The Motion of Falling Bodies in free space and down inclined planes.

HYDROSTATICS, HYDRAULICS, AND PNEUMATICS. The pressure of fluids is equally diffused, and varies as the depth. The surface of a fluid at rest is horizontal. Specific Gravity. A floating body displaces exactly its weight of the fluid, and is supported as if by a force equal to its weight pressing upwards at the centre of gravity of the displaced fluid. The Common Pump and the Forcing-Pump. The Barometer. The Air-Pump. The Steam-Engine.

ASTRONOMY. The apparent motion of the heavens round the earth. The apparent motion of the sun through the fixed stars. The phenomena of Eclipses. The Regression of the Planets. Proofs of the Copernican system.

Animal Physiology.

The mechanical, chemical, and vital properties of the several elementary Animal Textures.

General principles of Animal Mechanics.

Outline of the processes subservient to the Nutrition of the body; and general plan of structure of the Organs of Assimilation. Nature of Digestion; course of the Lacteal Absorbents. Structure of the Organs of Circulation. Principal varieties in the plan of circulation in the great divisions of the animal kingdom; viz. Mammalia, Birds, Reptiles, Fishes, Mollusca, Articulated, and Radiated Animals.

Mechanism of Respiration in the several classes of animals; chemical effects of respiration in the several classes of animals. Chemical properties of the Secretions; structure of secreting organs. Functions of the Nervous System. The Sensorial Functions, comprehending the physiology of the external senses, especially Vision and Hearing.

Logic and Moral Philosophy.*

Names, Notions, and Propositions.
Syllogism.
Induction and Subsidiary Operations.
The Senses.
The Intellect.
The Will, including the Theory of Moral Obligation.

On Tuesday morning, at nine o'clock in the following week, the Examiners shall arrange in two divisions, each in alphabetical order, such of the Candidates as have passed.

Any Candidate who has passed may be examined on subsequent days specially appointed, for Honours in Mathematics and Natural Philosophy, Classics, Logic and Moral Philosophy, Chemistry, Animal Physiology, and Vegetable Physiology and

* The extent of acquirement expected in Logic and Moral Philosophy is such as may fairly be attained by a course of instruction in a Class, during the year preceding Examination. The Senate think it better to leave the choice of Books to the respective Professors.

Structural Botany. The names of the successful candidates for honours are arranged in the order of proficiency.

Arrangements may be made for holding pass examinations for Matriculation, and the first and second pass examinations for the B.A. degree, at a distance from the Metropolis, under the superintendence of a Sub-Examiner, specially commissioned to superintend a provincial examination. The provincial examinations will be held simultaneously with similar examinations in London, on the same days, and at the same hours, and copies of the examination papers are intended to be sent down in sealed packets, and the answers returned to the University of London.

Master of Arts.

The Examination for the Degree of Master of Arts shall take place once a year, and commence on the first Monday in June.

No Candidate shall be admitted to the Examination for the Degree of M.A. until after the expiration of One academical Year from the time of his obtaining the Degree of B.A. in this University, or in one of the Universities of Oxford, Cambridge, Dublin, and Durham, nor unless he have shown evidence of having completed his Twentieth year.

The Fee for the Degree of M.A. shall be Ten Pounds.

Candidates for the Degree of M.A. shall be examined in one or more of the following branches of knowledge :—

I. CLASSICS.
II. MATHEMATICS AND NATURAL PHILOSOPHY.
III. LOGIC AND MORAL PHILOSOPHY, POLITICAL PHILOSOPHY, HISTORY OF PHILOSOPHY, POLITICAL ECONOMY.

No Candidate shall be approved by the Examiners unless he show a competent knowledge in one of these branches of knowledge.

The Candidates who pass to the satisfaction of the Examiners shall be arranged in the order of proficiency.

Number of Candidates for Matriculation and Degrees in Arts in the University of London.

Year.	Matriculation.		Bachelor of Arts.		Master of Arts.	
	No. of Candidates.	No. passed.	No. of Candidates.	No. passed.	No. of Candidates.	No. passed.
1838	23	22				
1839	31	30	17	17		
1840	77	69	32	30	4	3
1841	89	64	40	35	1	1
1842	82	66	33	20	4	3
1843	96	80	29	28	1	0
1844	95	79	33	30	3	3
1845	113	103	40	37	1	1
1846	110	99	32	30	2	2
1847	161	151	44	36	3	3
1848	171	161	47	41	4	4
1849	181	167	63	53	7	7
1850	206	190	70	58	10	10
1851	241	214	67	49	2	2
1852	244	206	62	49	8	6
1853	218	201	81	64	10	8
1854	241	199	93	73	8	8
1855	209	172	75	63	3	3
1856	255	209	71	58	10	10
1857	266	224	75	66	5	5
1858	299	248	72	59	10	10

COMMITTEE OF COUNCIL EXAMINATIONS FOR TEACHERSHIPS.

Considerable attention has been given by successive Committees of Council on Education to the training and examination of Teachers for Elementary Schools. The gradual elevation of youthful Monitors in Schools to the important and salaried position of Pupil-Teachers was accomplished, and arrangements were entered into with most of the larger ecclesiastical bodies of the United Kingdom, for the inspection, improvement, and increase of their schools, when Sir James Kay Shuttleworth, Bart., occupied the office of Secretary to the Committee of Council. His successor, Mr. Lingen, carries on the work of endeavouring to improve the mass of the people by local improvements in parochial and other schools, inspection of all departments of public instruction under the Committee of Privy Council, and a constant system of liberally assisting local exertions for education within the limits assigned to that Committee's supervision.

Candidates for apprenticeship as Pupil-Teachers, under the Committee of Council on Education, are required to be at least thirteen years of age, and must not be subject to any bodily infirmity likely to impair their usefulness as Pupil-Teachers. The Master or Mistress of the School to which such candidates belong is expected to be either certificated or registered, as competent to conduct the apprentice through the course of instruction required by the Committee of Council; and the school is to be well furnished, well supplied with books and apparatus, and divided into classes, with a graduated system of instruction, so that equal attention may be bestowed on each class.

Annual Reports are made by the Inspectors of Schools, relative to the progress of the Pupil-Teachers in the art of teaching.

The following secular subjects of examination are appointed for the election of Pupil-Teachers, and for each successive year during their apprenticeship :—

SECULAR EXAMINATION.	READING.	GRAMMAR.	WRITING AND COMPOSITION.	ARITHMETIC AND MATHEMATICS.		GEOGRAPHY.
				Male Pupil-Teachers.	*Female Pupil-Teachers.*	
For Election of Pupil-Teachers.	To read with fluency, ease, and expression.	To point out the Parts of Speech in a Simple Sentence.	To write in a neat hand, with correct spelling and punctuation, a simple narrative slowly read to them.	To write from dictation sums in the first four Rules of Arithmetic, Simple and Compound, and to work them correctly, and to know the Tables of Weights and Measures.		To have an elementary knowledge of Geography.
End of First Year of Apprenticeship.	Improved articulation and expression in reading.	The Noun, Verb, and Adjective; with their relations in a Simple Sentence.	To write from memory the substance of a more difficult narrative.	Practice and Proportion.	Practice and Bills of Parcels.	The British Isles. [Maps to be drawn in this and the following years.]
End of second year of Apprenticeship.	Improved articulation and expression in reading.	The Pronoun, Adverb, and Preposition; with their relations in a Sentence.	Composition of a Class Report, or the Abstract of a Lesson.	Vulgar Fractions.	Simple Proportion.	Europe and ancient Palestine.

	Improved articulation and expression in Reading.	The Conjunction; with the Analysis of Sentences.	Composition of the Notes of a Lesson on a subject selected by the Inspector.	Decimal Fractions; and Euclid, Book I., to end of XVth Proposition.	Vulgar Fractions.	The Colonies.
End of Third Year of Apprenticeship.						
End of Fourth Year of Apprenticeship.	Improved articulation and expression in Reading.	More advanced exercises in preceding subjects; with a knowledge of Prefixes and Affixes. [*As an alternative exercise, the regular declensions of Nouns, Pronouns, and Adjectives in Latin.*]	Composition of an account of the Organization of the School, and of the Methods of Instruction used.	Simple Interest; Euclid, Book I.; and Algebra, first four rules.	Compound Proportion, and recapitulation of preceding exercises.	Asia and Africa.
End of Fifth Year of Apprenticeship.	Improved articulation and expression in Reading.	The same subjects. [*As an alternative exercise, the government of Prepositions, and the regular conjugations of Verbs in Latin.*]	Composition of an Essay on some subject connected with the Art of Teaching.	Problems in Arithmetic; Euclid, Book II., and Algebra, to the end of Simple Equations.	Decimal Fractions and Simple Interest.	America and the Oceans.

An examination in English History commences at the end of the third year of the apprenticeship of Pupil-Teachers, and a similar examination is continued at the end of the fourth and fifth years of apprenticeship; the whole course includes the succession of sovereigns, with dates, from the reign of Egbert to the present time, as well as the outlines of British History, at first to the accession of Henry VII., and finally, from that period to our own days.

Where suitable means of instruction exist, Drawing and Music form subjects of examination for Pupil-Teachers. At the end of the first year, the apprentices are examined, relatively to Music, in the shapes of notes and rests, the stave, and the places of notes on the treble stave; at the end of the second year, the musical examination includes dotted notes and rests, various kinds and signatures of time, and the diatonic scale; in the third year, the Pupil-Teachers are examined in intervals, sharps and flats, and accidental intervals; and in the fourth year, they have to prove their acquaintance with the places of notes on the bass stave, major and minor scales, and the common characters in music. The examination at the end of the fifth year of apprenticeship comprises transposition and modulation, the alto and tenor staves, and a recapitulation of the preceding exercises.

Candidates above fourteen years of age may be apprenticed for four years, beginning with the emoluments of the second year if they pass the requisite examination.

For the admission of apprenticed Pupil-Teachers in Church of England Schools, a certificate is required from the Clergyman and Managers of the School to which the Candidates belong, assuring the Committee of Council that the moral character of the candidates and their families justifies an expectation that the instruction and training of the school will be seconded by their own efforts and the example of their parents. In schools not connected with the Church of England, a similar certificate is expected from the Managers of the school to which the candidates belong.

At the end of each of the five years of apprenticeship, certificates are required from the Managers of the school in which Pupil-Teachers are instructed, that the conduct of the apprentices has been good; in the case of Church of England Schools, a certificate from the Clergyman is expected, that the Pupil-Teachers have been attentive to their religious duties; and in schools not connected with the Church of England, similar certificates are required from the Managers. An additional certificate is required from the Master or Mistress of the School, that the apprentices have been punctual, diligent, obedient, and attentive to their duties. The annual payments granted by the Committee of Council to the Pupil-Teachers consist of £10 at the end of the first year, £12. 10s. for the second year, £15 for the third year, £17. 10s. for the fourth year, and £20 for the fifth year.

At the close of the apprenticeship every Pupil-Teacher who has passed the annual examination is entitled to refer to the Committee of Council any person who may, as an employer or otherwise, be properly interested in knowing his character, for a certificate, declaring that he has successfully completed his apprenticeship. But further than this, one of her Majesty's Inspectors, shortly before Christmas in each year, holds a public examination at each of the Training Schools under inspection, at which all those Pupil-Teachers who have successfully completed their apprenticeship are allowed to compete.

The Committee of Council on Education, on comparison of the testimonials and examination papers of these apprentices, awards exhibitions to as many qualified candidates (thenceforth denominated "Queen's Scholars") as answer to the total number of vacancies in all the Training Schools under inspection.

Each Queen's Scholar will be at liberty to go to any of the Normal Colleges under inspection, the authorities of which may consent to receive him. The exhibition granted to a Normal College, for each of the Queen's Scholars, is £23 in the case of males, and £17 in the case of females; and in consideration of this payment the Normal Colleges, in admitting any Queen's Scholar, are understood to agree thereby to provide tuition, lodging, board, washing, and medical attendance for the Queen's Scholar, without further charge. A Queen's scholarship is renewable for a second year.

The secular subjects of Examination for Queen's Scholarships are those of the Pupil Teachers' course, which have been already detailed in this pamphlet, pp. 34, 35, and 36.

There are schools in which, according to a Minute of the Committee of Council, dated 10th July, 1847, grants may be made for Pupil-Teacherships, though the Managers object on religious grounds to make a Report concerning the religious state of such schools.

Religious Examinations for Pupil-Teachers generally include the following subjects:—

End of First Year of Apprenticeship.	The Holy Scriptures and Catechism, with illustrations by passages from Holy Writ.	The Holy Scriptures and the Assembly's Shorter Catechism, with illustrations by passages from Holy Writ.	Certificate from the Managers of the School that the Religious Knowledge of the Pupil-teacher is satisfactory to them.
End of Second Year.	The Holy Scriptures, Liturgy, and Catechism, more fully than in the preceding year.	The Holy Scriptures, and the Assembly's Shorter Catechism, more fully than in the preceding year.	Same as above.
End of Third Year.	More fully in the Holy Scriptures, Liturgy, and Catechism.	More fully in the Holy Scriptures, and the Assembly's Shorter Catechism.	Same as above.
End of Fourth Year.	More fully in the Holy Scriptures, Liturgy, and Catechism.	More fully in the Holy Scriptures, and the Assembly's Shorter Catechism.	Same as above.
End of Fifth Year.	More completely in the Holy Scriptures, Liturgy, and Catechism.	More completely in the Holy Scriptures, and the Assembly's Shorter Catechism.	Same as above.

The scale of annual payments from the Committee of Council to the Masters or Mistresses of Schools for instructing Pupil-Teachers in the subjects of Examination, commences with £5 per annum for one apprenticed Pupil-Teacher; £9 per annum for two apprentices; £12 per annum for three; and £3 more annually for each additional apprentice. These payments are considered as due for whole years only, and Teachers who voluntarily quit the charge of apprentices before the termination of a year do not receive these gratuities.

Thirty-five Training Schools for the education of Masters and Mistresses of Schools, have been connected with the Committee of Council, and have received from that Committee the following grants:—

Fifteen Training Schools for Masters only.

	Grants.
Battersea (National Society's)	£22,449
Carmarthen (National Society's)	7,919
Carnarvon (Church of England)	1,503
Chelsea, St. Mark's (National Society's)	21,064
Chester (Diocesan)	9,805
Chichester (Diocesan)	2,988
Culham (Oxford Diocesan)	10,517
Durham (Diocesan)	6,378
Edinburgh, Scottish Episcopal	298
Exeter (Diocesan)	5,875
Hammersmith, St. Mary's (Roman Catholic)	5,076
Metropolitan (Church of England)	12,446
Saltley (Worcester Diocesan)	7,011
Winchester (Diocesan)	2,893
York and Ripon (Diocesan)	14,010

Thirteen Training Schools for Mistresses only.

Bishop's Stortford (Rochester Diocesan)	6,083
Brighton (Chichester Diocesan)	2,887

	Grants.
Bristol, Gloucester, and Oxford (Diocesan)	£5,164
Derby (Lichfield Diocesan)	4,182
Gray's Inn Road (Home and Col. Society's)	15,175
Liverpool Roman Catholic (96, Mount Pleasant)	956
Norwich (Diocesan)	2,310
Saint Leonard's-on-Sea (Roman Catholic)	645
Salisbury (Diocesan)	5,955
Truro (Exeter Diocesan)	—
Warrington (Chester Diocesan)	8,160
Whitelands (National Society's)	17,466
York and Ripon (Diocesan)	—

Seven Training Schools for both Masters and Mistresses.

Borough Road (Brit. and For. School Society's)	£16,703
Cheltenham (Church of England)	26,713
Edinburgh, Castle-hill-terrace (Est. Church)	13,399
Edinburgh, Moray House (Free Church)	17,934
Glasgow, Dundas Vale (Est. Church)	13,709
Glasgow (Free Church)	12,025
Westminster (Wesleyan)	14,420

The majority of these Training Schools are connected with the Church of England, but the plan of instruction includes a variety of subjects equally valuable and interesting to the members of all religious denominations, and the subjects of Examination in a Church of England School during the three years of study of the candidates may be seen in the following table:—

Subjects in which Students in Church of England Training Schools, and other Candidates for Certificates of Proficiency, as Teachers in Elementary Schools connected with the Church of England, are examined under the Committee of Privy Council on Education.

FIRST YEAR.

Reading. Penmanship. Usual Rules of Arithmetic. Mechanics. School Management. English Grammar. Geography.

Outlines of the History of England. First four Books of Euclid. Algebra, as far as Quadratic Equations. Drawing. Vocal Music. St. Luke's Gospel, and History of the Bible. Catechism and Liturgy. Church History, at the time of the Reformation.

SECOND YEAR.

Reading. Penmanship. Arithmetic (higher branches). School Management. English Grammar and Composition. Geography. History of England. Drawing. Vocal Music. Acts of the Apostles. Epistle to the Galatians. Church History, to the Council of Chalcedon.

SECOND YEAR.—*Alternative Subjects, in one only of which Students will be examined.*

Physical Science. Higher Mathematics, and Mathematical Physics. English Literature. Latin.

THIRD YEAR.

School Management. Vocal Music. Drawing. The Bible generally. Evidences of Christianity.

THIRD YEAR.—*Alternative Subjects; one to be selected at the option of each Student.*

Mental Science, as applied to Education. Experimental Science. Higher Mathematics. Ancient or Modern Language. History (selected Works, such as Hallam's 'Constitutional History of England'). English Literature.

The Training Institution for Teachers, in connection with the British and Foreign School Society, in the Borough Road, Southwark, has outgrown the accommodation afforded by the original design. Mr. Bowstead, in his Report on this Institution, dated January, 1858, observes, that "several candidates who successfully passed the recent examination for Queen's Scholarships, have been unable to obtain admittance, and some even of those Students who were 'scheduled,' or permitted to pass at the close of their first year, cannot be allowed to return for the purpose of completing their studies, and ultimately obtaining certificates of merit."

"It has become necessary," remarks Mr. Bowstead, "to rent two separate houses, one for the male and the other for the female students, at a distance from the main building, in order to provide sufficient sleeping-apartments; and additional lecture-rooms, class-rooms, and examination-halls are urgently needed, especially on the female side." Mr. Bowstead is of opinion that it is not possible to suggest any unobjectionable mode of providing additional accommodation in the female department upon the present confined site. There is but one class-room and one large lecture-room for the use of the female students. The class-room is inconveniently situated, and the lecture-room is also used as a dining-room. As this apartment is not large enough to admit the whole of the female students to dinner at once, it is necessary to have two dinners in succession every day, and to follow up the second dinner, after a very short interval, by a lecture.*

Mr. Bowstead states that he has been assured by Mr. Wilks, the secretary of the British and Foreign School Society, that the present state of things is to be regarded as merely temporary, and that active measures are in progress with a view to provide greatly extended accommodation. An infant-school may also probably be annexed to the female department of the Training Institution in the Borough Road, Southwark, among the contemplated new arrangements.

* Reports by her Majesty's Inspectors of Schools for 1857-8, p. 768.

Government liberality has already been manifested towards the Training College of the British and Foreign School Society, by the grant of £5000 from the Committee of Council on Education, for the enlargement and improvement of the buildings in the Borough Road. A similar amount of assistance has been twice accorded to the Education Committee of the General Assembly of the Established Church of Scotland, in a grant of £5000 to enable that Committee to erect a building for Model and Normal Schools in Edinburgh, and £5000 to aid in the expenses of founding Model and Normal Schools in Glasgow. An annual grant of £500 is further made to each of these two Scotch institutions, from the Committee of Council on Education.

As a general rule, when the Committee of Council are satisfied with respect to a Normal or Training School, their Lordships appear willing to award a grant not exceeding one-third of the outlay on the site, buildings, and fixtures, and estimated at the rate of £50 for every student accommodated, where the students are lodged on the premises. In the case of the Normal Schools of the Established Church of Scotland, the General Assembly's Education Committee accepted the grants made to them on the following principle: that "the standard of acquirements for certificates (of teachers) should not be ordered so as to interfere with the studies pursued in any Normal School, but should be adapted to those studies, so however as to apply impartially to all such Normal Schools an equal incentive to exertion, by requiring efficiency in a sufficient number of the studies pursued in them."[*]

Separate negotiations have hitherto been usual in re-

---

[*] Consolidation of Minutes and Regulations of the Committee of Privy Council on Education, p. 38.

gard to any fresh application to the Committee of Council for assistance in establishing Normal Colleges, and so large an increase of population and of schools has taken place, of late years, in the manufacturing districts of the North of England, that the time has probably now arrived for the formation of a new Training College in one of the great centres of English manufacturing industry. Lancashire and Yorkshire contain, at the present day, a larger number of inhabitants than the whole of Scotland. Many of the schools in these two great counties are conducted on plans which are not connected specially with any one religious denomination, and are usefully adapted to the communities among whom they are located. There are nearly a thousand Pupil-Teachers in the schools of the northern counties of England, connected with the British and Foreign School Society's system, for the scriptural education of the children of the poor, without distinction of sect or party. Of these one-half, or five hundred Pupil-Teachers, are males, and a hundred youths of this number may probably be prepared to become students if a Normal College on a liberal basis can be organized in the city of Manchester, where the distinguished talents of resident Professors may assist in its establishment.

On the 31st December, 1857, the total number of Pupil-Teachers in England amounted nearly to 10,000, including both males and females. They are thus classified in the Tables published in the last Report of the Committee of Council on Education, comprising Pupil-Teachers in all the English schools under that Committee.

Pupil-Teachers in England, December 31, 1857.

	First Year.			Fourth Year.
Male	1410		Male	810
Female	1298		Female	742
Total	2708		Total	1552
	Second Year.			Fifth Year.
Male	1195		Male	695
Female	1157		Female	653
Total	2352		Total	1348
	Third Year.			Total of the Five Years.
Male	904		Male	5014
Female	863		Female	4713
Total	1767		Total	9727

The number of certificated Teachers under the Committee of Council in England, on the 31st of December, 1857, was as follows:—

	Male.	Female.	Total.
	2310	1670	3980
Assistant-Teachers	140	42	182
Total	2450	1712	4162

History, English Literature, Geography, Physical Science, and Applied Mathematics, are considered by the Committee of Council to be of sufficient importance to merit a grant in aid of £100 annually, to each of a number not exceeding three of the resident professors in a Normal School, who teach these branches of knowledge, provided that the salaries of such lecturers, independently of any augmentation from Government, shall amount to not less than £150 a-year in each case, and that their Lordships receive satisfactory evidence of the attainments of the Teachers, and of their skill in adapting their acquirements to the purposes of elementary instruction.

Annual examinations for Teacherships are held in the different Normal Colleges under the inspection of the Committee of Council on Education, at which certificates of merit are given to the successful candidates, who exhibit a competent ability in the examination subjects, when they have been for two years in charge of the same elementary school, and have been twice reported on, as the teachers of such a school, by her Majesty's Inspector.

Part of the examination in presence of the Inspector consists in the candidate teaching a class, and he is expected to manifest skill in keeping the class attentive and active, as well as a power of addressing the understandings of the children, so that they may be likely to carry away clear ideas of their lessons.

Training Colleges receive grants from the Committee of Council, for the students under their care, according to the proficiency exhibited in the examinations; and these grants are made upon the following scale.

At the end of the first year, the Training College receives for each male student—

> In the First Class £20
> In the Second Class 16
> In the Third Class 13

Grants of two-thirds of these amounts respectively are made to the Normal Colleges for females, the same proportion of two-thirds being observed in successive years, for the grants to female students.

At the end of the second year of residence in the Training School, each male student receives—

> In the First Class £24
> In the Second Class 20
> In the Third Class 16

And at the end of the third year of residence, each male student receives—

In the First Class	£24
In the Second Class	20
In the Third Class	16

A considerable increase may be observed in the number of students passed at the examinations of the various Training Colleges. In 1856, there were in all 1449 students passed, and 1475 Queen's scholars admitted in Normal Colleges, for whom the sum of £24,000 was paid by the Committee of Council. In 1857, there were in all 1728 students passed, and 2000 Queen's scholars admitted, at the examinations of the different Training Colleges connected with the Committee of Council, and an estimate has been formed of £42,520, to be paid in 1858 for these.

In 1839, the Committee of Council commenced their grants to Normal Schools, by recommending £10,000 to be given in equal proportions to the National Society and the British and Foreign School Society, towards the erection of Normal Schools. The total amount of grants for Training Colleges to the National Society, numerous Church of England Training Colleges, and similar institutions connected with the Wesleyan Methodists, Roman Catholics, Established and Free Churches of Scotland, and Scotch Episcopal Church, between 1839 and 1857 inclusive, has risen to £330,300, whilst the total amount of grants for the Training College of the British and Foreign School Society, during the same period, is only £16,700, or about one-twentieth part of the whole sum, £347,000, granted to Training Colleges, by the Committee of Council.

MEMORIALS

RELATING TO ACADEMICAL IMPROVEMENT.

1. *Memorial in favour of an Inquiry into the Universities of Oxford and Cambridge ; presented in* 1848.

To the Right Honourable LORD JOHN RUSSELL, M.P., First Lord of the Treasury, etc. etc.

The Memorial of the undersigned Graduates and former Members of the Universities of Oxford and Cambridge with some of the Fellows of the Royal Society,

Showeth,—That the present system of the ancient English Universities has not advanced, and is not calculated to advance, the interests of religious and useful learning to an extent commensurate with the great resources and high position of those Bodies.

That the constitution of the Universities of Oxford and Cambridge and of the Colleges (now inseparably connected with their academical system) is such as in a great measure to preclude them from introducing those changes which are necessary for increasing their usefulness and efficacy.

That under these circumstances, believing that the aid of the Crown is the only available remedy for the above-mentioned defects, your Memorialists pray that your Lordship will advise her Majesty to issue her Royal Commission of Inquiry into the best methods of securing the improvement of the Universities of Oxford and Cambridge.

N. W. Senior, M.A., Magd. Coll., Oxford.
J. S. Henslow, (Rev.,) M.A., St. John's Coll., Camb.
B. Powell, (Rev.,) F.R.S., M.A., Oriel Coll., Oxford.
B. Price, M.A., Worcester Coll., Oxford.
T. J. Phillips, M.A., late Fellow of Trin. Coll., Cambridge.
James Heywood, M.P., F.R.S., Trin. Coll., Cambridge.
Edmund Head,(Bart.,)M.A., late Fell. Mert. Coll.,Oxford.
T. J. Agar Robartes, M.P., B.A., Christ Church, Oxford.
Ph. Le Breton, (Rev.,) M.A., Exeter Coll., Oxford.
Nugent, (Lord,) M.P., Brasenose Coll., Oxford.
Charles Lyell, F.R.S., M.A., Exeter Coll., Oxford.
Harry Verney, (Bart.,) M.P., Downing Coll., Cambridge.
P. J. Locke King, (Hon.,) M.P., M.A., Trin. Coll., Camb.
H. R. Yorke, M.P., Christ's Coll., Cambridge.
Joseph Kay, B.A., Trin. Coll., Cambridge.
E. F. Percival, M.A., Brasenose Coll., Oxford.
E. Horsman, M.P., Trin. Coll., Cambridge.
Erasmus Darwin, M.B., Christ's Coll., Cambridge.
Charles Darwin, M.A., Christ's Coll., Cambridge.
H. Wedgwood, M.A., late Fellow of Christ's Coll., Camb.
Thomas H. Farrer, B.A., Balliol Coll., Oxford.
W. P. Wood, M.P., M.A., late Fellow of Trin. Coll., Camb.
W. Ewart, M.P., B.A., Christ Church, Oxford.
F. W. Newman, B.A., late Fellow of Balliol Coll., Oxford.
A. De Morgan, Trin. Coll., Cambridge.
T. Hewitt Key, Trin. Coll., Cambridge.
E. P. Bouverie,(Hon.,) M.P., M.A.,Trin.Coll.,Cambridge.
J. Bonham Carter, M.P., Trin. Coll., Cambridge.
G. R. Philips, (Bart.,) M.P., M.A., Trin. Coll., Cambridge.
Duncan, (Viscount,) M.P., M.A., Trin. Coll., Cambridge.
W. Duckworth, Trin. Coll., Cambridge.
E. H. Bunbury, M.P., M.A., late Fell. Trin. Coll., Camb.
D. T. Ansted, M.A., F.R.S., Fellow of Jesus Coll., Camb.
J. Moultrie, (Rev.,) M.A., Trin. Coll., Cambridge.

Charles Anstey, (Rev.,) M.A., Trin. Coll., Oxford.
H. J. Buckall, (Rev.,) M.A., Queen's Coll., Oxford.
G. L. Cotton, (Rev.,) M.A., late Fellow Trin. Coll., Camb.
R. Congreve, (Rev.,) M.A., Fellow Wadham Coll., Oxford.
C. T. Arnold, (Rev.,) M.A., Balliol Coll., Oxford. .
J. C. Shairp, B.A., Balliol College, Oxford.
Granville Bradley, M.A., Fellow of Univer. Coll., Oxford.
John E. Blunt, M.A., Trin. Coll., Cambridge.
F. Dumergue, M.A., Trin. Coll., Cambridge.
John F. Hargrave, M.A., Trin. Coll., Cambridge.
Robt. R. A. Hawkins, M.A., Trin. Coll., Cambridge.
John Romilly, M.P., M.A., Trin. Coll., Cambridge.
W. M. Thackeray, Trin. Coll., Cambridge.
Ebrington, (Viscount,) M.P., Trin. Coll., Cambridge.
Richard Owen, F.R.S., M.D., D.C.L., Edinburgh.
E. H. Maltby, M.A., Trin. Coll., Cambridge.
Robert Sayer, M.A., Trin. Coll., Cambridge.
Charles Beavan, Caius Coll., Cambridge.
J. H. Law, M.A., Fellow of King's Coll., Cambridge.
G. M. Giffard, B.C.L., Fellow of New Coll., Oxford.
Thomas E. Headlam, M.P., M.A., Trin. Coll., Cambridge
Melgund, (Viscount,) M.P., M.A., Trin. Coll., Cambridge
James Haylock, M.A., Exeter Coll., Oxford.
H. Highton, (Rev.,) M.A., late Fell. Queen's Coll., Oxford
T. C. Evans, (Rev.,) M.A., St. John's Coll., Cambridge.
G. R. Porter, F.R.S.
T. Milner Gibson, (Rt. Hon.,) M.P., Trin. Coll., Camb.
J. Carrick Moore, Queen's Coll., Cambridge.
G. Poulett Scrope, M.P., St. John's Coll., Cambridge.
Charles Babbage, F.R.S., M.A., Trin. Coll., Cambridge.
W. F. Chambers, M.D., Trin. Coll., Cambridge.
John Crawford, F.R.S.
E. C. Tufnell, B.A., Balliol Coll., Oxford.
E. S. Creasy, M.A., late Fellow of King's Coll., Camb.
Oliver Arthur Heywood, M.A., Christ's Coll., Cambridge
Edward King Tenison, M.P., M.A., Trin. Coll., Cambridge
Edward Ryan, Rt. Hon., (Knt.,) M.A., Trin. Coll., Camb

Thomas B. Birch, (Bart.,) M.P., M.A., Jesus Coll., Camb.
William Ayrton, F.R.S., F.S.A.
Martin Thackeray, M.A., formerly King's Coll., Camb.
A. W. Kinglake, M.A., Trin. Coll., Cambridge.
Edward Romilly, B.C.L., Trin. Hall, Cambridge.
W. Lloyd Birkbeck, M.A., late Felllow of Trin. Coll., Camb.
W. Spence, F.R.S., President Entomological Soc., Lond.
J. W. Mylne, M.A., Balliol Coll., Oxford.
Edward Ellice, Jun., M.P., M.A., Trin. Coll., Cambridge
William Marshall, M.P., M.A., St. John's Coll., Camb.
C. P. Grenfell, M.P., Christ Church, Oxford.
Chichester Fortescue, M.P., M.A., Christ Church, Oxford.
George Cornewall Lewis, M.P., M.A., Christ Church, Oxf.
W. G. Hayter, M.P., B.A., Trin. Coll., Oxford.
R. B. Smithies, (Rev.,) B.A., Emmanuel Coll., Camb.
E. J. Rose, (Rev.,) Trin. Coll., Cambridge.
J. B. Blackett, M.A., late Fellow of Merton Coll., Oxford.
L. C. H. Hansard, B.A., University Coll., Oxford.
J. S. Hodgson, (Rev.,) M.A., Caius Coll., Cambridge.
Joseph Prendergast, D.D., Queen's Coll., Cambridge.
John Buckle, M.A., Trin. Coll., Cambridge.
Gray Skipwith, (Bart.,) M.A., Trin. Coll., Cambridge.
T. E. Dicey, M.A., Trin. Coll., Cambridge.
A. H. Clough, M.A., Fell. and late Tutor Oriel Coll., Oxf.
M. Arnold, B.A., Fellow of Oriel Coll., Oxford.
R. G. Latham, M.D., Fellow of King's Coll., Cambridge.
William Molesworth, (Bart.,) M.P., F.R.S.
Henry B. Faulkner, (Rev.,) M.A., Brasenose Coll., Oxford.
B. Hall, (Bart.,) M.P., Christ Church, Oxford.
M. T. Baines, M.P., Trin. Coll., Cambridge.
James Clark, (Bart.,) M.D., F.R.S. (Physician to Queen).
John Kenyon, St. Peter's Coll., Cambridge.
John Forbes, M.D., F.R.S.
L. Horner, F.R.S.
Edward Forbes, F.R.S., King's Coll., London.
W. H. Smyth, (Capt. R.N., Hon. D.C.L., Oxford,) F.R.S.
Charles Wheatstone, F.R.S., King's Coll., London.

Robert Brown, D.C.L., Oxford; LL.D., Edinburgh; F.R.S.
Thomas Graham, F.R.S., University Coll., London.
Eaton Hodgkinson, F.R.S., University Coll., London.
R. Pashley, M.A., late Fellow of Trin. Coll., Cambridge.
Herman Merivale, M.A., late Fell. Balliol Coll., Oxford.
Henry Warburton, F.R.S., M.A., Trin. Coll., Cambridge.
Edward Strutt, (Rt. Hon.,) M.A., Trin. Coll., Cambridge.
E. Sabine, (Lieut.-Col.,) Foreign Sec. to Royal Society.
James Yates, F.R.S., M.A., Glasgow.
John P. Boileau, (Bart.,) F.R.S., Merton Coll., Oxford.
C. Eyres, (Rev.,) M.A., Fellow of Caius Coll., Cambridge.
Richard Denman, (Hon.,) M.A., Trin. Coll., Cambridge.
W. Charles Henry, F.R.S., M.D., Edinburgh.
T. Law Hodges, M.P., M.A., Emmanuel Coll., Camb.
A. Thurtell, (Rev.,) M.A., Fellow Caius Coll., Cambridge.
D. Maude, M.A., late Fellow of Caius Coll., Cambridge.
W. R. Crompton Stansfield, M.P., M.A., Jesus Coll., Camb.
W. Ord, M.P., M.A., Trin. Coll., Cambridge.
Hugh Edward Adair, M.P., M.A., St. John's Coll., Oxford.
William Hutt, M.P., M.A., Trin. Coll., Cambridge.
C. P. Villiers, (Hon.,) M.P., M.A., St. John's Coll., Camb.
Charles Towneley, M.P., F.R.S.
Peter Heywood, M.A., Christ's Coll., Cambridge.
W. A. Collins, M.A., late Fellow Christ's Coll., Camb.
Henry Allen Wedgwood, B.A., Jesus Coll., Cambridge.
Osmond de Beauvoir Priaulx, M.A., Catharine Hall, Camb.
Francis Wedgwood, Peterhouse, Cambridge.
Henry Wrightson, M.A., (Rev.,) Queen's Coll., Oxford.
T. B. Wrightson, B.A., Brasenose, Oxford.
John T. Graves, F.R.S., M.A., Oriel Coll., Oxford.
Mont. J. Cholmeley, (Bart.,) M.P., Magdalen Coll., Oxford.
J. Robley, M.A., Trin. Coll., Cambridge.
Laurence Sulivan, M.A., St. John's Coll., Cambridge.
W. R. Grove, M.A., F.R.S., Brasenose Coll., Oxford.
Richard Partridge, F.R.S.
W. Sharpey, M.D., F.R.S.
George Newport, F.R.S., F.L.S.

J. Forbes Royle, M.D., F.R.S.
H. T. De la Beche, (Sir,) F.R.S., President Geological Soc.
W. Allen Miller, M.D., F.R.S., King's Coll., London.
W. Darwin Fox, M.A., Christ's Coll., Cambridge.
T. B. Burcham, M.A., late Fellow of Trin. Coll., Camb.
Tom Taylor, M.A., Fellow of Trin. Coll., Cambridge.
E. H. Crawfurd, M.A., Trin. Coll., Cambridge.
J. R. Bulwer, M.A., Trin. Coll., Cambridge.
F. Solly Flood, M.A., Trin. Coll., Cambridge.
R. Trott Fisher, M.A., late Fell. Pembroke Coll., Camb.
Francis Offley Martin, M.A., late Fell. Caius Coll., Camb.
George B. Maule, M.A., late Student Christ Church, Oxf.
W. Hayward Cox, (Rev.,) M.A., late Fell. Queen's Coll.
J. Wilkinson, (Rev.,) M.A., Merton Coll., Oxford.
St. John Wells Lucas, (Rev.,) M.A., Downing Coll., Camb.
John P. Gassiot, F.R.S.
P. E. Crofts, (Rev.,) M.A., Queen's Coll., Cambridge.
John Barlow, (Rev.,) F.R.S., M.A., Trin. Coll., Camb.
John Scobell, (Rev.,) M.A., Balliol Coll., Oxford.
T. G. James, (Rev.,) M.A., Brasenose Coll., Oxford.
Edward James, M.A., Brasenose Coll., Oxford.
J. B. S. Bradfield, B.A., Jesus College, Cambridge.
Joseph Hume, M.P., F.R.S.
J. C. Blair Warren, (Rev.,) M.A., Sidney Sussex Coll. Cam.
John Charles Thorold, (Bart.,) Christ Church Oxford.
Robt. Heron, (Bart.,) St. John's Coll., Cambridge.
Rowland Alston, Christ's Coll., Cambridge.
Thos. Neville Abdy, M.P., B.A., St. John's Coll., Camb.
B. C. Brodie, B.A., Balliol Coll., Oxford.
H. T. Erskine, Balliol Coll., Oxford.
John Wickens, M.A., Balliol Coll., Oxford.
Henry Thring, M.A., Fellow of Magdalen Coll., Camb.
Arthur Hobhouse, M.A., Balliol Coll., Oxford.
Edward Vansittart Neale, M.A., Oriel Coll., Oxford.
Richard Bartlett, B.A., St. John's Coll., Cambridge.
Robert William Mackay, M.A., Brasenose Coll., Oxford.
Peter Mark Roget, M.D., Secretary of Royal Society.

George Denman, (Hon.,) M.A., Fellow Trin. Coll., Camb.
George Elliot, (Hon.,) M.A., Trin. Coll., Cambridge.
W. Michell, M.D., Emmanuel Coll., Cambridge.
W. Calverley Trevelyan, (Bart.,) M.A., Univer. Coll., Oxf.
David Brewster, (Knt.,) F.R.S., M.A., Edinb. & Camb.
Alexander Roselles Brown, M.D., Trin. Coll., Cambridge.
Peter Le Neve Foster, M.A., late Fell. Trin. Hall, Camb.
T. F. Lewis, Rt. Hon., (Bart.,) M.P., Christ Church, Oxf.
Ralph W. Grey, M.P., B.A., Trin. Coll., Cambridge.
Joseph Alfred Hardcastle, M.P., M.A., Trin. Coll., Camb.
Nassau John Senior, M.A., Christ Church, Oxford.
J. W. Lubbock, (Bart.,) F.R.S., M.A., Trin. Coll., Camb.
J. M. Kemble, M.A., Trin. Coll., Cambridge.
Woronzow Greig, F.R.S., M.A., Trin. Coll., Cambridge.
W. James Farrer, B.A., Balliol Coll., Oxford.
R. A. Ferguson, (Bart.,) M.P., M.A., Trin. Coll., Camb.
J. R. Eustace, Knt., (Col.,) M.A., St. Peter's Coll., Camb.
Ch. Delibere Jones, Jesus Coll., Oxford.
Charles J. Thrupp, M.A., Trin. Coll., Cambridge.
J. C. Conybeare, M.A., Downing College, Cambridge.
John Riley, M.A., Trin. Coll., Cambridge.
Francis Gisborne, B.A., St. Peter's Coll., Cambridge.
George Hibbert Deffell, M.A., Trin. Coll., Cambridge.
Francis Morse, (Rev.,) M.A., St. John's Coll., Cambridge.
George Chance, M.A., Trin. Coll., Cambridge.
James F. Hore, M.A., Trin. Coll., Cambridge.
Charles Langton, (Rev.,) M.A., Christ Church, Oxford.
George Baugh Allen, M.A., Trin. Coll., Cambridge.
C. Wentworth Dilke, LL.B., Trin. Hall, Cambridge.
F. I. Lace, B.C.L., University Coll., Oxford.
John Lee, LL.D., St. John Coll., Cambridge.
Joseph G. Cumming, M.A., F.G.S., Emmanl. Coll., Camb.
W. D. Christie, B.A., Trin. Coll., Cambridge.
William Weld, B.A., St. John's Coll., Oxford.
James White, (Rev.,) B.A., Pembroke Coll., Oxford.
N. Arnott, M.D., F.R.S.
Theodore Dury, (Rev.,) M.A., Pembroke Coll., Cambridge.

H. A. Aglionby, M.P., M.A., St. John's Coll., Cambridge.
Gordon Whitbread, M.A., Brasenose Coll., Oxford.
T. P. L. Willett, LL.B., late Fellow of Trin. Hall, Camb.
F. T. Serjeant, M.A., Corpus Christi Coll., Camb.
James B. Davidson, B.A., Trin. Coll., Cambridge.
Joseph Hardcastle, M.A., St. Peter's Coll., Cambridge.
Edward Oldfield, M.A., Fellow Worcester Coll., Oxford.
John L. Kennedy, B.A., Trin. Coll., Cambridge.
James Clay, M.P., B.A., Balliol Coll., Oxford.
John Parker, M.P., M.A., Brasenose Coll., Oxford.
Robert Perfect, M.P., M.A., Queen's Coll., Oxford.
H. Johnson, (Rev.,) M.A., Trin. Coll., Cambridge.
W. Scurfield Grey, M.A., St. John's Coll., Cambridge.
James Lea, M.A., Worcester Coll., Oxford.
W. S. Wilson, Queen's Coll., Cambridge.
T. Ivory, M.A., Balliol Coll., Oxford.
John Hamerton, B.A., Trin. Coll., Cambridge.
T. P. E. Thompson, M.A., Queen's Coll., Cambridge.
Charles Otter, M.A., late Fellow of Christ's Coll., Camb.
J. R. Marshman, M.A., Trin. Coll., Cambridge.

---

2. *Petition for an Enlarged System of Granting Degrees in the University of Cambridge; forwarded to the Vice-Chancellor of the University of Cambridge, in January*, 1854.

To the Vice-Chancellor, and the other Syndics appointed by the Senate of the University of Cambridge, to take into consideration such parts of the Letter addressed on the 12th December, 1853, to the Chancellor of the University, by her Majesty's Secretary of State for the Home Department, as relates to the University, and to make such remarks thereon as they may deem fit for the purpose of their being transmitted by the Vice-Chancellor to his Royal Highness.

>The Undersigned, who have been educated in the University of Cambridge, respectfully submit the following Petition :—

That your petitioners observe with pleasure the earnest hope of her Majesty's Government, as expressed in the recent Letter of her Majesty's Secretary of State for the Home Department, to H. R. H. the Chancellor of the University of Cambridge, that they may find on the part of the University, "such mature views, and such enlarged designs of improvement, as may satisfy the reasonable desires of the country."

That among the enlarged designs of academical improvement, requisite to satisfy the reasonable desires of the country, is the restoration of the ancient custom of degrees being granted by the University of Cambridge, solely as the rewards of merit.

That academical statutes directing religious tests to be subscribed on graduation, have hitherto prevented your petitioners from taking the degrees in the faculty of Arts, to which they are entitled by academical standing, and for which they became duly qualified by residence in their respective Colleges, and by success in the various examinations required at Cambridge for the degree of Bachelor of Arts.

That in 1772, the Senate of the University of Cambridge altered the religious test for the degree of Bachelor in the faculties of Arts, Law, and Medicine, by substituting a declaration of *bonâ fide* membership with the Church of England in place of the previous subscription to the three articles of the 36th canon, relating to the Royal Supremacy, the Book of Common Prayer, and the

Thirty-nine Articles,—and that a similar substitution is now recommended for higher degrees in Arts, Law, and Medicine.

That on comparing the number of the degrees of Bachelor of Arts, granted by the University of Cambridge, in the early part of the seventeenth century, with the number of students who successfully pass the examination for the B.A. degree at the present time, it appears that in the five years from 1624 to 1628 inclusive, there was an annual average of 285 B.A. degrees granted at Cambridge, and in the five years from 1844 to 1848 inclusive, there was an annual average of 332 students who successfully passed the B.A. degree examination, thus showing an increase of only one-sixth in the annual average of Bachelors of Arts, at Cambridge, in 220 years.

That in 1794, his late Majesty, King George the Third, was graciously pleased to grant and ordain, by a Royal Letter, that Roman Catholics should be admitted into Trinity College, Dublin, and should obtain degrees in the University of Dublin; which was followed by the admission of students of all religious denominations into Trinity College, Dublin, with the privilege of taking degrees, and of voting in the election of the members who are returned by the University of Dublin to Parliament.

That comparing, for five successive years, the numbers of students annually admitted, and the number who receive testimonials for Orders, in Trinity College, Dublin, and in thirteen Cambridge Colleges* preserving records

* The thirteen Cambridge Colleges which preserve records of the testimonials granted for Holy Orders, are, St. Peter's, Clare Hall, Pembroke, Caius, Trinity Hall, Corpus Christi, Queen's, Jesus, Christ's, Magdalen, Trinity, Sidney, and Downing. No record of testimonials is kept in King's, St. John's, and Emmanuel Colleges. See the returns presented to Parliament in 1850, from the Universities of Oxford, Cambridge, and Dublin.

of their College testimonials, it appears that between 1844 and 1849 inclusive, Trinity College, Dublin, has an annual average of 353 students admitted, and 111 testimonials granted for Orders; whilst thirteen Cambridge Colleges preserving records of their testimonials, have an annual average of 379 students admitted, and 184 testimonials for Orders. Of these Cambridge Colleges, the largest and the most open has an annual average of 153 students admitted, and 56 testimonials for Orders, showing that about two-thirds of its students are intended for lay professions.

That in the Parliamentary debates of 1834, on the removal of subscription tests in the Universities, the Earl of Derby remarked, that the Churchman and Dissenter, by early association, might form those habits of friendship which would soften the animosities which prevailed between the two parties; and Lord Holland, in protesting against the rejection of the Bill for the opening of the Universities, by the House of Lords, observed, that excellence in the learned and liberal professions of law and medicine in no degree depended upon religious belief, and that Providence had not annexed the avowal of any peculiar tenets in religious matters as the condition of obtaining human knowledge.

That the ancient statutable course of academical instruction in the faculties of Arts, Law, and Medicine, at Cambridge, was of a secular or general character; that the compulsory attendance at the Sacrament of the Church of England is no longer usual in any of the College Chapels at Cambridge, with respect to students who are not members of the Church Establishment, and that the final examination for the degree of Bachelor of Arts, with honours, is strictly mathematical and scientific.

That the opening of the University as a national institution, and the consideration of the terms on which this important measure of academical improvement should be carried into effect, are alluded to with approbation in the report of the Royal Commissioners on the University and Colleges of Cambridge.

That your petitioners earnestly request your Syndicate to take into consideration such an enlarged system of granting degrees, as may satisfy the reasonable claims of your petitioners, and may be carried into effect consistently with the maintenance of the dignity of the University.

> James Heywood, M.P., F.R.S., Senior Optime in 1833, of Trinity College, Cambridge.
>
> Henry A. Bright, 1852, of Trinity College, Cambridge.
>
> J. J. Sylvester, Second Wrangler in 1837, formerly of St. John's College, Cambridge, F.R.S.—("Who signs this, not from the motive of desiring a Degree for himself, but from that of wishing to see the University of Cambridge become truly a University for the people of England, as such.")
>
> W. B. Coltman, Thirteenth Wrangler, in 1851, of Trinity College, Cambridge.
>
> Arthur Cohen (1853), of Magdalen College, Cambridge.
>
> William Aldam, Jun., Fourth Wrangler in 1838, of Trinity College, Cambridge (formerly M.P. for Leeds). "I sign this, not as being now prevented from taking a Degree, being now a member of the Church of England, but so far as it prays that the University be open to Dissenters in the matter of taking Degrees." —W. A. Jun.

3. *Memorial in favour of the Free Admission of Students to Matriculation and Graduation in the Ancient Universities of Oxford and Cambridge, without the imposition of any Religious Test; presented on the 3rd March,* 1854.

To the Right Honourable LORD JOHN RUSSELL, M.P., etc. etc.

The Memorial of the undersigned Members of the House of Commons,

Showeth,—That your Memorialists are grateful to your Lordship for the advice which, as Prime Minister, you gave to her Majesty in 1850, for the appointment of Royal Commissioners to inquire into the state, discipline, studies, and revenues of the Universities and Colleges of Oxford and Cambridge; and they are glad to learn that the Reports of the University Commissioners have led to the preparation of Bills, which your Lordship intends shortly to place on the table of the House, for an alteration in the constitution of the ancient Universities, a modification of the rules regarding College fellowships, and an application of some portion of College property to the general purposes of each University.

Your Memorialists desire to call your Lordship's notice to the fact, that the ancient Universities have long been recognized as national institutions; and that the Royal Commissioners describe the Colleges connected therewith as having now become such.

Your Memorialists beg to remind your Lordship, that by the volume of the census on religious worship of 1851, the number of the members of the Church of England cannot be estimated to exceed 6,000,000,—the total population of England being 17,927,609; and it is hardly necessary to observe, that the above numbers cannot justify the exclusive enjoyment, by the members of that Church, of institutions designed for the benefit of the entire community.

In the opinion of your Memorialists, strict justice, sound policy, and the principles of religious liberty, would alike require the admission of any of her Majesty's subjects, duly qualified by intellectual attainments, to all the advantages of these venerable seats of learning, without the imposition of any religious test.

Your Memorialists, however, are compelled to remind your Lordship, that at Oxford a copy of the Thirty-nine Articles is inserted at the commencement of the matriculation-book, and that young students are thus compelled to subscribe their formal assent to a number of theological propositions, which they cannot have studied; and that further, this form of subscription excludes a large portion of her Majesty's subjects from the advantages of the collegiate education there given; while at Cambridge, though no obstacle is imposed to matriculation, none but members of the Church of England are admitted to degrees or fellowships.

Your Memorialists rejoice to observe that, among the suggestions of the Oxford Commissioners, the two following are submitted to your Lordship's consideration:—

1. The Royal Commissioners recommend the practice of using a selection of prayers in the College chapels at Oxford, rather than the whole morning and evening services of the Book of Common Prayer, as evidently more

suitable to the age and character of the students; and they remark, that "authority, if needed, may doubtless be obtained for such a deviation from the Act of Uniformity, as would permit a short form of prayer to be used in the College chapels."

2. The Oxford Commissioners express their conviction, that the imposition of subscription to the Thirty-nine Articles at matriculation, "in the manner in which it is now imposed in the University of Oxford, habituates the mind to give a careless assent to truths which it has never considered, and naturally leads to sophistry in the interpretation of solemn obligations;" and, they further notice, that the subscription to the three Articles of the thirty-sixth Canon at graduation in Oxford, is a form especially intended for the clergy of the Church of England at their ordination, and not for lay graduates.

And your Memorialists would further beg to call your Lordship's notice to the fact, that the Cambridge Commissioners advert to the admission of persons who are not members of the Church of England to degrees at that University, in Arts, Law, and Medicine, as a concession to public opinion, which is left by them to the effect of time, to the wisdom of the Legislature, and to the gracious consideration of her Majesty.

On these grounds, and encouraged by these indications of opinion, your Memorialists respectfully request your Lordship, that in any Bill which may be brought forward by her Majesty's Government during the present Session, regarding either of the Universities of Oxford or Cambridge, due provision, where required, may be made therein for the free admission of any of her Majesty's subjects duly qualified by intellectual attainments to matriculation and graduation at both these ancient Universities without the imposition of any religious test.

James Heywood.	William Clay.	Joseph Hume.
S. Morton Peto.	Edward Miall.	Joshua Walmsley.
Goderich.	John B. Blackett.	H. Gore Langton.
William Biggs.	S. Gregson.	P. J. Locke King.
Robert Milligan.	M. J. Fielden.	G. F. Muntz.
James Bell.	C. Howard.	Charles Hindley.
Walter Coffin.	John Cheetham.	William Scholefield.
William Fagan.	James Anderson.	J. Duff.
Joseph Crook.	Lawrence Heyworth	G. S. Duff.
Hastings Russell.	Edward Ellice.	Shelburne.
Thomas Thornely.	George Hadfield.	J. Townshend.
Lloyd V. Watkins.	T. Milner Gibson.	W. B. Wrightson.
G. Poulett Scrope.	George H. C. Byng.	F. W. Russell.
J. Macgregor.	James Kershaw.	B. W. Willcox.
Apsley Pellatt.	Edward Ellice, Jun.	David Morris.
James Pilkington.	Thos. E. Headlam.	Charles Geach.
W. Massey.	De Lacy Evans.	George Thompson.
George Duncan.	H. Rich.	John Esmonde.
William Brown.	Thomas Phinn.	J. M. Caulfeild.
W. J. Fox.	J. Villiers Shelley.	Joseph Ferguson.
Richard Cobden.	F. H. F. Berkeley.	J. Duke.
Thomas Barnes.	J. A. Roebuck.	Alexander Hastie.
George Moffatt.	Benjamin Oliveira.	A. Murray Dunlop.
George Carr Glyn.	George Strickland.	Charles Cowan.
R. Grosvenor.	John Greene.	William Hutt.
John Ball.	Ouseley Higgins.	John O'Connell.
J. Forster.	W. Marshall.	Thos. S. Duncombe.
E. H. J. Craufurd.	W. P. Murrough.	William P. Price.
Edward Ball.	Arthur Otway.	Thomas Challis.
J. B. Smith.	Daniel O'Connell.	Frank Crossley.
Charles Forster.	T. J. Agar Robartes.	J. D. Fitzgerald.
William Williams.	William Kirk.	John Brocklehurst.
Joseph Locke.	H. M. Clifford.	John M. Cobbett.
Monck.	Francis Scully.	H. R. F. Davie.
O. Ricardo.	C. S. Butler.	R. A. Thicknesse.
T. A. Mitchell.		

4. *Memorial presented in July*, 1858, *to the Cambridge University Commission, in favour of the free holding of Scholarships in the Colleges of Cambridge, and of the institution of an open College in the University of Cambridge, by the gradual concentration and amalgamation of the Endowments of some of the smaller Colleges.*

The Memorial of the undersigned Friend of Religious Liberty

Showeth,—That the Cambridge University Act of 1856 provides that "it shall not be necessary for any person, on obtaining any Exhibition, Scholarship, or other College Emolument, available for the assistance of an undergraduate student in his academical education, to make or subscribe any declaration of his religious opinion or belief, or to take any oath, any law or statute to the contrary notwithstanding."

Your Memorialist notices with pleasure that Scholarships are conferred without any religious test at Cambridge, and he prays your Honourable Board to revise the College rules, so as to render Scholarships in all cases available for the assistance of undergraduate students in their academical education; especially he requests the attention of your Honourable Board to the conscientious scruples of students who are not members of the Church of England, with respect to taking a part in the Church of England services of the College Chapels, or wearing a surplice, or being present at the ordinary or full services of the Church of England.

During the seventeenth century the College Chapel arrangements of the University of Cambridge attracted the attention of the Legislature, and on the 17th February, 1642–3, the House of Commons declared "that the statute made in the University of Cambridge, which imposeth the wearing of surplices upon all graduates and students, under several pains, and reinforced by the Canons made 1603, ought not to be pressed or imposed upon any student or graduate, it being against the law and the liberty of the subject. And it is therefore ordered, that it shall not, for time to come, be pressed or imposed upon any student or graduate whatsoever."

Your Memorialist is not aware that this resolution of the House of Commons has ever been rescinded; but in 1662, the Act of Uniformity directed that no form or order of common prayers should be openly used in any Chapel of any College at Oxford or Cambridge, or of the Colleges of Westminster, Winchester, or Eton, other than what was prescribed and appointed to be used in and by the Book of Common Prayer.

At the present day, grave inconveniences are felt from the length and sameness of the daily liturgical services in the College Chapels at Cambridge.

A member of your Honourable Board, the Dean of Ely, formerly one of the most successful and popular tutors of Trinity College, Cambridge, remarks on the attendance of students at College Chapels, that "those persons who have been most intimately concerned with the superintendence of young men at the University, will be best able to appreciate the painful measures which are not unfrequently necessary to secure regularity of attendance." The learned Dean adds, that "there is little doubt but that the substitution of a shorter Service would remedy many evils of a very embarrassing and distressing nature."

The Bishop of St. David's, at a time when he held the office of Assistant Tutor in Trinity College, observed, with reference to College Chapels at Cambridge, "that if one-half at least of our present daily congregations were replaced by an equal number of Dissenters, they would not have come with greater reluctance, nor pay less attention to the words of the service, nor be less edified or more delighted at its close."

A daily roll-call, carried into effect by the marking with a pin of the names of persons present at the College Chapel Service, has long been characteristic of the Colleges in the University of Cambridge; but it is not requisite that the forms of prayer should comprise the expression of dogmatic sentiments.

Short prayers which do not involve dogmatic formularies are daily read in Parliament, and no conscientious objection to them is expressed by members of different religious denominations, who have been present at the time of prayers.

Considerable advantage has been derived by the University of Cambridge from the amalgamation of three of the older and smaller Colleges in the formation of Trinity College, under the authority of King Henry VIII. and the Parliament of 1545.

Similar benefits may be anticipated from the creation of a national institution, by the amalgamation of some of the smaller foundations at Cambridge, and the gradual concentration of their endowments. The new College might be alike independent of the Act of Uniformity of 1662, and of the University statute of compulsory celibacy for College Fellows.

A census of the resident academical population at Cambridge, taken in May, 1841, which is probably nearly correct for the present time, shows that there are eight Colleges,—King's, Downing, Trinity Hall, Sidney, Clare Hall, Jesus, Pembroke, and Magdalene,—which only contain, on an average, twenty-seven undergraduates for each College, so that the number of resident students must be too limited in these institutions to induce first-rate men to remain in such Colleges as tutors.

Fresh arrangements appear to be requisite with respect to the smaller Colleges of Cambridge on another ground, as the proposed University Statutes direct that the most important officers of the University, the Examiners, shall be nominated by the Colleges in succession,—two Examiners by each College; and it occasionally happens, that in a small College there is a very insufficient number of graduates who are competent to fill these responsible offices.

Academical place and power are largely vested in the existing Colleges at Cambridge: the Colleges form in fact the constituent parts of the University; on all occasions of academical visitations they have been subject to the control of University Commissioners; regulations for the Colleges occupy a part of the Cambridge University code, which Whitgift prepared and Queen Elizabeth enforced in 1570, and which the Parliament has decided to repeal in 1860. Both severally and collectively the arrangements of the Colleges are now under your consideration. For the improvement of these important institutions, your Memorialist recommends to your Honourable Board that regulations should be framed under your sanction to ensure the free holding of College Scholarships at Cambridge, and that an open College should be instituted in that University, by the gradual concentration and amalgamation of the endowments of some of the smaller Colleges.

JAMES HEYWOOD, B.A.,
Trin. Coll. Cambridge.

The Act of Parliament of 1545, alluded to in this Memorial (p. 67), is printed at length in the folio editions of the statutes at large. It is there entitled, " A Bill for Colleges, Chantries, etc.," and was passed in the 37th Henry VIII. The beneficial effects of that Parliamentary enactment was experienced at Oxford, in the dissolution of the three foundations of Cardinal College, Peckwater Inn, and Canterbury College, and the union of their endowments in Christ Church; as well as at Cambridge, by the exercise of Parliamentary and Royal power in the formation of Trinity College from the united endowments of King's Hall, Michael House, and Physwick Hostel.

The most important provision of cap. 4, 37th Henry VIII. was to the following effect. King Henry VIII. obtained power by this Act of Parliament, which was passed near the close of his life, to appoint Royal Commissions, under his Great Seal, by virtue of a warrant signed with his Grace's own hand, to enter into all colleges and other similar institutions, as well as into all their houses, lands, and estates, and to "seise and take" any of them into the King's possession, "to have and to hold the same to the King's Highness and to his heirs and successors for ever." Trinity College was thus founded, by Parliamentary and Royal authority, in the last year of the reign of Henry VIII., and received its earliest code of statutes from the following Royal Commissioners, who were appointed, under his successor, King Edward VI., to amend the state of the University of Cambridge:—Thomas Goodrich, Bishop of Ely; Sir John Cheke, tutor to the youthful Sovereign; William Mey, Dean of St. Paul's; and Thomas Wendye, physician to the King.

Under the statutes of these Commissioners, a liberal system for the election of college officers was established, by which the appointment of the President or Master of Trinity College was reserved to the Crown, without any restrictions as to compulsory ordination, academical degree, or even University.

Power to elect the subordinate officers of the College was vested in the Fellows who were Masters of Arts, and who were directed to meet annually, after the audit of the College accounts, under the chairmanship of the President, to elect the Vice-President, the Deans, the Examiners, and the Chapel-Warden for the ensuing year. A similar form of election was ordained for the choice of the Preachers of the College, the Master and Examiners of the Hall, and the Examiners of Latin and Greek translations. The title of "Scholars" was, according to the same statutes, given to Bachelors of Arts intended to hold Fellowships, as well as to undergraduate scholars who were on the foundation.

In the case of Fellowships, compulsory ordination at the end of seven years from the degree of Master of Arts, was regarded by Bishop Goodrich and his colleagues on the Royal Commission, as an important condition of tenure. Their statutes direct that the Fellows of Trinity College "shall be free for seven years after they have taken the degree of Master of Arts; in the eighth year, any one shall be immediately expelled from the College who shall not have become either a Deacon or a Priest, according to the custom of the kingdom, unless he has been prevented from taking orders, either by old-age or by a public profession in the Schools, or by being the Master of the Hall, or by the studies of civil law and medicine, or by the office of the daily reading in the Bible. But he who has devoted himself to the studies of civil law and medicine, shall remain in the College for twelve years after having taken his Master's degree. In the thirteenth year, he shall be expelled, unless he shall have departed of his own accord."

Archbishop Parker, Sir William Cecil, and other Cambridge University Commissioners under Queen Elizabeth, repeated the above regulation of their predecessors in the following terms:—" The Fellows who are Masters of Arts, after they have completed seven years from taking that degree, shall be ordained Priests; and if they refuse, within three months after the complete expiration of the aforesaid number of years, they shall be for ever excluded from the College, the two who profess medicine and the civil law being excepted."

Compulsory ordination statutes, according to Professor Vaughan, of Oxford, have prevented "some laymen from devoting themselves to literary and scientific pursuits, who may have had a real call to such occupations, without feeling any such call to 'preach the gospel' as ordination presupposes." "Is it not," remarks the anonymous writer of a pamphlet against compulsory ordination, "a solemn mockery, that men should declare before God, that they take orders, by the call of Christ, and by the inward impulse of the Holy Ghost, for the promotion of God's glory and service, when it is visible that they do it to save a poor place in a college, without any other view, present or future, of doing God glory or religion service, or of helping themselves by that character?"

Among the reasons for the repeal of compulsory ordination statutes in colleges, which have been urged in the pamphlet just mentioned, the author ingeniously argues that the Act of Uniformity "which establishes the present form of ordination, does in effect most plainly require that men should enter into orders upon the impulse of the Holy Ghost, to promote God's glory, that is, with a view to do service to God's religion, and his Church, in accepting and executing the duties of their order in some ecclesiastical employment. And consequently the local Statutes of Colleges which require the taking of orders upon other considerations and views, that is, upon the prospect of saving a Fellowship, are repugnant to the Act of Uniformity, which establishes this form of ordination, and are in reason repealed by it."

The same earnest writer is of opinion, that the only service rendered by a compulsory ordination statute, is to arm the governors of colleges with the means of arbitrary power. "Those good men, in regard to the change of times, and to the different reason of things, find themselves obliged in conscience upon some occasions, and to some persons, to remit the execution of these statutes. But at other times or to other men they hold it to be the indispensable duty of their office to pay a strict obedience to the letter of their founder's statute, and to enforce it with great rigour, but never without crafty distinction. This loose dealing in the execution of these statutes, which is managed by some governors of colleges with the utmost dexterity and subtlety, to serve their own purposes either of profit or power, has in some cases been the occasion of gentlemen's entering upon studies with assurance of security in them, which they have been called upon to relinquish, under danger of expulsion, after they had made such progress, as to render it some difficulty to them, whether to lose their present means of subsistence, or to relinquish the benefit of so much labour and time. These are the things that create heats and animosities in colleges, and render those little societies unquiet and unfit for the true ends of them, either in the promotion of study or virtue; instead of honourable principles and designs, which it is of great concern that men's minds should be strongly tinctured with in their younger years, they learn tricks, and artifice, and mean compliances to serve unworthy purposes."

Of the sixty Fellows of Trinity College, Cambridge, two only, by Archbishop Parker's statutes, are allowed to be permanently Lay Fellows, one of whom is permitted to study civil law, and the other, medicine, according to the judgment of the Master of the College. A similar arbitrary power of allowing a small number of laymen to retain their fellowships, is vested in the Provóst of Trinity College, Dublin. The late Archbishop of Dublin, Dr. Magee, was in early life a fellow of Trinity College, Dublin, and at a contest for the representation of the University of Dublin in Parliament, he declined to vote for the son of the Provost, who was a candidate. Mr. Magee was especially qualified by his reasoning talents, for distinction at the Bar, and on applying, after the election, to the Provost for permission to become a Lay Fellow, he was at once met by the polite refusal, " I cannot think, Mr. Magee, of depriving the Church of so great an ornament as you will be." The previous independent conduct of the Fellow had neither been forgotten or forgiven.

An oath is still retained on the statute-book of Trinity

College, Cambridge, for newly elected Fellows, in which a young man who had, perhaps, already entered on legal studies in the Metropolis, swears, as a Fellow of the College, that he "will make theology the end of his studies, and that when the time prescribed in the college statutes shall arrive, he will either take holy orders, or quit the college." Such an oath, under existing circumstances, cannot be defended, and that portion of the Fellowship oath is proposed by the Cambridge Parliamentary Commissioners to be omitted.

The Commissioners of the Cambridge Act have given much attention to the arrangement of suitable conditions for the tenure of College Fellowships, in place of compulsory ordination and compulsory celibacy, and they have judiciously suggested the term of ten years, after the M.A. degree, as under ordinary circumstances sufficient for the holding of this academical emolument; accompanied by the following regulations :—

"*Of the Conditions of Tenure of Fellowships.*

"Every Fellow hereafter elected shall vacate his Fellowship (whether in Holy Orders or not) at the end of ten years after attaining the full standing of Master of Arts, except in the following cases, namely :—

"First. Every Fellow who shall, at the expiration of such period of ten years, be actually holding any Professorship or Public Lectureship in the University, or the office of Public Orator, Librarian, or Registrar in the same, shall be allowed to retain his Fellowship so long as he holds such Professorship or public Lectureship, or such office in the University, but no longer; unless he shall be further empowered to retain it under the provisions hereinafter contained.

"Secondly. Every Fellow who shall, at the expiration of such period of ten years, be actually holding the office of Tutor, or Assistant Tutor, or Bursar in the College, and shall have actually held such office or any of such offices for the space of at least *two* years before the expiration of such period, shall be allowed to retain his Fellowship so long as he shall continue to hold such office, or any one of such offices, but no longer, unless he shall be further empowered to retain it under the provisions hereinafter contained.

"Thirdly. Every Fellow who shall have actually discharged, during the space of ten years, the duties of Tutor, Assistant Tutor, Lecturer, or Bursar, or of any one of such offices, or of a Professor or Public Lecturer in the University, shall be at liberty to retain his Fellowship thenceforward, whether resident or not, unless he shall vacate the same under the other provisions of these Statutes.

"Fourthly. Every Fellow not included in any of the above classes may be permitted by a special vote of two-thirds of the Master and *sixteen* Senior Fellows of the College, and with the sanction of the Visitor, to retain his Fellowship on account of his literary or scientific reputation or labours: provided that not more than *four* Fellows of the College be allowed to enjoy this privilege at the same time. Such Fellows to forfeit the privilege so conferred on them if they cease to be resident in College.

"Every Fellow hereafter elected shall vacate his Fellowship upon marriage, except in the following cases, namely:—

"1st. If he holds any University Professorship or Public Lectureship or one of the three offices in the University above specified.

"2ndly. If he be one of the three Tutors of the College, (or, if there be more than three, one of the three who have longest held that office in the College,) and has discharged the duties of Tutor or Assistant Tutor in the College for the space of not less than ten years.

"Any Fellow who shall have served the University or the College for a period of not less than *twenty* years in one of the offices of Professor, Public Lecturer, or Tutor, may, by a vote of not less than two-thirds of the Master and sixteen Senior Fellows, and, with the sanction of the Visitor, be allowed to retain his Fellowship after ceasing to hold such office, even though married, as a mark of distinction in consideration of eminent services rendered to the College or University; but the number of Fellows so retaining their Fellowships in virtue of this Statute shall never exceed *four* at one time.

"No married Fellow shall in any case reside in College."

---

5. *Memorial to the Cambridge University Commissioners; presented in* 1857, *in favour of changes in the present conditions of the tenure of Fellowships, relating especially to the condition of compulsory Celibacy.*

GENTLEMEN,

We, the undersigned Graduates of the University of Cambridge, beg leave respectfully to address you upon the subject of the compulsory celibacy of Fellows of Colleges.

The time is approaching when you, in conjunction with the governing Bodies of the several Colleges, will be called upon to carry the Cambridge University Act into effect.

Among the many questions which will be submitted to you for deliberation and decision, we feel that none is more important in all its bearings, whether academical or social, than that affecting the restriction upon marriage, to which the tenure of Fellowships is now subject.

We therefore venture to solicit your earnest consideration of the subject, and to express the hope, that you will give your sanction to such changes in the present "conditions of the tenure of Fellowships," as are calculated to augment the influence and extend the utility of the Colleges and University of Cambridge.

We have the honour to be, Gentlemen,
Your obedient Servants,

Ashby, Samuel, (Rev.,) M.A., Fellow of Pembroke Coll., and Vicar of Saxthorpe and Corpusty, Norfolk :—B.A. 1835; M.A. 1838.

Barrett, Richard Arthur Francis, (Rev.,) B.D., Senior Fellow of King's College :—B.A. 1835; B.D. 1850.

Budd, Francis Nonus, M.A., Senior Fellow of Gonville, and Caius College :—B.A. 1846; M.A. 1849.

Brodribb, William Jackson, M.A., Fellow of St. John's College :—B.A. 1852; M.A. 1855.

Berry, Robert, M.A., Fellow of Trinity College :—B.A. 1848; M.A. 1851.

Bell, John, (Rev.,) M.A., Fellow of Clare College, Assistant Classical Master in King Edward's School, Birmingham :—B.A. 1850; M.A. 1853.

Besant, William Henry, M.A., Fellow and Assistant Tutor of St. John's College :—B.A. 1850; M.A. 1853.

Booth, Charles, M.A., Fellow of King's College :—B.A. 1853; M.A. 1856.

Brown, William Henry, (Rev.,) B.A., Fellow of Gonville and Caius College, and Curate of Bradsby, Yorkshire: —B.A. 1854.

Callendar, Hugh, (Rev.,) M.A., Fellow and Tutor of Magdalene College :—B.A. 1851 ; M.A. 1854.

Clayton, Charles, (Rev.,) M.A., Senior Fellow and Tutor of Gonville and Caius College; Examining Chaplain to the Lord Bishop of Ripon :—B.A. 1836; M.A. 1839.

Crompton, Charles, B.A., Fellow of Trinity College :— B.A. 1855.

Davies, John Llewelyn, (Rev.,) M.A., Fellow of Trinity College. Rector of Christ's Church, Marylebone, London :—B.A. 1848; M.A. 1851.

Drosier, William Henry, M.D., Senior Fellow of Gonville and Caius College :—B.A. 1839; M.D. 1847.

Droop, Henry Richmond, M.A., Fellow of Trinity College :—B.A. 1854; M.A. 1857.

Drury, Benjamin Heath, (Rev.,) M.A., Fellow of Gonville and Caius College, one of the Masters at Harrow School :—B.A. 1840; M.A. 1843.

Dusautoy, Francis Peter, (Rev.,) M.A., Fellow of Clare College :—B.A. 1851 ; M.A. 1854.

Fawcett, Henry, B.A., Fellow of Trinity Hall :—B.A. 1856.

Hanson, Stephen, M.A., Fellow and Senior Dean of Gonville and Caius College :—B.A. 1848 ; M.A. 1851.

Hayward, Robert Baldwin, M.A., Fellow of St. John's College, and Professor of Natural Philosophy in the University of Durham :—B.A. 1850; M.A. 1853.

Hue, Corbet, M.A., Fellow of Gonville and Caius College: —B.A. 1840; M.A. 1843.

Johnson, William John, M.A., Fellow of Gonville and Caius College :—B.A. 1836; M.A. 1839.

Liveing, George Downing, M.A., Fellow of St. John's College :—B.A. 1850; M.A. 1853.

Long, Andrew, M.A., Senior Fellow of King's College :—
B.A. 1836; M.A. 1839.
Maxwell, James Clerk, M.A., Fellow of Trinity College; Professor of Natural Philosophy, Mareschal College, Aberdeen :—B.A. 1854; M.A. 1857.
Porter, James, M.A., Fellow and Senior Dean of St. Peter's College:—B.A. 1851; M.A. 1854.
Phear, John Budd, M.A., Fellow (late Assistant Tutor) of Clare College; 7, Fig-tree Court, Temple, London: —B.A. 1847; M.A. 1850.
Phear, Samuel George, (Rev.,) M.A., Fellow of Emmanuel College :—B.A. 1852; M.A. 1855.
Porter, William Archer, M.A., Fellow (late Tutor) of St. Peter's College :—B.A. 1849; M.A. 1852.
Roberts, John, M.A., Fellow of Magdalene College :—B.A. 1847; M.A. 1850.
Roby, Henry John, M.A., Fellow and Assistant Tutor of St. John's College :—B.A. 1853; M.A. 1856.
Stokes, George Gabriel, M.A., Fellow of Pembroke College, and Lucasian Professor of Mathematics, F.R.S., and Secretary of the Royal Society :—B.A. 1841; M.A. 1844.
Sykes, John, M.A., Fellow of Pembroke College; Privy Council Office, Whitehall, London :—B.A. 1841; M.A. 1844.
Simonds, Henry John, M.A., Fellow of King's College:—
B.A. 1851; M.A. 1854.
Sprague, Thomas Bond, M.A., Fellow of St. John's College :—B.A. 1853; M.A. 1856.
Todhunter, Isaac, M.A., Fellow of St. John's College :—
B.A. 1848; M.A. 1851.
Watson (the late), Richard, (Rev.,) M.A., Fellow and Tutor of Queen's College :—B.A. 1847; M.A. 1850.
Wolfe, Arthur, (Rev.,) M.A., Senior Fellow and Tutor of Clare College :—B.A. 1842; M.A. 1845.
Westlake, John, M.A., Fellow of Trinity College, Lincoln's Inn, London :—B.A. 1850; M.A. 1853.

Wiglesworth, Thomas Walker, M.A., Fellow of Gonville and Caius College:—B.A. 1848; M.A. 1851.
Ware, Henry, M.A., Fellow of Trinity College:—B.A. 1853; M.A. 1856.

Ackland, T. S., (Rev.,) M.A., late Fellow of Clare Coll.
Amps, John, (Rev.,) M.A., Emmanuel Coll.
Atkinson, Anthony, M.A., Clare Coll.
Adams, Samuel, (Rev.,) M.A., Sidney Sussex Coll.
Abbott, Jabez, B.A., Queen's Coll.
Atkinson, Henry, (Rev.,) B.A., Magdalene Coll.
Allison, Henry, (Rev.,) B.A., Clare Coll.
Allen, Ebenezer Brown, (Rev.,) B.A., Queen's Coll.
Atkinson, Frederick, (Rev.,) M.A., Trinity Coll.
Ayerst, William, (Rev.,) M.A., Gonville and Caius Coll.
Bosworth, Joseph, (Rev.,) D.D., Trinity Coll., F.R.S.
Brett, Francis Henry, (Rev.,) M.A., St. John's Coll.
Bromley, John William, (Rev.,) M.A., Gonv. & Caius Coll.
Baxter, Robert Dudley, M.A., Trinity Coll.
Baker, William Samuel, (Rev.,) M.A., Clare Coll.
Bromby, John Edward, (Rev.,) D.D., late Fellow of St. John's Coll.
Butterton, George Ash, (Rev.,) D.D., late Fellow of St. John's Coll.
Budd, George, M.D., late Senior Fellow of Gonville and Caius Coll., F.G.S.
Barclay, Andrew Whyte, M.D., Gonville and Caius Coll.
Blackburn, Hugh, M.A., late Fellow of Trinity Coll.
Bernard, Samuel Edward, (Rev.,) M.A., Magdalene Coll.
Ballance, Josiah, (Rev.,) M.A., Trinity Coll.
Bates, William, (Rev.,) B.D., late Fellow and Tutor of Christ's Coll.
Badger, Albert, (Rev.,) M.A., Trinity Coll.
Briant, Henry, (Rev.,) M.A., Queen's Coll.
Bowstead, Joseph, M.A., late Fellow of Pembroke Coll., one of H.M. Inspectors of Schools.
Buxton, Charles, M.A., Trin. Coll., M.P. for Newport.

Bridge, Stephen, (Rev.,) M.A., Queen's Coll.
Bally, William Ford, M.A., Downing Coll.
Bellingham, John George, (Rev.,) M.A., Trinity Coll.
Beecheno, James, (Rev.,) M.A., Queen's Coll.
Blackden, Charles, (Rev.,) M.A., Queen's Coll.
Booty, Miles Galloway, (Rev.,) M.A., Trinity Coll.
Blomefield, John, M.A., Trinity Coll.
Bryan, Guy, Sen., (Rev.,) M.A., late Fell. of St. Peter's Coll.
Bryan, Guy, Jun., (Rev.,) M.A., St. Peter's Coll.
Bryan, Wilmot Guy, (Rev.,) M.A., St. Peter's Coll.
Bryan, Reginald Guy, (Rev.,) M.A., Trinity Coll.
Bellman, Augustus Frederick, (Rev.,) B.A., St. Peter's Coll.
Burbidge, Thomas, B.A., Trinity Coll., Cambridge.
Birch, Charles, (Rev.,) B.A., St. John's Coll.
Bolton, James Jay, B.A., Corpus Christi Coll.
Braithwaite, Henry Thomas, B.A., Clare Coll.
Bampton, John Black, (Rev.,) B.A., Christ's Coll.
Bonnin, Thomas Scott, (Rev.,) B.A., Queen's Coll.
Bourn, John George, (Rev.,) M.A., Corpus Christi Coll.
Bull, Alfred Nicholas, (Rev.,) M.A., Sidney Sussex Coll.
Bruce, William, (Rev.,) M.A., Queen's Coll.
Bateman, Gregory, (Rev.,) M.A., Trinity Coll.
Bolton, William Jay, (Rev.,) M.A., Gonville and Caius Coll.
Boyce, William, (Rev.,) M.A., Trinity Coll., Cambridge.
Beresford, Gilbert, (Rev.,) B.D., late Fell. of St. John's Coll.
Boyer, Richard, (Rev.,) M.A., Trinity Coll.
Broughton, Henry Vivian, (Rev.,) M.A., St. Peter's Coll.
Banham, William, (Rev.,) B.A., Sidney Sussex Coll.
Carver, Alfred James, (Rev.,) M.A., late Fellow of Queen's College.
Cox, Homersham, M.A., Jesus Coll., Cambridge.
Clutton, Ralph, (Rev.,) B.D., late Fellow of Emmanuel Coll.
Croker, Joseph Morrison, (Rev.,) M.A., late Fellow of Gonville and Caius Coll.
Cotton, George Edward Lynch, (Rev.,) M.A., late Fellow of Trinity Coll.
Chapman, Matthew James, M.A., Trin. Coll., M.D. [Edin.]

G

Carrow, Harry, (Rev.,) M.A., Trinity Coll.
Childs, John Glynn, (Rev.,) B.A., Trinity Coll.
Cumming, Joseph George, (Rev.,) M.A., Emmanuel Coll.
Clarryvince, John, (Rev.,) M.A., Gonville and Caius Coll.
Crump, Frederick William, M.A., Gonville and Caius Coll., one of the Mathematical Masters of Eton Coll.
Cockerton, John, (Rev.,) M.A., St. John's Coll.
Crewe, Henry Robert, (Rev.,) M.A., Trinity Coll.
Crewe, Henry Harpur, (Rev.,) M.A., Trinity Coll.
Chatfield, Robert Money, (Rev.,) M.A., Trinity Coll.
Coombs, William, (Rev.,) M.A., St. John's Coll.
Carr, Edmund, (Rev.,) M.A., St. John's Coll.
Carus Wilson, William, (Rev.,) M.A., Trinity Coll.
Charlton, Robert, (Rev.,) B.A., Queen's Coll.
Casher, Charles Edward, B.A., Gonville and Caius Coll.
Childs, Thomas Cave, (Rev.,) M.A., Sidney Sussex Coll.
Chance, Henry, M.A., Trinity Coll.
Crowther, Henry Martyn, (Rev.,) M.A., St. John's Coll.
Daubeny, Henry Jones, (Rev.,) M.A., late Fellow of Jesus Coll.
Dalton, James Edward, (Rev.,) B.D., late Fellow of Queen's Coll.
Dodwell, George Branson, (Rev.,) M.A., of Clare Coll.
Dixon, William, (Rev.,) M.A., Trinity Coll.
Drake, Thomas Rompe, (Rev.,) M.A., Corpus Christi Coll.
Deck, Henry, (Rev.,) M.A., Corpus Christi Coll.
Dumergue, Walter Scott, (Rev.,) M.A., Corpus Christi Coll.
Dickson, Thomas Miller, (Rev.,) M.A., Clare Coll., Camb.
Dumergue, Francis, M.A., Trinity Coll., Cambridge.
Dearsly, William Henry, (Rev.,) B.A., Sidney Sussex Coll.
Dusautoy, William Stevens Oliver, (Rev.,) M.A., St. John's College.
Deck, John, (Rev.,) M.A., Christ's Coll.
Doria, Samuel, (Rev.,) M.A., St. John's Coll.
Douglas, Robert Archibald, M.A., St. John's Coll.
Dixon, John Jones, (Rev.,) B.A., Magdalene Coll.
Davies, Frederick, (Rev.,) B.A., Gonville and Caius Coll.

Downing, Josiah, (Rev.,) B.A., Corpus Christi Coll.
Dicey, Thomas Edward, M.A., Trinity Coll.
Day, Henry, (Rev.,) LL.B., Trinity Hall.
Dalton, Samuel Neale, (Rev.,) M.A., Gonv. and Caius Coll.
Dalton, Edward, M.A., Pembroke Coll.
Eyres, Charles, (Rev.,) M.A., late Fellow of Gonville and Caius Coll.
Earnshaw, Samuel, (Rev.,) M.A., St. John's Coll.
Elliott, Edward Bishop, (Rev.,) M.A., late Fellow of Trinity Coll.
English, John Francis Hawker, (Rev.,) LL.D., Christ's College.
Edwards, Edward Lloyd, M.A., St. John's Coll.
Elliott, Edward King, (Rev.,) M.A., Trinity Coll.
Evered, Charles William Henry, (Rev.,) B.A., Corpus Christi Coll.
Evans, Charles, (Rev.,) M.A., St. John's Coll.
Eaton, John, (Rev.,) M.A., Trinity Coll.
Edwards, John, (Rev.,) M.A., St. John's Coll.
Evelyn, Frederick Massey, M.A., Trinity Coll.
Fowler, Hugh, (Rev.,) M.A., late Fellow of Sidney Sussex College.
Fearon, Henry, (Rev.,) B.D., late Fellow of Emmanuel College.
Fuller, Frederick, M.A., late Fellow and Tutor of St. Peter's Coll.
Fuller, Henry William, M.D., Gonville and Caius Coll.
Finley, John, (Rev.,) M.A., Trinity Coll.
Franks, James Clarke, (Rev.,) B.D., late Chaplain of Trinity Coll.
Finch, Matthew Isaac, (Rev.,) M.A., St. Catharine's Coll.
Fowke, William Lyme, (Rev.,) B.A., Queen's Coll.
Furnivall, Frederick James, M.A., Trinity Hall.
Fisher, Charles John, (Rev.,) M.A., Jesus Coll.
Fisher, William, (Rev.,) M.A., Gonville and Caius Coll.
Grant, Alexander Ronald, (Rev.,) M.A., late Fellow of Trinity Coll., H.M. Assistant-Inspector of Schools.

Gifford, Edwin Hamilton, (Rev.,) M.A., late Fellow of St. John's Coll.
Gedge, Sidney, (Rev.,) M.A., late Fellow of St. Catharine's Coll.
Griffith, John, (Rev.,) M.A., St. John's Coll.
Gaskin, Thomas, (Rev.,) M.A., late Fellow and Tutor of Jesus Coll., F.R.S.
Gwyther, Henry, (Rev.,) M.A., Trinity Coll.
Gurney, Thomas, (Rev.,) M.A., St. John's Coll.
Gibbins, Henry Thomas, (Rev.,) M.A., late Chaplain of Trinity Coll.
Greaves, Talbot Aden Ley, (Rev.,) M.A., St. John's Coll.
Gibbon, William Wynter, (Rev.,) M.A., Christ's Coll.
Gibson, Christopher Mends, (Rev.,) B.A., Jesus Coll.
Gowring, John William, (Rev.,) B.A., Trinity Coll.
Grignon, Robert Scarlett, (Rev.,) B.A., Trinity Coll.
Gibbs, Michael, (Rev.,) M.A., late Fellow of Gonville and Caius Coll.
Goodeve, Thomas Minchin, M.A., St. John's Coll.
Gall, James, (Rev.,) B.A., Gonville and Caius Coll.
Griffith, George Sandham, (Rev.,) M.A., Clare Coll.
Horner, Joseph, (Rev.,) M.A., late Fellow of Clare Coll.
Hildyard, James, (Rev.,) B.D., late Fellow and Tutor of Christ's Coll.
Hutchinson, Christopher Blick, (Rev.,) M.A., late Fellow of St. John's Coll.
Holmes, Timothy, M.A., Pembroke Coll.
Hyde, John Thomas, M.A., Emmanuel Coll.
Hobson, Alfred William, (Rev.,) M.A., of St. John's Coll.
Hulbert, Charles Augustus, (Rev.,) M.A., Sidney Sussex College.
Haddon, Thomas Cornfield, (Rev.,) LL.B., St. John's Coll.
Haworth, Richard, (Rev.,) M.A., Queen's Coll.
Hedgeland, John White, (Rev.,) M.A., Emmanuel Coll.
Heywood, James, B.A., Trinity Coll., (late M.P. for North Lancashire.)
Hoskin, Peter Charles Mellish, (Rev.,) M.A., Jesus Coll.

Hebert, Charles, (Rev.,) M.A., Trinity Coll.
Hutchins, Richard Masters, (Rev.,) M.A., Trinity Coll.
Harper, Robert, M.A., Corpus Christi Coll.
Head, George, (Rev.,) M.A., Trinity Coll.
Harris, James, (Rev.,) M.A., St. Catharine Coll.
Harris, Robert, (Rev.,) M.A., Trinity Coll. *
Holford, George, B.A., Emmanuel Coll.
Hogg, John Roughton, (Rev.,) M.A., Christ's Coll.
Hill, John Smith, (Rev.,) M.A., Gonville and Caius Coll.
Humphry, George Murray, M.B., Downing Coll.
Harriss, Joseph, (Rev.,) M.A., Pembroke Coll.
Henslow, John Stevens, (Rev.,) M.A., St. John's Coll.
Howes, Charles, (Rev.,) M.A., late Fellow of Clare Coll.
Hewett, John William, (Rev.,) M.A., Trinity Coll.
Hill, John Smith, (Rev.,) M.A., Gonville and Caius Coll.
Hamilton, Robert, M.A., Trinity Coll.
Iliff, Frederick, (Rev.,) D.D., Trinity Coll.
Isaacson, Stuteville William, (Rev.,) M.A., Sidney Sussex College.
Ingram, Rowland, (Rev.,) M.A., Trinity Coll.
Jex-Blake, Charles Thomas, (Rev.,) M.A., Jesus Coll.
Jones, William Taylor, (Rev.,) M.A., Queen's Coll.
Johnson, Frederick, (Rev.,) M.A., St. Catharine's Coll.
Jackson, Albert Francis, M.A., Gonville and Caius Coll.
Jones, Charles William, (Rev.,) M.A., Gonville and Caius College.
Kelland, Philip, (Rev.,) M.A., late Fellow and Tutor of Queen's Coll.
Kearney, John Batchelor, (Rev.,) M.A., St. John's Coll.
King, John, (Rev.,) M.A., Queen's Coll.
Kemp, Henry William, (Rev.,) B.A., Corpus Christi Coll.
Knight, William, (Rev.,) M.A., St. Catharine's Coll.
Kirwan, Edward Dominic Galf. Martin, (Rev.,) M.A., late Fellow of King's Coll.
Killick, Richard Henry, (Rev.,) M.A., Queen's Coll.
Kelk, Theophilus Henry Hastings, B.A., Jesus Coll.
Kingston, Edward, (Rev.,) M.A., Gonville and Caius Coll.
Loftus, Lord Adam, (Rev.), M.A., Trinity College.

Lushington, Edmund Law, M.A., late Fellow of Trinity Coll., Cambridge.
Locock, Charles Brodie, M.A., Trinity College.
Lestourgeon, Charles, M.A., Trinity College.
Langshaw, Thomas Wall, (Rev.,) B.A., St. John's College.
Largé, W. J. Agg, (Rev.,) B.A., Gonville and Caius Coll.
Lewis, James, M.A., Christ's College.
Lewis, W. S., (Rev.,) M.A., late Chaplain of Trin. Coll.
Levingston, Charles, (Rev.,) M.A., St. John's College.
Luckock, Thomas Gilbert, (Rev.,) B.A., St. John's Coll.
Lloyd, Julius, M.A., Trinity College.
Leathes, Frederic, (Rev.,) B.A., Emmanuel College.
Litchfield, Richard Buckley, M.A., Trinity College.
Lloyd, Albany Rossendale, (Rev.,) B.A., Trinity College.
Lushington, Vernon, B.A., Trinity College.
Lindsay, James, (Rev.,) M.A., Trinity College.
Michell, B., (Rev.,) B.D., late Fellow of Emmanuel Coll.
Martineau, A., (Rev.,) M.A., late Fellow of Trin. Coll.
Mather, Frederick Vaughan, (Rev.,) M.A., Trinity Coll.
MacMichael, John Fisher, (Rev.,) B.A., Trinity Coll.
Mathias, George, (Rev.,) M.A., St. John's College.
Montague, H., (Rev.,) M.A., St. Catharine's College.
Money, James Drummond, (Rev.,) B.A., Trinity College.
Meggison, Septimus Stanley, (Rev.,) B.A., Trin. Coll.
Meade-King, W. T. P., (Rev.,) M.A., Trinity College.
Morewood, Robert, (Rev.,) M.A., Queen's College.
Margetts, Henry, (Rev.,) M.A., St. John's College.
Maule, Henry Augustus, M.A., St. Peter's College.
Molyneux, Henry George, (Rev.,) B.A., Magdalene Coll.
Mothersole, William Frederick, B.A., Trinity College.
Moncrieff, William Scott, (Rev.,) M.A., Trinity College.
Mayor, John Eyton Bickersteth, (Rev.,) M.A., Fellow and Assistant Tutor of St. John's College.
Merriman, S. W. J., M.D., Gonville and Caius College.
Montagu, E. W., (Rev.,) M.A., Gonville and Caius Coll.
Marsh, Theodore Henry, (Rev.,) M.A., Pembroke Coll.
Nightingale, Thomas, (Rev.,) M.A., St. John's College.
Nixson, Joseph Mayer, B.A., Clare College.

Noel, Leland, Hon. and Rev., M.A., Trinity College.
Norman, John Manship, M.A., Trinity College.
Owen, Joseph Butterworth, (Rev.,) M.A., St. John's Coll.
Pullen, Joseph, (Rev.,) B.D., late Fellow and Tutor of Corpus Christi College.
Parish, W. S., (Rev.,) M.A., late Fellow of St. Peter's Coll.
Pryme, George, M.A., late Fellow of Trinity College.
Pine, Sir Benjamin Chilly Campbell, Knt., M.A., Trinity College, Governor and Commander-in-Chief and Vice-Admiral of the Gold Coast, Western Africa.
Prendergast, Joseph, (Rev.,) D.D., Queen's College.
Pitman, Henry Alfred, M.D., Trinity College.
Peill, John Newton, (Rev.,) B.D., late Fellow and Tutor of Queen's College.
Phear, John, (Rev.,) M.A., late Fellow and Tutor of Pembroke College.
Phear, Henry Carlyon, M.A., late Fellow of Gonville and Caius College.
Potts, Robert, M.A., Trinity College, Cambridge.
Pearson, John, (Rev.,) M.A., Trinity College.
Parkin, John, (Rev.,) M.A., Queen's College.
Price, James, M.A., St. John's College.
Price, Thomas Jones, B.A., St. John's College.
Pratt, Charles, Junior, (Rev.,) B.A., Trinity College.
Penny, Samuel Stansfield, (Rev.,) M.A., St. John's Coll.
Pilling, C. R., (Rev.,) B.A., Gonville and Caius College.
Paske, Theophilus John, (Rev.,) B.A., Clare College.
Pashley, Robert, Q.C., M.A., late Fellow of Trinity College, Cambridge.
Punnett, John, (Rev.,) M.A., late Fellow of Clare Coll.
Penruddocke, J. H., (Rev.,) M.A., Clare College.
Quick, Charles Thomas, (Rev.,) M.A., St. John's Coll.
Robinson, Hastings, (Rev.,) D.D., late Fellow of St. John's College.
Relph, J., (Rev.,) M.A., late Fellow of St. Peter's Coll.
Rackham, R. A., (Rev.,) M.A., late Fellow of Jesus College.

Russell, Richard Norriss, (Rev.,) M.A., late Fellow of Gonville and Caius College.
Roscow, Thomas Tattersall, M.D., Downing College.
Ramsay, William, M.A., Trinity College, Cambridge.
Richards, T. W., (Rev.,) M.A., Sidney Sussex College.
Reynolds, William James, M.A., Queen's College.
Rooker, John, (Rev.,) M.A., Christ's College.
Richings, Alfred Cornelius, (Rev.,) B.A., Christ's Coll.
Ramsay, Alexander, (Rev.,) M.A., Clare College.
Ralph, Henry Francis William, M.A., Trinity College.
Ramsden, Robert John, M.A., Trinity College.
Robinson, Disney, (Rev.,) M.A., St. John's College.
Robinson, W. W., (Rev.,) M.A., St. John's College.
Ripley, W. N., (Rev.,) M.A., Gonville and Caius Coll.
Roberts, Henry Seymour, LL.B., Queen's College.
Smith, C. L., (Rev.,) M.A., late Fellow of Christ's Coll.
Stephenson, Lawrence, (Rev.,) D.D., late Fellow of St. John's College.
Smith, John James, (Rev.,) M.A., late Fellow and Tutor of Gonville and Caius College.
Suffield, George, M.A., late Fellow of Clare College.
Sargant, Henry, M.A., Trinity College, Cambridge.
Sealy, Sparks Bellet, (Rev.,) M.A., St. Peter's College.
Stokes, George, (Rev.,) LL.B., Trinity Hall, Cambridge.
Smith, Sydney, (Rev.,) M.A., Trinity College.
Spencer, Charles, (Rev.,) M.A., Pembroke College.
Sanders, James, (Rev.,) M.A., Queen's College.
Scudamore, Lewis Wallere, B.A., St. Catharine's Coll.
Smith, Alfred Fowler, (Rev.,) B.A., Pembroke College.
Streeter, George Thomas Piper, B.A., Clare College.
Scargill, John James, (Rev.,) B.A., Clare College.
Sharp, William, B.A., Trinity College.
Southwood, Thomas Allen, (Rev.,) M.A., Emmanuel Coll.
Smyth, George Watson, M.A., Trinity College.
Selwyn, Edward, (Rev.,) M.A., St. Catharine's College.
Selwyn, Edward Jasper, (Rev.,) M.A., Trinity College.
Seaman, Shadrack, (Rev.,) M.A., Queen's College.

Sadler, William, (Rev.,) B.A., Queen's College.
Soames, Charles, (Rev.,) M.A., Gonville and Caius Coll.
Salisbury, Edward Lister, (Rev.,) B.A., Trinity Hall.
Tate, Alexander, (Rev.,) B.D., late Fellow and Tutor of Emmanuel College.
Thurtell, Alexander, M.A., late Fellow and Tutor of Gonville and Caius College.
Thomson, William, M.A., late Fellow of St. Peter's College, Cambridge.
Turnbull, Joseph Corbett, (Rev.,) M.A., Trinity College.
Tooke, Thomas Hammond, (Rev.,) M.A., Trinity Coll.
Tottenham, Robert Loftus, (Rev.,) M.A., St. John's Coll.
Titcomb, Jonathan Holt, (Rev.,) M.A., St. Peter's Coll.
Tracy, Frederick Francis, (Rev.,) M.A., Christ's Coll.
Tayler, George Wood Henry, (Rev.,) B.A., Trinity Coll.
Tebay, Septimus, (Rev.,) B.A., St. John's College.
Thornton, John, M.A., Trinity College.
Townsend, William Manifold, (Rev.,) B.A., Queen's Coll.
Venn, John, (Rev.,) M.A., late Fellow of Queen's Coll.
Voigt, George, M.A., Clare College.
Whiston, Robert, M.A., late Senior Fellow of Trinity College, Cambridge.
Walker, Edward, M.A., late Fellow and Assistant Tutor of Trinity College.
Watt, Robert, (Rev.,) M.A., late Fellow of Trinity Coll.
Wisken, J., M.A., late Fellow of Gonville and Caius Coll.
Wilkinson, John Brewster, (Rev.,) B.D., late Fellow of St. John's College.
Walker, J. K., M.D., Gonville and Caius Coll., Cambridge.
Wilson, Richard, (Rev.,) D.D., late Fellow of St. John's College, Cambridge.
Wilson, J., (Rev.,) D.D., St. Catharine's Coll., Cambridge.
Whitley, Charles Thomas, (Rev.,) M.A., late Fellow of St. John's College.
Warren, William Newton, M.A., late Fellow of Clare College, Cambridge.
Whitley, John, (Rev.,) M.A., Queen's College.
Wawn, Edward Bickersteth, M.A., St. John's College.

Whieldon, Edward, (Rev.,) M.A., St. John's College.
Wharton, George, (Rev.,) M.A., St. John's College.
Wardroper, Cutfield, (Rev.,) M.A., Trinity Hall.
Williams, W. R., (Rev.,) M.A., Sidney Sussex College.
Wright, Robert Henry, (Rev.,) M.A., Trinity College.
Williams, B. H., (Rev.,) M.A., St. John's College.
Waddingham, T., M.A., late Fellow of St. John's Coll.
Westbrook, Stephen, (Rev.,) M.A., St. Catharine's Coll.
Warner, George Townsend, (Rev.,) M.A., Trinity Coll.
Whish, John Matthew Hale, (Rev.,) B.A., Trinity Coll.
Ward, William Fisher, (Rev.,) B.A., St. John's College.
Wanton, Joseph Atherton, B.A., Christ's College.
White, Charles, (Rev.,) B.A., St. John's College.
Wilkinson, M., (Rev.,) D.D., late Fellow of Clare Coll.
Wharton, James, B.A., St. John's College.
Wilmot, John Bramston, M.D., Gonville and Caius Coll.
Woodhouse, Walter Webb, (Rev.,) M.A., Queen's Coll.
Wardale, J., (Rev.,) M.A., late Fellow of Clare College.
Yorke, Charles Isaac, (Rev.,) M.A., Trinity College.

OBSERVATIONS.

It may be interesting to remark, that of the foregoing list of 371 Graduates who signed the Memorial, 107 are present or late Fellows, and

110 were admitted to their first Degree between the years	. .	1857 and 1848
114	. . . . . .	1847 and 1838
102	. . . . . .	1837 and 1828
27	. . . . . .	1827 and 1818
13	. . . . . .	1817 and 1808
5	. . . . . .	1807 and 1803

The following observations were circulated at the time of obtaining signatures to this Memorial:—

"A Fellowship is now regarded in general as a reward for Academical distinction. It may be questioned whether, under the existing tenure, a Fellowship be not too ample and permanent a reward for such distinction. It may be suggested, whether the tenure of such Fellowships with an annual stipend for a fixed number of years, and free from the restraint of celibacy, would not be an ample reward for Academical distinction, irrespective of future exertion and success; and the number of such rewards might perhaps be considerably increased. We scarcely think that Founders intended Fellowships to be premiums to celibacy, or comfortable sinecures for men of large Professional income, or of independent fortunes; or even to be enjoyed by distinguished students who are not promoting in some way the legitimate objects of the University. The Cambridge University Act appears to recognize something unsatisfactory in the existing tenure of Fellowships, as it gives the power 'to make fresh provision respecting the *duration and conditions* of the tenure of Fellowships and emoluments, so as to ensure such Fellowships and emoluments being conferred according to personal merits and fitness, and being retained *for such periods* as are likely to conduce to the better advancement of the interests of Religion and Learning.'

"The University of Cambridge is recognized as a place of 'Sound Learning and Religious Education,' and professes to give to its students a literary, scientific, and Christian education in its highest form. It claims to educate the man, as well as to instruct the student. It aims to exercise over every individual member a transforming influence which shall extend to all the relations of life, so that neither his principles of action, his general habits, nor his outward demeanour, shall escape the force of good impressions. It proposes to do more than other institutions, but it seems to place itself in a position to do less. The objects of education are certainly not best attained by excluding those who teach and those who are taught from the softening and elevating influence of domestic life. This is an element which cannot be abstracted from any Society without lowering its tone of purity and diminishingi ts refinement; and consequently its absence must be injurious both to the interests of Morality and Religion. We consider that the moral tone of feeling which pervades the body of teachers would be raised, and the powerful influence which their position gives them in guiding the intellect and forming the habits of young men (many of them destined to occupy hereafter positions of importance), during the most critical period of life, would be more beneficially exercised if the unnatural restriction of celibacy were abolished. We cannot doubt the impolicy of that restriction which sometimes brings the most blameless characters under suspicion, and thus lessens their moral influence and impedes their usefulness. The Fellows of Colleges, who remain as Tutors, foresee for themselves no prospect of a home at Cambridge. No College Tutor ever views the work of Education as his profession for life, but regards it as a temporary occupation, till a desirable College living falls, or till the irksomeness of his unnatural position impels him to forsake it. Is it not desirable to retain the most able and best qualified men to conduct the work of Education at Cambridge? If the University is to exercise its legitimate share of influence in leading the age, it must not be deprived of the presence and labours of the leading minds of the age. The concession of marriage to Fellows, under judicious regulations, would not discourage literary and scientific merit, nor check the advancement of science, for it can scarcely be imagined that circumstances which call forth energy and exertion in every other profession and employment in life, should be less influential on men engaged in education or in scientific and literary pursuits."

An arrangement to meet the scruples of Dissenters in the draft of Statutes for Trinity College was suggested by the Parliamentary Commission, as follows:—"That if any member of Trinity College 'in statu pupillari,' shall not be a member of the Church of England as by law established, he shall not be required to attend at the celebration of Divine service according to the Liturgy of the Church of England in the College Chapel." This proposition did not receive the approval of the meeting of Masters and Fellows of Colleges, recently assembled at Cambridge, but it may be of interest to remark, that a similar plan has been for some time successfully in operation in Trinity College, Dublin.

Religious liberty has, in the last ninety years, made considerable progress in Cambridge, which will be manifest from the following incident, illustrative of the state of Cambridge intolerance in the last century. Mr. Samuel Heywood was an undergraduate at Trinity Hall, Cambridge, in the year 1772, and being a Dissenter, absented himself from the sacramental service in the chapel of that College. About the same time, on Whitsunday, Dr. Hallifax, the Tutor of Trinity Hall, remarked to Mr. Heywood that a few days previously, the question had been put to some of the Heads of Houses in the Caput, as to whether Dissenters who would not attend the Sacrament, or prayers, in their College, should be expelled, and the answer given was, that they should. "I have consequently thought it my duty," said the Doctor, "to give you notice. No Dissenters shall come to this College, and you must go. Dissenters have no business at the University. In disputing about the non-agreement of the Articles and the Liturgy between themselves, as to the nature of the Sacrament, and the grace that falls on the communicants, you are far too wise for your years. However, you may write to me your sentiments upon the subject, that I may take them into consideration, although I do not mean this as a punishment. Now go; but remember you do not spread these principles in the College."

In the afternoon of Whitsunday, another conversation occurred between Dr. Halifax and Mr. S. Heywood, when the Doctor said:—

"It was expected that those who came to the university should conform to the Liturgy of the Church of England, and receive the Sacrament.

"This place was never designed by our benefactors for such as you; it is a charitable institution, but not founded for the instruction of Dissenters.

"When you came here," continued Dr. Halifax, "you entered into an implied contract to conform to the rules of the place."

"To conform to the rules, or pay the penalty," replied his pupil. "I am ready to perform any punishment you may please to inflict."

"Penalty! yes, yes," responded the tutor, "you are ready to do anything as a penalty, but I understand you; and as this is your first offence of the kind, nothing more shall be said about it."

Mr. S. Heywood has recorded in his private papers, which he preserved with great care, another instance of persecution, to which he had been subjected at Trinity Hall, on account of his conscientious convictions.

The College butler one day confronted Mr. Heywood as he was coming out of Hall, from dinner, with the other Pensioners, and, in an unaccustomed and insolent manner, demanded of him the payment of a pecuniary fine* for non-attendance at Sacrament, and desired the instant payment of the penalty.

On the following morning Mr. Heywood stopped Dr. Hallifax on leaving the chapel, to request to know why he had been thus treated, and what the footing was upon which he was permitted to remain in the College; whether, in fact, he was supposed to be excused from the attendance upon the administration of the Sacrament, on account of his religious principles, or whether, by keeping away, he was still liable to penalty and punishment.

The tutor told his pupil that "he never saw such a man;" that "he ought to attend;" that "he had been treated with great lenity, and ought to submit." During his conversation, Dr. Hallifax seemed exceedingly uneasy, and kept creeping all the time towards his own room, for he had been speaking with Mr. Heywood at the bottom of the staircase.

On the same evening Dr. Hallifax referred, in the College Chapel, to the 23rd Canon of the Church of England, relative to the receiving of the Sacrament in the Colleges, and which is thus worded:—

CANON 23. *Students in Colleges to receive the Communion Four times a Year.*

"In all Colleges and Halls within both the Universities, the Masters and Fellows, such especially as have any pupils, shall be careful that all their said pupils, and the rest that remain amongst them, be well brought up, and thoroughly

---

* Probably amounting to sixpence.

instructed in points of religion, and that they do diligently frequent public Service and Sermons, and receive the holy Communion; which we ordain to be administered in all such Colleges and Halls the first or second Sunday of every month, requiring all the said Masters, Fellows, and Scholars, and all the rest of the Students, Officers, and all other the servants there, so to be ordered, that every one of them shall communicate four times in the year at the least, kneeling reverently and decently upon their knees, according to the order of the Communion Book prescribed in that behalf."

So serious was the annoyance of College bigotry to Mr. Heywood, that he visited London, and consulted Sir William Meredith, Bart., M.P., a leading friend of religious liberty, who expressed his willingness to bring the subject before Parliament: but the father of the young student deemed it more prudent for his son not to have his name thus brought before the public in early life. Mr. Heywood shortly afterwards commenced his legal studies, and became a Serjeant-at-Law, and one of the Welsh Judges.

It is remarkable, that the College of which he was a member, had been designed by Bishop Bateman, its founder, chiefly for the encouragement of the studies of Canon and Civil Law: at the Reformation, the study of Canon Law was suppressed, and at the present time, the study of Civil Law in England has very nearly ceased on account of altered circumstances, so that the principal objects of the worthy Founder in the fourteenth century, cannot now be advantageously carried into effect, and the Parliamentary Commissioners may have to consider the adaptation of the endowments of Trinity Hall to the requirements of modern times.

On the large question of Religious Ordinances for

England, Mr. Charles James Fox said, in 1791, "that the religious establishment of any country is to be governed, not so much with regard to the purity of the precepts and truth of a religion, as with a view to that sort of religion which is most likely to inculcate morality and religion in the minds of a majority of its inhabitants."*

The Report of the Oxford Royal Commission, in 1852, thus commented on the internal state of the Colleges and Halls in that University, with reference to religious services in the Chapels, all of which are more or less regulated by the Act of Uniformity of 1662 :—

"The College authorities might consider how far the directly religious services of the place are so regulated as to promote the spirit of true religion, which ought to be the most powerful means of counteracting vice. We fear that these services are not turned to so much advantage as they might be. The obvious mode of appealing to the moral and religious feelings of the Students, by short practical addresses in the College Chapels, has not been so generally adopted as might naturally have been expected. The mischievous practice of forcing the Students to participate in the Holy Communion, though less frequent than formerly, seems not to have been altogether disused. That of making attendance on Divine Service a penalty for College offences, has been discontinued to a great extent since notice was called to it by Lord Stanley in 1834, but it is not entirely abolished. The Aularian Statutes, re-enacted by the University in 1835, impose on the members of Halls the necessity of communicating three times a year.

"The practice of using a selection of prayers, rather than the whole Morning and Evening Service, which prevails in Christ Church, Worcester College, and, on some days, in

---

* Referred to by Lord John Russell, M.P., in his Speech on the Repeal of the Test and Corporation Acts, Feb. 26, 1828.

Wadham College, has been followed nowhere else, though it is evidently suitable to the age and character of the Students. The College Statutes furnish no defence of the existing practice, having reference either to Roman Catholic services which have ceased to be observed, or in other cases enjoining an amount of attendance which is now nowhere enforced. Authority, if needed, might doubtless be obtained for such a deviation from the Act of Uniformity as would permit a short form of prayer to be used in College Chapels. This permission would be amply justified by the example set in so many of the chapels attached to episcopal palaces."

At Cambridge, Dissenters are not expected to attend the Sacrament in College Chapels, and a valuable suggestion has been made by the late lamented Dr. Peacock, Dean of Ely, who for many years held a Tutorship in Trinity College, that the use of shorter forms of prayer on ordinary week-days, so as to make the chapel services approximate in their character to family worship, would be advantageous to the cause of religion and good order.

The learned and excellent Dean remarks that the public worship of the Church of England is nowhere more decorously or more solemnly performed than in the College Chapels of the University of Cambridge, but he continues: "Those persons who have been most intimately concerned with the superintendence of young men at the University will be best able to appreciate the painful measures which are not unfrequently necessary to secure regularity of attendance. There is little doubt but that the substitution of a shorter service would remedy many evils of a very embarrassing and distressing nature."*

* Observations on the Statutes of the University of Cambridge, p. 127.

Probably, the most simple compilation of a short form of public prayer is contained in the daily service read, previous to the commencement of business, in Parliament. Five minutes usually suffice for the solemn reading of the 67th Psalm and the accompanying prayers. No one is fatigued, and the language is so general that Members of Parliament of all religious denominations can listen to it in comfort.

It may be worthy of consideration, if short forms of prayer can be adapted to the circumstances and position of College students at Cambridge, in the same manner as the following prayers have been adapted to the Parliament:—

PRAYERS FOR THE PARLIAMENT.

Psalm lxvii.

1. GOD be merciful unto us, and bless us: and shew us the light of his countenance, and be merciful unto us;

2. That thy way may be known upon earth: thy saving health among all nations.

3. Let the people praise thee, O God: yea, let all the people praise thee.

4. O let the nations rejoice and be glad: for thou shalt judge the folk righteously, and govern the nations upon earth.

5. Let the people praise thee, O God: let all the people praise thee.

6. Then shall the earth bring forth her increase: and God, even our own God, shall give us his blessing.

7. God shall bless us: and all the ends of the world shall fear him.

¶ *After the Psalm these Suffrages, and the Prayers following, shall be used.*

The Lord be with you.

ANSWER. And with thy Spirit.

¶ *Let us pray.*

Our Father, which art in Heaven, Hallowed be thy Name. Thy kingdom come. Thy will be done in earth, As it is in Heaven. Give us this day our daily bread. And forgive us our trespasses, As we forgive them that trespass against us. And lead us not into temptation; But deliver us from evil: For thine is the kingdom, The power and the glory, For ever and ever. *Amen.*

O Lord our heavenly Father, high and mighty, King of kings, Lord of lords, the only Ruler of princes, who dost from thy throne behold all the dwellers upon earth; Most heartily we beseech thee with thy favour to behold our most gracious Sovereign Lady, Queen *VICTORIA;* and so replenish her with the grace of thy Holy Spirit, that she may alway incline to thy will, and walk in thy way: Endue her plenteously with heavenly gifts; grant her in health and wealth long to live; strengthen her that she may vanquish and overcome all her enemies; and finally, after this life, she may attain everlasting joy and felicity; through Jesus Christ our Lord. *Amen.*

Almighty God, the fountain of all goodness, we humbly beseech thee to bless the Prince Consort, Albert Prince of Wales, and all the Royal Family: Endue them with thy Holy Spirit; enrich them with thy heavenly grace; prosper them with all happiness; and bring them to thine everlasting kingdom; through Jesus Christ our Lord. *Amen.*

Almighty God, by whom alone kings reign, and princes decree justice; and from whom alone cometh all counsel, wisdom, and understanding; we thine unworthy servants here gathered together in thy Name, do most humbly beseech thee to send thy heavenly wisdom from above, to direct and guide us in all our consultations: And grant that we, having thy fear always before our eyes, and laying aside all private interests, prejudices, and partial affections, the result of all our counsels may be to the glory of thy blessed Name, the maintenance of true religion and justice, the safety, honour and happiness of the Queen, the public wealth, peace and tranquillity of the realm, and the uniting and knitting together of the hearts of all persons and estates within the same in true Christian love and charity one towards another, through Jesus Christ our Lord. *Amen.*

O ALMIGHTY GOD, who art a strong tower of defence unto thy servants against the face of their enemies; we yield thee praise and thanksgiving for our deliverance from those great and apparent dangers wherewith we were compassed in this place: we acknowledge it thy goodness that we were not delivered over a prey unto them; beseeching thee still to continue such thy mercies towards us, that all the world may know that thou art our Saviour and mighty Deliverer, through Jesus Christ our Lord. *Amen.*

PREVENT us, O Lord, in all our doings with thy most gracious favour, and further us with thy continual help; that in all our works begun, continued, and ended in thee, we may glorify thy holy Name, and finally by thy mercy obtain everlasting life; through Jesus Christ our Lord. *Amen.*

2 *Cor.* xiii.

The grace of our Lord Jesus Christ, and the love of God, and the fellowship of the Holy Ghost, be with us all evermore. *Amen.*

Enlarged plans of competitive examinations for Trinity College Scholarships have been promulgated by the Cambridge Parliamentary Commissioners, in their draft report, and provisions have been proposed by them for setting apart, in each year, seven Scholarships, the examination for which shall be held about the time when students usually begin their residence in the University. The Commissioners were of opinion that these Scholarships should be open to all students who had not yet commenced residence in the University, or who were in their first term of residence, and that in the case of candidates who were not members of Trinity College, testimonials should be sent in from the College or Hostel to which such candidates belonged.

A preference might be given for any of these Scholarships to excellence in one or more of the learned or Oriental languages, or in special departments of Mathematics or Physical Science.

The remaining Scholarships of Trinity College, which are numerous, and of which a portion become annually vacant, are confined to students of that College who are in their second or third year of residence. The Master and Senior Fellows, in adjudging these Scholarships, would be enabled, under the draft statutes, to give a preference to excellence in one or more of the learned or Oriental languages, or in special departments of Mathematics, or of Physical or Moral Science.

6. *Memorial presented July* 15*th*, 1858, *to the Right Honourable Spencer Horatio Walpole, M.P., Secretary of State for the Home Department, on the setting of Questions, at the ordinary Bachelor of Arts Examination, in Cambridge, respecting the History of the Thirty-nine Articles and of the Book of Common Prayer.*

The Memorial of the undersigned Friends of Religious Liberty humbly showeth,—

That the Statutes for the future government and regulation of the University of Cambridge, now before

Parliament, do not contain suitable provisions for the practical working of the academical changes introduced by the Cambridge University Act of 1856.

From the earliest period, it has been the custom of the University of Cambridge, emphatically expressed in the Statutes prepared by Whitgift and enforced by Queen Elizabeth in 1570, that a course of secular study in the University shall precede instruction in theological learning.

The system of examining all the students who are candidates for the ordinary degree of Bachelor of Arts, in the History of the Reformation, and in the Acts of the Apostles in Greek, is inconsistent with the removal of the Church of England Subscription Test from that degree, as the answers to divinity questions are expected to be in accordance with the tenets of the Church of England, and some of the questions are framed for students who are supposed to be familiar with the various services of the Book of Common Prayer, and to be in the habit of regarding that liturgy as their own.

A reduction of the compulsory period of residence at Cambridge to six academical terms, or two years, for the ordinary degree of Bachelor of Arts, and the postponement of the Divinity Examinations to a time subsequent to the Degree Examination, so as to render attendance on what is now the Theological portion of the ordinary Degree Examination optional on the part of the students, would meet those University requirements which necessarily follow the abolition of religious tests for secular degrees at Cambridge.

Your Memorialists therefore pray, that you will be pleased to advise her Majesty to withhold her Majesty's approbation, so far as the candidates for the ordinary Bachelor's degree in Arts are concerned, from that portion of Chap. 2, Sect. 1, of the New Statutes, in which *nine* terms of compulsory academical residence are directed for the B.A. degree ; and that *six* terms* may be substituted for nine terms of residence for the candidates for the ordinary B.A. degree ; and arrangements be adopted for the postponement of what is now the Theological portion of the ordinary Degree Examination in Arts, at Cambridge, until after the examination in secular subjects; and for the classification of the names of the Candidates for that Degree according to their success in passing the general or secular examination in Arts, so as to ensure the same religious equality among the students in the ordinary Bachelor of Arts Examination, which the Legislature has already conferred on the graduates when they take their Degrees in Arts.

James Heywood, F.R.S., B.A., Trinity College, Camb.
L. L. Dillwyn, M.P.
Chas. J. Foster, LL.D., University of London.
Wm. Ewart, M.P., B.A., Christ Church, Oxford.
John Cheetham, M.P.
Robert N. Philips, M.P.
Charles Paget, M.P.
John D. Harris, M.P.
J. Aspinall Turner, M.P.
Thomas Thornely, M.P.
M. J. O'Connell, Barrister-at-Law.
Melgund, (Viscount,) M.P., M.A., Trinity Coll., Camb.
J. Locke King, M.P., M.A., Trinity College, Cambridge.
J. Bonham-Carter, M.P., Trinity College, Cambridge.
H. W. Wickham, M.P.

* This part of the Memorial, on the reduction of the period of Undergraduate residence at Cambridge to six terms, was not pressed at the time of the presentation of the above Memorial.

105

G. Hadfield, M.P.
W. J. Fox, M.P.
Adam Black, M.P.
H. Morgan Clifford, (Col.,) M.P.
Ed. Holland, M.P., M.A., Trinity College, Cambridge.
William Brown, M.P.
James Duke, (Baronet,) M.P.
William Scholefield, M.P.
J. B. Smith, M.P.
S. Gregson, M.P.
Frank Crossley, M.P.
James Kershaw, M.P.
Joseph Crook, M.P.
William Tite, M.P.
William P. Price, M.P.
James Pilkington, M.P.
J. C. Ewart, M.P.
J. W. Donaldson, D.D., Trinity College, Cambridge.
Henry Rich, M.P., B.A., Trinity College, Cambridge.
Charles Cowan, M.P.
Hastings Russell, M.P.
E. J. Hutchins.
S. E. De Vere, M.P.

The Memorial was accompanied by a copy of the following selection of questions on the History of the Reformation, which had been set at the ordinary Bachelor of Arts Degree Examination, in Cambridge, January, 1858, and which were manifestly not consistent with the removal of religious tests from the B.A. degree.

" Sketch the history of the origin and successive alterations in the English Articles of Religion.

" Mention the chief Continental Confessions of Faith. From which of these is any part of our Articles derived?

" What are the dates of the several Acts of Uniformity? What English Service-books were enforced by Royal Proclamation? When do the Roman Catholics seem first to have formed a separate religious body in England?

"Write a short history of the Church of England in the reign of Edward the Sixth. What is the history of the *Reformatio Legum Ecclesiasticarum*?

"Give an account of the steps by which the Latin Service-books were gradually altered into our present Book of Common Prayer. From what Continental Service-book were parts added to translations from the Latin?

"What parts of the public worship of the Church were used in English before the compilation of the first Prayer-book? What books were ordered to be set up in Churches before the same time?"

In the Examination-paper on the Acts of the Apostles, the following question presupposes a familiarity with the Book of Common Prayer, which students who are not members of the Church of England cannot be expected to possess: and is therefore unfair to such students.

"Translate Acts iii. 17–22. Its usual meaning being given to ὅπως ἂν (in the sentence [verse 19] μετανοήσατε οὖν, κ.τ.λ.), we have the expression of a similar sentiment in one of the prayers which conclude our Burial Service; can you call it to mind?"

---

7. *Memorial to the Senate of the University of London, for Degrees in Science, presented on the* 12*th of May,* 1858.

The undersigned persons, practically engaged in the pursuit of some branch of scientific inquiry, being informed that modifications of the regulations of the University of London are in contemplation, venture to draw the attention of the Senate of the University to the following expression of their views, as to the kind of alteration which would be most beneficial to the advance of Science in general, no less than to that of their own departments.

The branches of human knowledge at present academically recognized, are those of Arts, Theology, Law, and Medicine. But this fourfold division, though possibly sufficient in the age in which Universities took their rise, has become utterly inadequate as a recognition of the great classes of knowledge which at the present day subserve the discipline of the individual mind or promote the good of mankind. In fact, a fifth branch of knowledge,—Science,—the result of the search after the laws by which natural phenomena are governed, apart from any direct application of such laws to an art, —has gradually grown up, and being unrecognized as a whole, has become dismembered; some fragments, consisting of Mathematics and such branches of Physics as are capable of Mathematical treatment, attaching themselves to Arts; others, such as Comparative Anatomy, Physiology, and Botany, clinging to Medicine, amidst whose professors they took their rise.

No evil could result from this arrangement to the undeveloped Science of a century ago, when Electricity, Heat, Magnetism, Organic Chemistry, Histology, Development, Morphology, Geology, Palæontology, branches of knowledge which constitute the very essence of Science as distinguished from Arts and Medicine, were non-existent. Now, however, the attainment of proficiency in any one of these sciences is acknowledged to be the worthy object of a life's labour; and society, appreciating the value of their fruits in alleviating the wants of man, practically regards the pursuit of these sciences as Professions, and honours those who follow them.

The Academic bodies, on the other hand, continue to ignore Science as a separate Profession; and even the University of London, though specially instituted to meet the wants of modern times, can confer no Degree upon the first Chemist and Physicist of his age, unless he possess at the same time a more than average acquaintance with classical literature; nor would she acknowledge a Cuvier, unless he were also a surgeon and physician, far more highly accomplished than the majority of those in actual practice. We conceive such a state of things as this to be not only anomalous in itself, but in the highest degree injurious to the progress of Science; for those who have the direction of youth, finding Science unrecognized as a profession, discourage it as a pursuit; and the Englishman who pursues a purely scientific career is obliged, if he desire a Degree in Science as an evidence of his qualifications, to obtain it in a foreign University.

The remedy for these evils appears to us to be, that the Academic Bodies in this country should (like those of France and Germany) recognize "Science" as a Discipline and as a Calling, and should place it on the same footing with regard to Arts, as Medicine and Law. We therefore most strongly urge upon the Senate of the University of London the propriety of establishing Degrees in Science equivalent to those in Medicine. The details of the scheme of Examination are matters for ulterior discussion; but it is suggested that after a common preliminary Examination, Candidates should be allowed to make their election between the two great natural divisions of Science, and should ultimately take their Degree either in the Physico-Chemical or in the Biological Sciences.

Rod. I. Murchison.	Henry Bence Jones.
Charles Lyell.	Thomas H. Huxley.
Richard Owen.	R. G. Latham.
Andrew C. Ramsay.	J. Lubbock.
Arthur Farre.	John Lindley.
Jos. D. Hooker.	J. Beete Jukes.
George Busk.	R. E. Grant.
P. M. Grey Egerton.	Thomas Bell, Pres. L.S.
W. Sharpey.	Arthur Henfrey.
W. Bowman.	George J. Allman.

A Committee was appointed by the Senate of the University of London, in 1858, consisting of the Chancellor, the Vice-Chancellor, Dr. Arnott, Mr. Braude, Sir James Clark, M.D., Dr. Faraday, Mr. Grote, and Mr. Walker, to consider the propriety of establishing a Degree or Degrees in Science, and the conditions on which such Degree or Degrees should be conferred.

Detailed views on the subject of graduation in Science were laid before this Committee by various eminent scientific gentlemen, and, in the course of evidence, the class of persons who were likely to desire a Degree in Natural Science, was described by Professor Sharpey, of University College, London, and Secretary to the Royal Society, in the following manner :—

" Amongst persons likely to desire a Degree in Natural Science, we may reckon gentlemen who are engaged in Analytical and Chemical laboratories, who make Chemistry a pursuit, and who eventually intend to become consulting chemists, chemical manufacturers, or chemical superintendents of manufactories. Again, those who study Chemistry with a view to its application to Agriculture and Rural Economy, which is now a growing science in this country. I should include also," continued Professor Sharpey, " the students in the School of Mines, who intend to become mineral and geological surveyors, either in this country or in the colonies, and probably also men who would eventually become directors of Astronomical Observatories in different parts of the world. I think, moreover, we might reckon that there are Medical Men who would desire to take the Degree in Science; those especially who, in this country, aim at becoming Officers of Health, to which office it would be probably a recommendation; or some of those intending to go abroad, especially to India, because it is well known that in India various scientific appointments are open to medical men, such, for example, as the offices of Superintendents of Botanical Gardens, Inspectors of Forests, or Directors of the Presidential Mints. I have known medical gentlemen holding all these appointments. Then I think that from all these classes there are men who probably would desire to have a Degree in Science with a view of teaching it in Colleges and in Schools, where it is likely to take a larger development than it has hitherto done. And finally, I think probably there are men of wealth, or who are to inherit wealth, who would pursue Science for its own sake, but might at the same time desire some public recognition of their proficiency in it. These being the classes who, I think, are likely now or henceforth to look forward to the Degree, and many others perhaps whom I have not thought of, I think it would be desirable that there should be a Junior Degree and a Senior Degree, so as to correspond with the Junior and Senior Degrees in Medicine and in Arts. The title might be B.S. for the Junior Degree, and M.S. or D.S. for the Senior Degree. The title is of no great moment to the University; but for the Senior Degree probably the title of 'Doctor' would be more coveted by most people, especially by young men."

Dr. Carpenter, F.R.S., and Registrar of the University of London, thus explained the results of his practical experience, which he had in part obtained as the Principal of University Hall, an institution intended for the residence of students connected with University College, London :—

"Having been an Examiner for many years in the Medical Faculty,, I have recognized very strongly, in the superior class of our graduates, the effects of the cultivation of those sciences, as having served as a most valuable mental discipline; and therefore I am strongly inclined to believe that, merely as a means of preparing a number of minds for the active business of life, and especially for entering into many pursuits in which scientific cultivation is required, a Degree in Science would be fully equal as an educational means to the training required for a Degree in Arts. I know that there are a number of young men who are preparing for various departments of business, who would gladly pass through such a course of education as might be required for a lower Degree in Science, such as B.S., but would think it a waste of time to go through the amount of literary study which is required for a Degree in Arts. At University Hall, I have under my constant observation a superior class of young men of this kind, who come to London for two or three years' study : some of them I have induced to pass the Matriculation Examination merely as a means of testing the value of their school acquirements, and of keeping them at work for the first session during which they are under my care; but I generally fail in inducing them to continue their literary studies sufficiently to pass the examination in Arts. I find that they would be glad to go on with Mathematics and with Latin perhaps, with Chemistry and Natural Philosophy; but they think it a waste of time to continue to study Greek, and the large amount of History that is required; and I find, therefore, that there is no academical distinction for that class of young men, which is at present a very large one. Mr. Warburton, it will be recollected, has adverted to that class several times, as one whose existence he had come to know in various ways. I therefore think that a Degree equivalent to the Degree of B.A.,—I mean, taking the same rank in the University as B.A., in which, without altogether leaving out literary study, scientific studies should constitute the principal qualification,—would be very useful as a means of directing the education of a large number of young men who are at present studying at various public institutions. I think also that such a Degree would be the best preparation for the higher Degree of D.S., which would attest the highest scientific qualifications."

Dr. Carpenter was of opinion that, "as a rule for the direction of the education of those who are to make Science their profession, a Matriculation Examination closely corresponding with our present one should be required. I say," continued the Doctor, "closely corresponding, because I rather agree with those who think that a little more option might be advantageously given: for example, I would suggest whether, in the place of requiring two Classical languages and one Modern, it might not be advantageous to give the option of one

Classical language and two Modern languages; and I suggest this particularly for this reason :—I have seen a good deal of the mode in which Greek is *crammed* for at the Matriculation Examination. I have known many instances in which young men who have not studied Greek at school, put themselves (I know one at the present time) under a crammer, and manage to get up their Greek in the course of about two months; that is, to get up enough to pass the Matriculation Examination. No one can now pass his examination in Greek who is absolutely ignorant of Greek; but I know that Greek is the subject most crammed for in the Matriculation Examination. On the other hand, there are many youths who go to a school in Germany (I know three or four such instances at the present time, among those who are going up for the next Matriculation Examination), and who there acquire a fair knowledge of German, and who also have a good knowledge of French; and it appears to me that such knowledge should be accepted as equivalent to that imperfect knowledge of Greek which is at present sufficient to pass a candidate. I do not think that a student who intends to go on in Arts would wish to avail himself of such an option, since he must apply himself seriously to Greek as a preparation for the Degree in Arts; but it might be taken by the Medical student, and by those who intend to go on for the Degree in Science; and to each of those classes it would have this special advantage, that a knowledge of German, as well as of French, is now really essential to every one who desires to keep up with the progress of Medicine, Physiology, Chemistry, and, in fact, of almost any department of scientific inquiry."

Dr. Frankland, F.R.S. and Lecturer on Chemistry at

St. Bartholomew's Hospital, stated his general approval of the present scheme of the Matriculation Examination of the University of London, but considered that it might be desirable to allow of the substitution of one or two modern languages for Latin and Greek. That is, he would allow a student to take Latin and French, for instance, or Latin and German; or he would allow him to take French and German, in place of Latin and Greek. He thought, in certain cases, that might be an advantage.

---

8. *Memorial to the Senate of the University of London, presented October, 1858, for a Degree of Bachelor in Moral and Economic Science, and for some liberty of alternation among the subjects required at the Matriculation Examination.*

To the Chancellor, Vice-Chancellor, and Senate of the University of London.

The Memorial of the undersigned, being Members of the Section (F) of Economic Science and Statistics, of the British Association for the Advancement of Science, assembled at Leeds, in September, 1858,

Showeth,—That, in the opinion of your Memorialists, the principle contained in the proposition recently submitted to your academical Senate by various eminent scientific men, and favourably considered by a Committee of your Honourable Body, for the establishment of Degrees for attesting proficiency in *Natural Science*, may with advantage be extended to other departments of knowledge.

For the benefit of students intending to enter on a Public or Commercial career, or whose inclination leads them towards Social or Political inquiries, your Memorialists respectfully recommend to your consideration the utility of establishing a Degree of Bachelor in *Moral and Economic Science* (or whatever other more appropriate designation your Honourable Senate may determine).

It appears to your Memorialists that the attainment of such scientific Degrees would be facilitated if some liberty of substitution were allowed, with reference to languages, at the Matriculation Examination; as, for example, by permitting a student to take up Latin and French, or Latin and German, or French and German, in place of Latin and Greek, or some such similar arrangement as might approve itself to your Honourable Senate.

Edward Baines, President of the Section of Economic Science and Statistics, at Leeds.
J. G. Marshall, Vice-President of the Association.
W. H. Sykes, M.P., Vice-President of the Section.
William Scrope Ayrton, Vice-President of the Section.
J. P. Kay Shuttleworth, Bt., Vice-Pres. of the Section.

William Newmarch,
John Strang, LL.D.,
John E. Cairnes, } *Secretaries of the Section.*
E. Jardine Fishbourne,
T. B. Baines,

Edwin Chadwick, C.B.,
C. Holte Bracebridge,
J. Shuttleworth, } *Members of the Committee.*
Robert Baker,
Joseph Bateman, LL.D.
Walter Lewis, M.B.

William Napier Molesworth, M.A.
William Camps, M.D., F.S.S.
William Neild.
J. H. Alexander, Professor of Physics in the University of Maryland, United States.
Richard M. Milnes, M.P.
W. Donelly, C.B., Reg.-Gen. in Ireland.
Horace Mann.
James Hole.
Thomas Bazley.
James Booth, LL.D., F.R.S.
} *Members of the Committee.*

Goderich, M.P.
Charles Cowan, M.P.
J. W. Fraser.
Joseph Locke, M.P.
P. Fairbairn, Mayor of Leeds.
Arthur Lupton, Leeds.
Thomas Avison, Liverpool.
Charles Frost.
Edmund Ashworth.
Frederick Watkins, H. M. Inspector.
Henry A. Bright, B.A., Liverpool.
George Hadfield, M.P.
High Sheriff of Yorkshire.
Robert Milligan, M.P.

---

9. *Memorial to the Senate of the University of London, in favour of arrangements for Provincial Matriculation Examinations, presented in* 1858.

To the Chancellor, Vice-Chancellor, and Fellows of the University of London.

MY LORDS AND GENTLEMEN,—We, the undersigned Professors in certain of the Northern Colleges of the University, beg to represent to the Senate, that in our opinion the Candidates from the Northern Counties seeking to undergo the Examinations of the University of London, would be yet larger, but for the expense and inconvenience attending the journey to, and residence in, London.

This difficulty presses, we believe, most seriously on the candidates for Matriculation: and we desire respectfully to submit to you that it would be removed if a Matriculation Examination were held, simultaneously with that in London, in Manchester or any other convenient central town: the printed papers, the same as those used in London, might be forwarded to a Committee of Professors, or others, delegated to conduct the Examination, in a sealed packet to be publicly opened on the morning of each day of the Examination, and the written answers returned, duly sealed in like manner, to the Examiners of the University on the evening of each day.

If, either in the way we have suggested, or by means of an independent Examination held in the North, either by the Examiners of the University, or by the authorities of the Colleges themselves, an obstacle which virtually closes the doors of the University against many young men living at a great distance from the Metropolis could be removed, we believe that the prosperity and usefulness of the University would be greatly promoted.

We are, my Lords and Gentlemen,

Yours very respectfully,

J. G. Greenwood, B.A., Lond., Principal of, and Professor of Classics in, Owens' College, Manchester.

A. J. Scott, M.A., Professor of Mental Philosophy and Comparative Grammar, Owens' College.

Richard Copley Christie, M.A., Oxon, Professor of History and Political Economy, Owens' College.

H. E. Roscoe, B.A., Lond., Prof. of Chem., Owens' Coll.
Henry Rogers, Principal of Lancashire Independent Coll., Manchester.
Theos. D. Hall, M.A., Lond., Professor of Greek and Latin at the Lancashire Independent College.
A. Newth, Prof. of Math. at Lancashire Independent Coll.

10. *Extract from a Letter, dated September 22nd, 1858, from the Rev. E. J. Purbrick, Præfect of Studies in Stonyhurst College, Lancashire, to Dr. Carpenter, Registrar of the University of London, containing a suggestion of arrangements for University Examinations at Stonyhurst College, under the care of an Examiner appointed by the University of London.*

"Hitherto, Candidates, say for B.A. honours, have had, after Matriculation, one journey to London, or at the most two, supposing their return to their College between the Pass and Honour Examinations. By the new arrangement* these expenses, and those of residence in London, are exactly doubled.

"This difficulty has been already represented to the Senate by the Professors of Owens' College and of the Lancashire Independent College, and a remedy has been proposed by them, viz. the creation of new centres of Examination. We declined joining in their Memorial, partly because the difficulty with us will not press so seriously on the Matriculators as on the Candidates for B.A., the very reverse of their case, and partly because, although the expense would by the proposed remedy be reduced by the difference of the journey, yet a sojourn

---

* Referring to the institution of an intermediate University Examination between Matriculation and the B.A. degree in the University of London.

in Manchester, with fewer advantages of other kinds, would be scarcely any, if any, saving upon the expenses incurred in London.

"I beg therefore to submit to the consideration of the Senate:—

"That an Examiner, who might be a neighbouring Clergyman or other person appointed by the University, should be delegated to conduct the Examinations at the College itself: the (duplicate) Examination-papers might be forwarded to him in a sealed packet to be publicly opened on the morning of each day of the Examination, and the written answers returned, in the same manner, to the Examiners of the University on the evening of each day, as proposed by the Professors of Owens' College.

"Of course every facility would be secured to the Delegate of carrying out his arrangements for the prevention of copying, and there would be no hesitation on the part of the College as to the payment of Fees or other remuneration to the Delegate."

---

11. *Memorial to the Senate of the University of London, from the Manchester Society of Middle-Class Teachers and others, presented in November,* 1858, *in favour of University Examinations for Matriculation being held in Manchester.*

To the Chancellor, Vice-Chancellor, and Fellows of the University of London.

We, the undersigned Members of the Manchester Society of Middle-Class Teachers and others, beg respectfully to memorialize the Senate of the University of

London on the desirableness of their making the city of Manchester a centre for holding Examinations of Candidates for Matriculation in the said University, simultaneously with those held in London.

We believe that the adoption of the plan just named would greatly extend the influence and very much increase the usefulness of the London University, by affording greater facilities to Candidates for presenting themselves at the Matriculation Examinations from North Wales, and from an extensive and populous district in the North-west of England, of which Manchester may be considered the metropolis.

The following statements in support of this view are submitted for consideration :—

1. The population contained within an area formed by a radius of fifty miles round Manchester is equal to, if not greater than, the population of an equal area having London for its centre.

2. Within this area around Manchester are situated ten Colleges, most of them affiliated to the London University, four Medical Schools, as well as numerous Grammar Schools and Private Schools from which pupils are frequently presented for Matriculation in London.

3. The expense attendant upon a journey to London and a week's residence there, we have reason to believe, prevents many students from being sent at all to the Matriculation Examination; for at present when a youth does go to London with this object, (in the majority of cases) a parent or guardian deems it requisite that some person should accompany him; and thus, the expense being doubled, the chief obstacle which prevents Candidates from going to this Examination from a distance is greatly increased.

4. The plan of holding such Matriculation Examinations in Manchester, simultaneously with those in London, would be attended with very little expense or inconvenience to the University, since sealed packets containing the Examination-papers might be entrusted to a Local Committee of Professors or other gentlemen appointed to superintend the Examination:—these packets might be publicly opened at the time they are required for the Candidates, and the written answers sealed up and sent to the Examiners in London at the end of each day.

From these considerations we, the undersigned, earnestly and respectfully pray that this Memorial may receive the early and serious attention of the Senate of the University of London.

 John Kendall, B.A., Chairman of the Manchester Society of Middle Class Teachers.
 Oct. A. Ferris, Treasurer of the above Society.
 J. M. D. Meiklejohn, M.A.,} *Secs. of the above Society*.
 C. J. Crawshaw,
 E. W. Makinson, M.A., Higher Broughton School, Manchester.
 V. E. Etienne, B.A., Stony Knolls High School, Manchester.
 John Thompson, Belfield House, Bowdon.
 John Atkinson, Daisy Bank House, Victoria Park.
 John F. Thomson, Fullarton House, Chorlton-on-Medlock, Manchester.
 Thomas Somerville, LL.D., Hawthorn Hall, Wilmslow, Manchester.
 A. C. O'Dwyer, Clifton View School, Prestwich, near Manchester.
 E. Hamilton Sharp, Old Trafford School, Manchester.
 H. I. Marcus, M.A., P.D., Upper Brook St., Manchester.
 W. J. Fertel, 36, Great Ducie Street, Manchester.

12. *Observations by Professor Greenwood, B.A., Lond., Principal of Owens' College, Manchester, in favour of Provincial Examinations under the care of the University of London, presented on the 2nd December, 1858, to the Committee of the Senate of the University of London, appointed for the purpose of considering the present system of Matriculation, and the other conditions of admissibility to Degrees in Arts.*

"For some years the Professors of Owens' College have felt that the expense and inconvenience attendant upon the repeated visits to London required from Candidates for Degrees in Arts, was a serious drawback on the advantages derived by the country Colleges from their affiliation to the University of London. These visits vary from *two* (in the case of those who merely pass) to *four* (in the case of those who seek honours), and at each visit a distance of nearly four hundred miles must be travelled. In this feeling both the late and the present Principal of the Lancashire Independent College have shared.

"Last summer a Memorial was forwarded to the Senate of the University, signed by the Professors of Owens' College and of the Lancashire Independent College, requesting the attention of the Senate to the grievance indicated, and pointing out a method by which, in the opinion of the Memorialists, it might be removed, to the great advantage both of the Colleges and of the University. It is right to add that others of the Colleges in Lancashire and Yorkshire had been communicated with, and from several an expression of adhesion to the proposals emanating from Owens' College was received: others partially adhered to them, suggesting various modifications.

"The strength of the reasons urged in the above Memorial is greatly increased by the proposal, in the new regulations, to institute an intermediate Examination between Matriculation and the final Examination for B.A. The expense and other inconveniences attendant on the series of University Examinations is hereby increased.

"We therefore earnestly ask the consideration of the Committee to the difficulty we have set forth, and to the remedy we venture to suggest, as far as regards the Matriculation Examination at least. In our opinion the best remedy would be, that an Examination identical with that held in London should be conducted at the same time in Manchester (which would perhaps be the most accessible centre for the Lancashire and Yorkshire Colleges), by an Examiner deputed from the University, assisted by a local body of Examiners connected with the Colleges. This course would better guard the character of the University certificates; and Matriculated students would not be disabled from afterwards competing at the consequent Examinations for Honours. It would also probably be more attractive to the Middle-Class Schools of the province, and would be free from any suspicion of laxity on the part of the Examiners, and from the difficulty attendant on Examinations conducted by Examiners who had been lecturing to some of the Candidates on the very subjects of examination.

"That the method we recommend is quite practicable, we think proved by the Oxford Examinations held in

Manchester and other towns in June last. The writer of this paper was frequently present during the course of those Examinations, and he was confirmed in his belief that the system could be successfully worked.

"We would point out that the carrying University Examinations into provincial towns, which is a pure extension grafted upon the older Universities, is in harmony with the very essence of the constitution of the University of London. It would therefore be a grievous anomaly if those Universities offered to Provincial *Schools*, unconnected with them, facilities greater than those which the University of London afforded to *Colleges* which were incorporated with her.

"We believe that not only will the privilege we are asking be a valuable boon to the Colleges which were affiliated to the University under its old constitution, but that it is a natural and almost necessary consequence of the change instituted under Sect. 36 of the New Charter. Opposed as we were to that change, we are yet anxious that, once adopted, it should have a fair chance of successful working, which it would scarcely have without some such measure as that suggested by us.

"The writer has seen a Memorial presented to the University by a number of Middle-Class Schoolmasters in Manchester: among the names appended to it are those of the Masters of the principal Unendowed Schools of that city; and there can be little doubt that the adoption of their prayer would be followed by a considerable increase in the number of Matriculated Students and, in proportion, of Graduates.

"As respects the details of such an Examination, a voluntary organization might be readily formed, under which the delegate from the University might be aided by representatives of the Colleges, and (should it be deemed expedient) of the Associated Schoolmasters who have addressed the Senate.

"If the method suggested should be found to work successfully for the Matriculation Examination, it might be found expedient to extend it so as to embrace the intermediate Examination also.

"J. G. GREENWOOD,
"*Principal of Owens' College.*"

Regulations of the Senate of the University of London, January, 1859, *with reference to Provincial Examinations for Matriculation and for the Degree of B.A.*

These Examinations will be carried on simultaneously with the Examinations in London; on the same days and at the same hours. Sealed packets containing the Examination-papers will be sent down from London, and publicly opened at the commencement of the Provincial Examination. These packets will be entrusted to a Sub-Examiner named by the Senate, and sent down expressly for the occasion, who will be responsible to the Senate for the proper opening of the Papers, for the conduct of the Examination, and for the collection and sealing-up of the answers at the close of each Examination. The answers will be brought back to London in sealed packets, so as to be reviewed by the Examiners in London at the same time with the answers of the London candidates; and the total results (including the local as well as the central) will be made known by the Examiners in London on the same day as they are at present.

Applications from any City, Town, or College, desiring the institution of Provincial Examinations in the present year, must be transmitted to the Registrar before May 1st.

13. *Extract from the Report of the Oxford University Commissioners, under the Act* 17*th &* 18*th Vict. c.* 81, *dated* 10*th June,* 1858, *to the Right Honourable the Secretary of State for the Home Department, relating to St. John's College, Oxford.*

"In the case of St. John's College, an ordinance framed and settled by us was objected to by two-thirds of the governing body of the College, as prejudicial to the College as a place of learning and education.

"After having been informed of the nature of the objections entertained to it, we framed and settled another ordinance, different from the first in some particulars, in which it appeared to us that these objections might be met without any sacrifice of the essential principles by which we have been guided, or of the objects which, under the Act, it is our duty to promote, but otherwise substantially the same.

"This ordinance has been laid before the College, as the Act directs, and we have since received from the President of the College an instrument, signed by him and by twenty of the thirty graduate Fellows, by which the power of veto is again exercised, and the second ordinance declared to be likewise prejudicial to the College as a place of learning and education.

"In dealing with the several Colleges, we have thought it right and desirable, before proceeding to settle any ordinance, to enter into free and unreserved communication with the College affected by it, to receive any proposals or representations which might be addressed to us, and to invite the full and friendly discussion of points in difference by personal conference as well as by letter. We have found this course most useful in removing difficulties and misapprehensions, and enabling the Colleges to co-operate with us in the work of reform. We have not deviated from it in the case of St. John's College, with which we have had much communication, by personal interviews and otherwise, at various times during the present and the three preceding years. The full substance of what has passed would not be fairly represented by the letters written and received, but we believe we are correct in stating, as the result of the whole, that the College would not have objected to the ordinance as prejudicial to it as a place of learning and education, if its wishes had been complied with on two points, and we shall therefore confine ourselves to a statement of these, and some brief observations upon each.

"One of these points, upon which the chief stress has been laid, relates to the Fellowships; the other, which is of less importance, to the Scholarships of the College. We shall advert to the latter first.

"According to the practice pursued under the existing statutes, thirty-seven out of the fifty Fellows and Scholars come from Merchant Taylors' School, a Scholar being ordinarily admitted to a Fellowship after he has been three years at College. It is proposed by the ordinance that twenty-one Scholarships shall be assigned to Merchant Taylors' School, tenable for seven years, if the College shall declare its satisfaction with the Scholar at the end of the first five, but otherwise terminable at the end of five years. According to this plan, whenever the tenure of a Scholarship ceased at the end of five years, or earlier, there would be a period of two years or more during which it would remain vacant. It was the wish of the College that the Scholarships should be filled up for such broken periods by open election, and to this wish we were at first disposed to accede; but we found that the Merchant Taylors' Company, who had, after much communication with us, signified their acquiescence in the rest of our scheme, attached great importance to the retention of such vacancies for the pupils of their own school; and, after giving due attention to their representations, it appeared to us to be fair and reasonable that Scholarships intended to serve for the benefit of the school during the whole seven years, should not, during a part of that time, be entirely lost to it through the fault of, or through any accident happening to, the individuals holding them. We deemed it therefore just to provide that Merchant Taylors' Scholarships vacated before the completion of seven years should be open, in the first instance, only to candidates educated at Merchant Taylors' School, but in default of qualified candidates from the School, should be thrown open to general competition. We are unable to understand how the ordinance can be considered open on this account to the charge of being prejudicial to the College as a place of learning and education.

"The question connected with the Fellowships is, as we have said, of much greater importance. The ordinance, it will be perceived, directs that half of the Fellowships shall be open, and half appropriated to Scholars of the College educated at the five schools of Merchant Taylors, Coventry, Bristol, Reading, and Tunbridge, which at present enjoy the privilege of sending Scholars. The main objection entertained by the College to the scheme we understand to be, that this part of the ordinance does not appropriate a clear majority of the Fellowships to the Scholars of the College educated at the five schools.

"We have regarded it as an essential part of the duty laid upon us by the Legislature to ensure that elections to Fellowships shall be determined, speaking generally, by the personal merits and fitness of the successful candidate, and not by the accident of his having been born at a particular place, or educated at a particular school. The removal for this purpose of school and local preferences in such elections, appears to us to be clearly indicated by the Act by which our duties are imposed, as one of the objects to be kept in view in the reform of the Statutes. In Section 28,* which contains an enumeration of these objects, power is expressly given to abolish or modify any preference, for the purpose of ensuring that College emoluments shall be conferred according to personal merits and fitness. Again, while a certain power of preventing the abolition of Scholarship preferences is given to the governing bodies of Schools, no similar power is given to them as regards Fellowships (Section 31); and the power given to Colleges of objecting to ordinances framed by us, is limited to cases in which it can be declared by two-thirds of the governing Body, that the ordinance would be prejudicial to the College as a place of learning and education (Section 29). It cannot be denied, we think, that the comparative efficiency of a College as a place of learning and education must depend in a great measure on the excellence

* Oxford University Act, 17 & 18 Vict. c. 81.

of the tutors; that this again must greatly depend on the character, learning, and ability of the Fellows; and these again on the principle upon which Fellows are elected, and the field from which the choice is made. We have accordingly provided for the total abolition of these preferences, except in the case of two Colleges, to which we were prepared to add St. John's, the peculiar circumstances of these Colleges appearing to warrant a difference of constitution. The two in which preferences continue to exist are New College and Jesus College. In the former, in which hitherto all the Fellows have been elected from the Foundation Members of Winchester College, half of the Fellowships are to be open to general competition, the other half are to be appropriated to persons educated at that College; the right of preference, however, will not be confined to Foundation Members; and at whatever College, or even at whatever University, such persons may have been after leaving Winchester, their right will be precisely the same. In Jesus College, where all the Fellowships, except two (and those locally limited), have hitherto been confined to Wales, they are henceforth to be divided, from time to time, as nearly as may be (the whole number is thirteen), into two moieties, one of which is to be open, the other confined to natives of Wales or Monmouthshire. We have, therefore, even in these cases, been careful to avoid giving the Colleges the character of close Colleges, both by making the number of the open Fellowships equal as nearly as may be to that of the appropriated, and by enlarging as widely as possible the limits of eligibility for the latter. We may add, that in the case of Christ Church, which in some respects resembles that of St. John's, no preference for the Senior Studentships, which will answer to Fellowships elsewhere, has been granted to the Westminster Students, who now form a considerable proportion of the whole. The utmost limitation, therefore, which we thought ourselves justified in allowing to St. John's College was, that half of the Fellowships should be appropriated to persons who are or have been Scholars of the College educated at the five schools. More than this we felt ourselves unable to concede, because to concede more would be to fasten upon the College the character of a close College; because we have dealt on different principles with other Colleges having special claims to exceptional treatment; and because St. John's, if its choice of Fellows is more restricted than that of other Colleges, must necessarily suffer in competition with them, as the best candidates will, when twenty or thirty Fellowships are open every year for competition, be unwilling to stand for Fellowships in that which, if the desired concession were made, would be the only close College in the University. Nor should it be forgotten that this College, retaining for itself a peculiar and exclusive position, would nevertheless share the benefit of the great changes which have been introduced into others. These Scholars of St. John's will be admitted to compete freely, not only for the Fellowships in their own College, but for those in other Colleges, a competition, it may be added, from which their own statutes have hitherto jealously excluded them.

"Lastly, we have seen in the peculiar circumstances of St. John's a further reason for insisting on at least an equal division of the Fellowships, because, though the founder's idea of preference in favour of London schools would, if it could have been carried out, have furnished an ample field, yet the number of boys destined for a liberal education at Merchant Taylors' School, the school from which the great majority of the Scholars will be elected, as well as the area and class of persons from whom they are drawn, is practically limited. The same observation applies in a great degree to the other four schools; and it appears to us most undesirable that a College should be permanently governed by a society of which the majority must be chosen from so confined a circle.

" We have therefore been unable to accede to the proposal made to us by the College, that of its eighteen Fellowships ten should always be appropriated to Scholars of the College educated at the five schools named in a former paragraph of this Report. Could we have approved of it, or could we have satisfied ourselves that the point in question was of little importance, we should gladly have avoided a difference which must interfere, greatly to our regret, with the completion of the work entrusted to us. The President and Fellows admit its importance by exercising mainly on this point their right of veto, and by objecting on this ground to the ordinance, as prejudicial to the College as a place of learning and education. Far from agreeing in this opinion, we can only regard their proposal as calculated to secure to the College the character of a close College, which we feel it our duty to refuse. Being thus at issue on an important principle, we have thought it right, though with much regret, to adhere to our judgment, and to persist in the ordinance, which we finally adopted."

A subsequent article in the 'Saturday Review' thus announces the desirableness of a special Act of Parliament with reference to St. John's College, Oxford:—

" St. John's College, from its extreme closeness, is too

much isolated from the rest of the University to be affected by general opinion, or to share in the pervading impression that it was necessary to submit to reasonable measures of reform. The Fellows of St. John's have demanded that they should be allowed to retain a clear majority of close Fellowships, the result of which would inevitably be to restore the general close character of the College; and this at the same time that the members of that College are admitted to free competition for all the other Fellowships which are thrown open in the University. The Commissioners considered that they could not, as trustees for the objects of the Legislature, accede to this demand, more especially as they had required even New College, in spite of its strong Wykehamist traditions, to open half its Fellowships; and the majority of the governing body of St. John's have in effect set their hands to a declaration, that to have half its Fellowships open to merit, would be 'injurious to the College as a place of learning and education.' The Commissioners, as prescribed by the Act in a case of final disagreement, have made a Report to the Home Secretary, which has been laid before Parliament; and a special Act will, no doubt, pass for St. John's College. It is absurd to suppose that the Legislature will allow this particular College to escape the provisions of the general Act."

Some idea of the predominance of the clerical element in the new constitution for St. John's College, Oxford, may be derived from the following Statutes, proposed by the Parliamentary Commissioners for this College.

"33. The Fellowships shall always be divided as nearly as may be into two classes, the one of which (being two-thirds of the whole) shall be called Clerical Fellowships, and the other (being one-third of the whole) Lay

Fellowships. No holder of any Lay Fellowship shall be required to take Holy Orders as a condition of retaining his Fellowship. No person shall be eligible to a Clerical Fellowship who shall not be a Priest or Deacon of the United Church of England and Ireland, or have declared that he intends to take Holy Orders in the said Church. Every person who shall have made such declaration shall be required to take Deacon's Orders at the least within one year after the time at which he shall be of sufficient standing to take the degree of Master of Arts by the statutes of the University, and in default thereof shall vacate his Fellowship: provided, that it shall be lawful for the President and Fellows, in case of sickness, or for any other very urgent cause, to grant a delay for a period not exceeding six months. If any holder of a Lay Fellowship shall take Holy Orders, his Fellowship shall be deemed a Clerical Fellowship, and a holder of a Clerical Fellowship not in Holy Orders may thereupon, with the permission of the President and Fellows, enter the class of Lay Fellows; or the next vacant Fellowship, which would otherwise be a Clerical Fellowship, shall be considered a Lay Fellowship, and be filled up accordingly.

"34. Every holder of a Clerical Fellowship shall be required to take the degrees of Master of Arts and Bachelor of Divinity within one year after the time at which he shall be of sufficient standing to take those degrees respectively by the statutes of the University: and every holder of a Lay Fellowship shall be required to take either the degree of Master of Arts, or the degrees of Bachelor and Doctor of Civil Law, or those of Bachelor and Doctor of Medicine, within one year after the time at which he shall be of sufficient standing to take those degrees respectively by the statutes of the

University. Any Fellow failing to comply with the foregoing provisions shall vacate his Fellowship: provided, that the President and Fellows may, whenever they shall deem it just on special grounds to do so, allow the taking of any such degree to be postponed for a period not exceeding, except in cases of unsoundness of mind, one year."

Sir Thomas White's Statutes of 1555, direct the President to be in Holy Orders, and attached to divine service, virtue, and learning; his academical degree was to be, at least, that of Master of Arts, or Bachelor of Divinity, and he was not allowed to be either a Bishop or a Monk. When a vacancy in the Presidential office occurs, the electors are the Vice-President and the Fellows of the College present in the University; and the Oxford Commissioners recommend that the person shall be chosen who, in the judgment of the electors, shall be most fit for the government of the College as a place of religion, learning, and education, *and* who shall be duly qualified, according to the statutes of the College in force for the time being,—so that the restriction of compulsory ordination is intended to be continued for the Presidency.

The qualifications of 1555, which do not appear to be repealed, for Scholarships, include a general clerical description of the Scholars as "*clerici*," either having the first clerical tonsure of the Roman Catholic Church, or about to adopt that tonsure, and a power of plain-singing, which was required in White's age for the performance of Mass in the College chapel. The ancient Scholarship oath also includes a clause that the young scholar entertained no objection in his mind to the order of the priesthood.

The Oxford Commissioners recommend the following rules on Divine service for St. John's College :—

"The President and Fellows shall, at the first stated general meeting, or as soon afterwards as conveniently may be, make regulations for the daily performance of Divine service according to the Liturgy of the United Church of England and Ireland, within the College, during full term, and at such other times as they shall think proper, and for attendance on the same, and may vary such regulations from time to time; but such regulations shall be made and varied at stated general meetings only, and the Visitor shall have power to disallow and annul any such regulations, or any variation thereof. In the meantime, and until such regulations can be made, the President and Fellows may at any ordinary meeting or meetings make provisional regulations for the same purposes. The provisions of the existing statutes relating to Divine service shall be henceforth void.

"In case the President or any Fellow of the College shall contumaciously cease to conform to the Liturgy of the United Church of England and Ireland, as by law established, such contumacious ceasing to conform shall be a cause for depriving the President of his Presidentship, and any such Fellow of his Fellowship."

All Colleges, both in Oxford and Cambridge, are subject to the provisions of the Act of Uniformity of 1662, with respect to the form of Common Prayers to be openly used in the College chapels,—which, according to that Act, is not to be any other than what is prescribed by the book of Common Prayer.

Masters, Tutors, Fellows, and Chaplains of Colleges, and University Professors, are required by the same Act to subscribe a declaration that they will conform to the

Liturgy of the Church of England, as it was by law established in 1662: the Heads or Masters of Colleges are further required, by the Act of Uniformity, to subscribe to the Thirty-Nine Articles and to the book of Common Prayer, and to declare their unfeigned assent and consent unto and approbation of the said Articles, and of the same book, and to the use of all the prayers, rites and ceremonies, forms, and orders in the said book prescribed and contained.

Such Parliamentary restrictions may give an interest to the following notice of important English Liturgical changes, from the Reformation under King Edward VI.

Archbishop Cranmer, the principal compiler of the English Liturgy, was never wholly satisfied with his work; and King Edward VI. lamented in his diary, that he could not restore the primitive discipline according to his heart's desire, "because of several of the Bishops; some of whom from age, some from ignorance, and some out of love to Popery, were unwilling to consent to it."

King Edward VI., with the advice of his uncle, the Lord Protector (Somerset), and other members of his Council, had appointed the Archbishop (Cranmer) of Canterbury, and certain of the most learned and discreet Bishops, and other learned men of this realm, to draw up and prepare a convenient and meet order, rite, and fashion of common and open prayer, and administration of the sacraments. The Liturgy thus prepared was delivered to the King, and the Parliament enacted penalties, in an Act of Uniformity, for those clergymen who declined to read it to their congregations.

Four years afterwards, in 1552, a second Act of Uniformity obtained the assent of the Legislature, (5th and

6th Edward VI. c. 1,) the preamble to which described the Prayer-book of the previous Act as "a very godly order, set forth by the authority of Parliament, for common prayer and the administration of the sacraments, to be used in the mother tongue, within the Church of England, agreeable to the word of God, and the primitive Church." Parliamentary authority for the revision of the first Book of Common Prayer was subsequently mentioned in the following terms:—

"The King's most excellent Majesty, with the assent of the Lords and Commons, in this present Parliament assembled, and by the authority of the same, hath caused the aforesaid order of common service, intituled 'The Book of Common Prayer,' to be faithfully and godly perused, explained, and made fully perfect, and by the aforesaid authority hath annexed and joined it, so explained and perfected, to this present statute, adding also a form and manner of making and consecrating of Archbishops, Bishops, Priests, and Deacons, to be of like force, authority, and value as the same like foresaid book intituled 'The Book of Common Prayer' was before, and to be accepted, received, used, and esteemed, in like sort and manner."

Early in the reign of Queen Mary, (1553,) both the Acts of Uniformity of King Edward VI. were repealed, and the forms of divine service and administration of sacraments, which had been used in the last year of King Henry VIII., were restored by Parliamentary authority, without any other kind of service or administration of sacraments being allowed in the churches of England and Wales.

At the commencement of the reign of Queen Elizabeth, (1558,) the power of Parliament was again employed to declare the statute of repeal passed under Queen Mary, to "be void and of none effect," and to sanction the restoration of the second Prayer-book of King Edward VI., already alluded to, and which had been authorized by Parliament in the fifth and sixth years of that monarch's reign.

All the ministers of cathedral or parish churches in England and Wales, were directed by the Parliament, under Queen Elizabeth, to employ this Book of Common Prayer, "with one alteration or addition of certain lessons to be used on every Sunday in the year, and with the form of the Litany altered and corrected, and two sentences only added in the delivery of the sacrament to the communicants, and none other (alteration) or otherwise" (stat. 1 Eliz. c. 2).

Stephens, in his edition of Statutes relating to Ecclesiastical Institutions (vol. i. p. 364), states that two years after the passing of this Act, Queen Elizabeth issued her Royal Commission to the Archbishop of Canterbury, and three others, to peruse the order of lessons throughout the whole year, and to cause some new calendars to be imprinted; which were finished and sent to the several Bishops to see them observed in their dioceses, in 1560.

The alteration of the form of the Litany alluded to in the Act, was the omission of a clause which had been adopted in the reign of Edward VI., for deliverance "from the tyranny of the Bishop of Rome, and all his detestable enormities." This clause was omitted in 1558, and other changes were made in accordance with the suggestions of the Royal Commission appointed previously to the passing of the Act.

Many earnest English Protestants had been compelled to take refuge on the Continent, from the persecution which raged in England under Queen Mary. On their return from Zurich, Geneva, and other towns, in which a simpler ritual had obtained public support, the Puritans became dissatisfied with the pompous ceremonial patronized by the Court of Queen Elizabeth. Archbishop Parker, of Canterbury, found it difficult to obtain a general use of the surplice, and a curious letter to his Grace has been preserved, in which Dr. Beaumont, the Master of Trinity College, Cambridge, informed the Archbishop, in 1564, that he had done what he could for the maintenance of orderly apparel in his College; but that he had obtained "from some, more from fear of punishment, than for love of good order."

On the 14th of April, 1571, Mr. Strickland, M.P., introduced a bill, which was read a first time in the House of Commons, for the Reformation of the Book of Common Prayer.

In the debate on this bill, the Treasurer of her Majesty's Household argued, that "if the matters mentioned to be reformed were heretical, then verily they were presently to be condemned; but if they were but matters of ceremony, then it behoveth us (the House of Commons) to refer the same to her Majesty, who hath authority, as chief of the Church, to deal herein. And for us to meddle with matters of her prerogative," quoth he, "it were not expedient."*

Mr. Snagg maintained the articles proposed by Strickland, especially approving of that which rendered it unnecessary to kneel at the sacrament. He wished "to set every man at liberty, and, in this behalf, to do according to his conscience and devotion; he judged it to be nothing derogatory or contrary to the prerogative; and

* Parliamentary History, vol. i. 1571, p. 746.

the direction, he thought fit to be left out of the book, which should be a law," etc.

The House of Commons agreed at the conclusion of the debate, that a Petition should be addressed by the House to the Queen's Majesty, "for her licence and privity to proceed in this bill, before it be any further dealt in."

Subsequently, under King Charles I., the tyrannical conduct of Archbishop Laud, in attempting to enforce the adoption of the Anglican Liturgy in Scotland, and in persecuting eminent Puritans in England, roused the national feelings in both countries to a state of exasperation. The English Parliament, aided by Commissioners from Scotland, set both Royal and Episcopal authority at defiance. In June, 1643, an ordinance was passed in both Houses of Parliament, for the assembly of a Synod of divines and laymen, "to settle the Government and Liturgy of the Church of England;" and the Westminster Assembly, which was, in fact, a Parliamentary commission, prepared a Directory for public worship.

On the 25th September, 1643, the Solemn League and Covenant was assented to by the divines of the Westminster Assembly and the Scotch Commissioners, and subscribed by the Members of both Houses of Parliament.* This document included a declaration on the part of those who subscribed it, that they would endeavour to bring the Churches of God in the three kingdoms (of England, Scotland, and Ireland), to the nearest conjunction and uniformity in religion, confession of faith, form of Church government, directory for worship, and catechizing.

* Parl. Hist. vol. i. p. 747.

In January, 1644–5, an Ordinance of Parliament was issued relative to the Directory for Public Worship, in which the Lords and Commons state, that after consultation with the reverend, pious, and learned divines of the Westminster Assembly, they judge it necessary that the Book of Common Prayer be abolished, and that the Directory for Public Worship be established and observed in all the churches in England and Wales.

The Parliament, in March, 1644–5, ordered an edition of this Directory for Public Worship to be published, and on the 23rd of August, 1645, a Parliamentary Ordinance was passed for the more effectual putting in execution the Directory for Public Worship, in all parish churches and chapels of England and Wales, and for the dispersion of copies in all places and parishes within this kingdom.

The knights and burgesses of the several English and Welsh counties were requested by this ordinance to send printed copies of the Directory for Public Worship to the Parliamentary Committees residing in the said respective counties; and the Committees, on the receipt of these books, were to forward them, with all convenient speed, to the constables, or other local officers of each separate parish or chapelry, within their province. Provision was further made for the copies of the Directory being delivered by the constables to the respective ministers of the different parishes, and any constable failing to obey this injunction, became liable to a fine of five shillings. A fine of forty shillings was ordered to be imposed on every minister who did not observe the Directory for Public Worship, according to the true meaning thereof, in all exercises of the public worship of God, and heavier fines and more severe punishments were ordained in cases of persons using the Book of Common Prayer. Fines of not less than five pounds, and not more than fifty pounds, were appointed to be levied on persons who might be convicted of preaching, writing, or printing in derogation of the Directory for Public Worship. Lastly, all the copies of the Books of Common Prayer remaining in the parish churches or chapels, were ordered to be carried to the Committees of the respective counties, where any such copies might be found, to be disposed of as the Parliament should direct.

Various reasons were urged in the Preface which accompanied the Directory, for the important Liturgical change of superseding the Book of Common Prayer, and replacing it by a manual of suggestions for public worship; and among the arguments brought forward in favour of the latitude thus allowed in the services of religion, the state of enlightenment at that period of religious history was alluded to, in which God had vouchsafed to his people more and better means for the discovery of error and superstition, and for the attainment of knowledge in the mysteries of godliness, and the gifts of preaching and prayer.

After the death of Oliver Cromwell, the Presbyterians united with the Episcopalian party on behalf of the restoration of the Stuart race to the throne of England. A gracious declaration of Royal intentions was issued at Breda, in April, 1660, in which King Charles II. promised liberty to tender consciences. At the Hague, a deputation of Presbyterian clergymen waited on the King, and were informed by him that he had referred the settling of all differences respecting matters of conscience to the wisdom of Parliament; that in his own chapel he would have no other form of prayer used than that of the Book of Common Prayer, and that he would never by his own practice discountenance the good old order of the Church with respect to the use of the surplice.

In October, 1660, a Royal Declaration of considerable liberality, concerning ecclesiastical affairs, was issued at Whitehall. Mr. Hale, M.P., proposed in the House of Commons, on the 6th of November, in the same year, that a bill should be passed on the basis of this Declaration; but on the following day he was made a judge, and as on his promotion, Sir Matthew Hale no longer remained in the House of Commons, the measure which he had initiated was easily defeated by the Church party.

King Charles II. agreed, in his Royal Declaration at Whitehall, to appoint an equal number of learned divines of both persuasions (the Episcopalians and Presbyterians) to review the Liturgy, and to make such alterations as should be thought most necessary. On the 25th of March, 1661, the Royal Commission for the conference on Liturgical alterations was issued; the Commission met in the Savoy, in the Strand, which gave its name to the conference. Some delay took place before any meeting was held, and on the 15th of April, Sheldon, Bishop of London, informed the Presbyterians that there was nothing to be done until they (the Presbyterians) had, in writing, brought in all they had to adduce against the Book of Common Prayer.

Royal orders had been sent out on the 11th of April, to the Archbishop of Canterbury, for the summoning of a convocation of the clergy, and no time was lost in thus superseding the Conference.

Calamy and Baxter were chosen on the 2nd of May, 1661, to sit as proctors for the clergy of the Archdeaconry of London in convocation; but as Bishop Sheldon had the power to select two out of four, or four out of six of the clergy nominated as proctors, he passed over the names of those two eminent divines, and selected others to attend the Convocation.

On the 4th of May, the Savoy Conference again met; the Presbyterians delivered in their liturgical objections, and Baxter presented his reformed Liturgy, which he wished to leave on record, as a witness that he and his friends were not adverse to a settled form of public worship.

Formal replies were prepared by the Bishops to the exceptions of the Presbyterians; but the conference terminated without any agreement on either side. A new Parliament met about the same time in Westminster, and all the influence of the Crown was given to the restoration of the Book of Common Prayer in the churches of England and Wales.

Letters patent were issued by the King in June, 1661, authorizing the Convocation to make canons and constitutions; but this inconsiderate stretch of arbitrary power does not appear to have been acted upon; indeed, the resolution of the House of Commons in 1640, prevented any such canons from being made, to bind the clergy or laity, "without consent of Parliament;" and practically no canons were promulgated by Convocation in 1661.

It is curious to observe the change of Royal policy from the declaration concerning ecclesiastical affairs in October, 1660, to the message to the House of Lords, in February, 1662, shortly before the introduction of the Bill for Uniformity, in Parliament. Ample evidence is thus afforded of the duplicity of the Government toward the Presbyterians of that period.

In the Declaration of 1660, King Charles II. observed, that the present jealousies would hardly agree upon a Synod, and that he would himself give some determination to the matters in difference, until such a Synod might be called, as might without passion or prejudice give him such further assistance towards a perfect union of affections, as well as submission to authority, as was necessary. With respect to the Book of Common Prayer, the King remarked, that since he found some exceptions had been made against several things therein, he would appoint an equal number of Divines of both persuasions (Episcopalians and Presbyterians) to review the same, and to make such alterations as should be thought necessary.

On the faith of the promises contained in his Declaration, Charles II. obtained possession of the crown of England; and having firmly grasped his sceptre, he became a bitter persecutor of the Presbyterian party, which had assisted in his elevation to the throne.

Without waiting for the result of the Savoy Conference of Episcopalians and Presbyterians, Charles II. summoned a Convocation of Clergy, actuated with the strongest desire for retaliation against the Presbyterian denomination; and having, in his Royal Message to the House of Lords, described the Savoy Conference as a Royal commission to "several Bishops and other divines, to review the Book of a Common Prayer," he informed the Peers that he had summoned a Convocation to review the Book of Common Prayer, and had approved their proceedings; and concluded with a recommendation for the adoption of the Prayer Book thus sanctioned by the Convocation into the intended Act of Uniformity.

Many of the clergy, in different parts of England, had

suffered under the Commonwealth, from their attachment to the forms of the Book of Common Prayer; and, when elected into an ecclesiastical Synod, and requested to revise the Liturgy, which Parliament would constitute as a test for the holding of rich benefices, they inserted whatever was most annoying to the Puritans in the revised Book of Common Prayer.

As soon as the Liturgy recommended by Convocation had obtained Parliamentary sanction in the Act of Uniformity of 1662, the wishes of the Episcopalians were gratified by the secession of about two thousand Nonconformist Ministers from the communion of the Church of England. Their benefices were filled by the adherents of the old Liturgy; and the Nonconformists of 1662 became the revered founders of Protestant Dissenting congregations in many parts of the country.

Mr. Hallam, on calmly reviewing the subscriptions imposed by the Act of Uniformity, remarks, of the "unfeigned assent and consent to all and everything contained in the Book of Common Prayer," that such a test seems to amount "to a complete approbation of an entire volume, such as a man of sense hardly gives to any book; and which, at a time when scrupulous persons were with great difficulty endeavouring to reconcile themselves to submission, placed a new stumbling-block in their way, which, without abandoning their integrity, they found it impossible to surmount."

The revolution of 1688 was a happy event in the annals of religious liberty: a toleration act for Protestant Dissenters passed both Houses of Parliament in 1689, and a bill was introduced into the House of Lords for the uniting of the Protestants of the kingdom. When this latter measure was under consideration, some amendments were proposed in the House of Lords, and the question was put on the 4th of April, (1689,) whether to agree with the Committee of the House in leaving out a clause about the indifferency of posture at the receiving the Sacrament; and the votes being equal, it was, according to ancient rule, carried in the negative. The next day, the Lords resumed the debate on the report of the same amendments, particularly of a clause concerning a Commission to be given out by the King to some Bishops and others of the Clergy; and it was proposed that some Laymen should be added in the Commission; upon which, the question being put, the votes, including the proxies, were equal, and so it was again carried in the negative; four Lords, the Marquis of Winchester, Lord Mordaunt, Lord Lovelace, and the Earl of Stamford, entering their dissent with the following reasons :*—

"1. Because the Act itself being, as the preamble sets forth, designed for the peace of the State, the putting the Clergy into the Commission, with a total exclusion of the Laity, lays this humiliation on the Laity, as if the Clergy of the Church of England were alone friends to the peace of the State; and the Laity less able or less concerned to provide for it.

"2. Because the matters to be considered being barely of human constitution, viz. the Liturgy and Ceremonies of the Church of England, which had their establishment from King, Lords Spiritual and Temporal, and Commons, assembled in Parliament, there can be no reason why the Commissioners for altering anything in that civil constitution should consist only of men of one sort of them; unless it be supposed that human reason is to be quitted in this affair, and the inspiration of spiritual men to be alone depended upon.

* From the life of Archbishop Tillotson, in vol. i. of his works, edited by the Rev. Thomas Birch, M.A.

"3. Because, though upon Romish principles the Clergy may have a title to meddle alone in matters of religion, yet with us they cannot, where the Church is acknowledged and defined to consist of Clergy and Laity; and so those matters of religion which fall under human determination, being properly the business of the Church, belong to both; for in what is of divine institution, neither Clergy nor Laity can make any alteration at all.

"4. Because the pretending that differences and delays may arise by mixing laymen with ecclesiastics, to the frustrating the design of the Commission, is vain and out of doors; unless those that make use of this pretence suppose, that the Clergy-part of the Church have distinct interests or designs from the Lay-part of the same Church; and this will be a reason, if good, why one or other of them should quit the House for fear of obstructing the business of it.

"5. Because the Commission being intended for the satisfaction of Dissenters, it would be convenient that Laymen of different ranks, nay, perhaps of different opinions too, should be mixed in it, the better to find expedients for that end, rather than Clergymen alone of our Church, who are generally observed to have very much the same way of reasoning and thinking.

"6. Because it is the most ready way to facilitate the passing the alterations into a law, that Lay Lords and Commons should be joined in the Commission, who may be able to satisfy both the Houses, of the reasons upon which they were made, and thereby remove all fears and jealousies which ill men may raise against the Clergy, of their endeavouring to keep up, without grounds, a distinct interest from that of the Laity, whom they so carefully exclude from being joined with them in consultations of common concernment, that they will not have those have any part in the declaration, who must have the greatest part in the determining.

"7. Because such a restrained Commission lies liable to this great objection, that it might be made use of to elude repeated promises, and the present general expectation of compliance with tender consciences, when the providing for it is taken out of the ordinary course of Parliament, to be put into the hands of those alone who were latest in admitting any need of it, and who may be thought the more unfit to be the sole composers of our differences, when they are looked upon by some as parties.

"Lastly, because, after all, this carries a dangerous supposition with it, as if the Laity were not a part of the Church, nor had any power to meddle in matters of religion; a supposition directly opposite to the constitution both of Church and State, which will make all alterations utterly impossible, unless the Clergy alone be allowed to have power to make laws in matters of religion; since what is established by law cannot be taken away or changed but by consent of Laymen in Parliament, the Clergy themselves having no authority to meddle in this very case, in which the Laity are excluded by this vote, but what they derive from Lay hands."

These reasons were signed by the Marquis of Winchester, and the Lords Mordaunt and Lovelace, and the Earl of Stamford wrote under them, that he dissented for the following, as well as other reasons, " because it is contrary to three statutes made in the reign of Henry VIII.* and one in Edward VI.† which empower thirty-two Commissioners to alter the Canon and Ecclesiastical Laws, etc., whereof sixteen to be of the Laity, and sixteen of the Clergy."

Bishop Burnet . . . argued warmly on the other side, imagining that the Clergy would have come into the design of the Bill with zeal and unanimity, and being apprehensive that the proposed amendment of the clause would be looked on by them as taking the matter out of their hands. But he was soon afterwards convinced that

* Stat. 25 Hen. VIII. c. 19 ; 27 Hen. VIII. c. 15 ; and 35 Hen. VIII. c. 16.
† Stat. 3 & 4 Edw. VI. c. 11, A.D. 1549.

he had taken wrong measures, and that the method proposed by the Lords on the other side was the only one likely to be effectual. Nor did his opposition to it so recommend him to the Clergy as to balance the censure which he fell under, for moving in another proviso in that Bill, that the subscription, instead of "assent" and "consent," should be only to "submit" with a promise of conformity; and for his zeal for the other clause above mentioned, of dispensing with the posture of kneeling at the Sacrament.

While the Bill [of Union] and that of Toleration were depending, Mr. Locke, whose opinions are well known to have been favourable to both, wrote a letter dated March 12th, 1688-9, to his friend Philip à Limborch, an eminent writer and professor of divinity among the Arminians in Amsterdam, in which he declares it as his opinion that the Episcopal Clergy were no great friends to those Bills, and other matters then in agitation in England; "whether," says he, "to their own or the nation's advantage, let them consider."

The Bill of Union as well as that of Toleration had been moved for by some of the Bishops, who afterwards scrupled the oaths; and they both were drawn and offered by the Earl of Nottingham, who had been appointed one of the principal Secretaries of State on the day of their Majesties' proclamation; and they were the same which had been prepared for the House of Commons in King Charles the Second's reign during the debates of the exclusion; but then considered rather as artifices to allay the heat of that time, and to render the Church party more popular. And even now, those who had moved for the Bill of Union, and afterwards brought it into the House, acted a very disingenuous part; for while they studied to recommend themselves by this show of moderation, they set on their friends to oppose it; and such as were sincerely and cordially for it, were represented as the enemies of the Church, who intended to subvert it. When the Bill had passed the Lords, and was sent down to the House of Commons, it was suffered to lie upon the table; and instead of proceeding in it, the House of Commons resolved upon an address to the King, in which they were joined by the Lords, and which was presented to his Majesty on the 20th of April, desiring him to continue his care for the Church of England established by law; and to issue forth writs, according to the ancient usage and practice of the kingdom in time of Parliament, for calling a Convocation of the Clergy, which practically defeated the measure.

In September, 1689, a Royal Commission was issued to ten Bishops and twenty Divines, to prepare matters to be considered by Convocation, and subsequently submitted to Parliament. The result of this step would not encourage a similar experiment at the present time. Convocation declined to enter on any of the topics prepared for them by the Royal Commission; although the propositions of Liturgical amendments proposed to be laid before them were of the mildest, and in some instances most insignificant, nature.

The alterations in the Book of Common Prayer, agreed upon by the Commission of 1689, were printed by order of the House of Commons, in a small Parliamentary volume, in June, 1854.

More important Liturgical reforms were carried into effect, in a Convention of the Protestant Episcopal Church of the United States, in 1785, by the union of divines and laymen in the same assembly.

A correspondence ensued with the Archbishops and Bishops of England, on the Liturgical alterations adopted by the Convention; and in October, 1768, votes were taken on two points proposed to be altered by the Americans.

The Convention agreed with the Archbishops of Canterbury and York, that the words, "he descended into hell" should continue to form a part of the Apostles' Creed for the Protestant Episcopal Church of the United States; but they declined to assent to the recommendation of the Archbishops, that the Athanasian Creed should continue as a part of the Book of Common Prayer for the Protestant Episcopal Church. A decided majority of the deputies from the Protestant Episcopal Churches of different States negatived the proposition to allow the Athanasian Creed a place in the revised Liturgy; and, in fact, the important Liturgical change of omitting the Athanasian Creed met with almost unanimous approbation.

Within the last few years, meetings of the English Convocation for the province of Canterbury have been revived in Westminster, but the assembly is wisely forbidden to prolong its sittings, and no power of action is allowed to it.

In the summer of 1855, the following correspondence took place between the Archbishop of Canterbury, as President of the Convocation of Clergy, and the Right Hon. Sir George Grey, Bart., M.P., Secretary of State for the Home Department; in which the venerable Primate was informed, that her Majesty the Queen had not been advised to comply with the prayer of the Convocation that a Royal License should be granted to them, to consider and agree upon a Canon or Constitution to modify the representation of the Clergy in the House of Convocation :—

"*Lambeth, July* 27, 1855.

"Sir,

"As President of the Convocation of Clergy recently assembled, I have the honour of enclosing to you an address to her Majesty, which passed both Houses, and which, in the name of the Convocation, I hereby offer to her Majesty's gracious consideration.

"I have, etc.

"*Right Honourable*   (Signed)   "J. B. CANTUAR.
Sir George Grey, Bart."

To the QUEEN's Most Excellent Majesty:

We, your Majesty's faithful subjects, the Archbishop, Bishops, and Clergy, of the province of Canterbury, assembled in Convocation, humbly represent to your Majesty:—

That Committees of Convocation have sat, and, after careful consideration, have reported to Convocation on various subjects deeply concerning the spiritual welfare of this realm, namely, on the measures needful for enforcing discipline amongst the Clergy; the extension of the Church; the modification of her Services, and the reform of the representation of the Clergy in the Provincial Synod of Canterbury.

We are convinced that the full consideration of these subjects is of great moment to the well-being of our Church; but in order that our deliberations on these, and any matters which your Majesty shall see fit to submit for our consideration, may be so conducted, as to give to the Church the fullest satisfaction, that in such deliberations the mind of the Clergy will be fairly expressed, we humbly submit to your Majesty, that it seems desirable to modify the representation of the Clergy in the Lower House of Convocation.

We venture therefore humbly to pray your Majesty to grant

us your Royal License to consider and agree upon a Canon or Constitution to be submitted to your Majesty's consideration, for effecting such modification.

(Signed)   J. B. CANTUAR., *President.*

"*Whitehall, August* 7, 1855.
"MY LORD ARCHBISHOP,
" I have had the honour to lay before the Queen the address transmitted to me by your Grace on the 27th ultimo, from the Archbishop, Bishops, and Clergy of the Province of Canterbury assembled in Convocation, praying her Majesty to grant them her Royal License to consider and agree upon a Canon or Constitution to be submitted to her Majesty's consideration, for effecting a modification in the representation of the Lower House of Convocation.

" I have the honour to inform your Grace that this address was graciously received by her Majesty, but that her Majesty has not been advised to comply with its prayer.

"I have, etc.
"*His Grace the Archbishop*   (Signed)   "G. GREY.*
of Canterbury."

Public opinion fully sanctions this determination of her Majesty's Government to permit no legislative power to a purely Clerical assembly. Commissioners appointed, either by the Crown or Parliament, constitute at the present day the legitimate organs for ecclesiastical improvement, and questions of grave importance with reference to the Church have been already considered by the Oxford and Cambridge University Commissioners.

A recent movement also manifests the progress of public opinion towards Liturgical reform, when, on the

* Paper printed by order of the House of Commons, August, 1855.

17th January, 1859, the following warrant was issued by the Queen, under her Majesty's Royal Sign Manual:—

"VICTORIA, R.—Whereas by our Royal Warrant of the 21st day of June, 1837, in the first year of our reign, we commanded that certain forms of prayer and service made for the 5th of November, the 30th of January, and the 29th of May, should be forthwith printed and published and annexed to the Book of Common Prayer and Liturgy of the United Church of England and Ireland, to be used yearly on the said days in all Cathedral and Collegiate Churches and Chapels, in all Chapels of Colleges and Halls within our Universities of Oxford, Cambridge, and Dublin, and of our Colleges of Eton and Winchester, and in all parish Churches and Chapels within those parts of our United Kingdom called England and Ireland.

"And whereas in the last Session of Parliament addresses were presented to us by both Houses of Parliament, praying us to take into our consideration our proclamation in relation to the said forms of prayer and service made for the 5th day of November, the 30th day of January, and the 29th day of May, with a view to their discontinuance.

"And whereas we have taken into our consideration the subject of the said addresses, and, after due deliberation, we have resolved that the use of the said forms of prayer and service shall be discontinued.

"Now, therefore, our will and pleasure is, that so much of our said Royal Warrant of the 21st day of June, 1837, in the first year of our reign, as is hereinbefore recited, be revoked, and that the use of the said forms of prayer and service made for the 5th of November, the 30th of January, and the 29th of May, be henceforth discontinued in all Cathedral and Collegiate Churches and Chapels, in all Chapels of Colleges and Halls within our Universities of Oxford, Cambridge, and Dublin, and of our Colleges of Eton and Winchester, and in all parish Churches and Chapels within the parts of our United Kingdom called England and Ireland, and that the said forms of prayer and service be not henceforth printed and published with, or annexed to, the Book of Common Prayer and Liturgy of the United Church of England and Ireland.

"Given at our Court, at St. James's, the 17th day of January, 1859, in the 22nd year of our reign. By her Majesty's command,

"S. H. WALPOLE."

In the House of Lords, on the 6th of May, 1858, Lord Ebury moved, that an humble address be presented to her Majesty, for a Commission to consider whether the Liturgy of the Church of England be not capable of such alterations as may render it more profitable than it now is for the religious instruction and education of the people. During his speech on this motion, his Lordship quoted the following recommendation from a report on Liturgical amendments, by a Committee recently appointed by the Convocation of the Clergy of the Province of Canterbury :—

"That a shorter order for daily prayer be compiled from the Book of Common Prayer, with a prescribed lesson or lessons of Holy Scripture, which might be used instead of the present order of daily morning and evening prayer."

At the close of the discussion on Lord Ebury's motion, Earl Granville observed, that "the subject was one that ought to be carefully considered before any positive step was taken." The motion was withdrawn by the leave of the House.

A few weeks after the publication of the above-mentioned Royal Warrant, it was followed by the introduction of a Bill into the House of Commons to repeal the Acts of Parliament, and parts of Acts, which relate to the use of special forms of Church Services for the

30th of January, the 29th of May, and the 5th of November, as well as to abrogate the enactments of the Irish Parliament, which required the observance of the 23rd of October, and the 29th of May as anniversary days. Parliament alone, without Convocation, is therefore manifestly sufficient for the removal of political Services from the Prayer-book.

The Dean of Bristol (Dr. Elliot), in a sermon preached on the 5th of November, 1854, in the cathedral of that city, referred to the influence of Parliament at the time of the Reformation, and to the "manly and most noble Statutes of Parliament, which thickly stud the annals of the reigns of Henry, and of Edward, and of Elizabeth," and thus explained the constitutional power in Clerical matters obtained by Parliament in the sixteenth century:—

"At the Reformation, and in these acts of their national legislature, the English people asserted their right to frame their ecclesiastical polity in such manner as to themselves should seem most fit, and wrested the usurped power, not only from the hands of the Pope of Rome, but of the Clergy also, despite of all their pretensions to be exclusively 'the Church,' to which Christ had assigned power, and to which he demanded also obedience. If you would see how this nation thus asserted its independence of priestly dominion, whether in the Pope solely, or in the Clergy collectively, and asserted further the right and duty of Christian peoples to take unto themselves authority in ecclesiastical matters within their own proper limits as a nation or people, you will possibly most easily and readily see it illustrated in that act of Elizabeth, which, in giving us our Book of Prayer, gave us that outward form of faith and of worship which we retain, with little change, unto this day.

"At that time, and on this very subject, the Bishops and Abbots then in Parliament (being all of them Romanists) earnestly contended against the reception of the Prayer-book, calling it, as did the Jews the faith of the Nazarenes, a heresy. At the same time the Clergy assembled in their Convocation, adopted and promulgated resolutions and declarations denouncing the tenets of the Reformation as heresy, and affirming, in the strongest manner possible, and in their very strictest sense, the peculiar and antagonistic doctrines of Rome.

"The answer of the English people to these reclamations of the Bishops and Clergy was given in the Act of Uniformity" (of Elizabeth).

In recent times, and with a view to the advancement of education, Parliament has made an onward movement towards religious liberty, by the abolition of scholarship oaths in the Colleges of Cambridge, and by enacting, in the Cambridge University Act, that there shall be no declaration of religious opinion or belief for a College scholarship in that seat of learning.

The portion of the scholarship oath, thus abrogated in Trinity College, Cambridge, and which dates from the sixteenth century, was as follows:—

"I, N. N., swear, and take God to witness, that I will embrace with my whole soul, the true religion of Christ; that I will place the authority of Scripture before the judgments of men; that I will take my rule of life, and sum of faith from the word of God; that I will account as human other matters which are not proved from the word of God; that I will hold the Royal authority supreme among men, and in no wise submitted to the jurisdiction of foreign Bishops; that I will refute with my whole will and mind opinions contrary to the will of

God; and that, in the matter of religion, I will prefer truth to custom, and things written to things not written."

---

14. *Extracts from the Memorial of the Mayor, Aldermen, and Burgesses of the Borough of Cambridge, in Council assembled, dated 5th of February, 1852, to her Majesty's Commissioners for inquiry into the State, Discipline, Studies, and Revenues of the University and Colleges of Cambridge, respecting the Proctors and Pro-proctors of the University, and the power of the University over the town.*

Under the head of "Search for Common Women," the Mayor and Town Council of Cambridge submitted to the Royal Commissioners, in 1852, the following important observations :—

"By various charters granted to the University, the officers of that body are empowered to search in this town (Cambridge) and suburbs, by day and night, for common women and persons suspected of evil, and to punish them by imprisonment, banishment, or otherwise.

"We have lately obtained a local Act, with which is incorporated 'The Town Police Clauses Act, 1847,' under which the magistrates of the town have power to punish 'every common prostitute or night-walker loitering and importuning passengers for the purpose of prostitution,' and this, with the power given by the Vagrant Act (5 Geo. IV. c. 83, sect. 3) to punish prostitutes behaving riotously or indecently, is amply sufficient to preserve decency in the streets.

"The police are vigilant in apprehending offenders against these Acts, who are duly punished by the magistrates.

"The Proctor and Pro-proctors of the University, however, still continue to exercise the powers of search given them by the University charters. Occasionally mistakes have been committed, and the general exercise of the powers in question tends to place all the unfortunate women of the class referred to on a level with the very lowest; to create strong popular feelings against the University authorities; and to subject the University to a large annual expenditure in the performance of duties which, as it appears to us, can be more efficiently and properly executed by a police force.

"Much of course must depend, in the exercise of such powers, on the discretion of the gentlemen who fill the Procuratoria' office, and we have no reason to believe that any just exception can be taken to the manner in which the present Proctors (of 1852) execute their office; we cannot, however, refrain from suggesting a doubt, whether duties of this kind are strictly compatible with the Clerical character, and the Proctors are, as you must be aware, with few exceptions, clergymen."*

A copy of this Memorial was forwarded by the Bishop of Chester, chairman of the Cambridge University Royal Commission, to the Vice-chancellor of the University, and a Syndicate, or Committee, was consequently appointed in the academical Senate, by whom remarks were made upon the various topics alluded to, which

---

* Evidence at the conclusion of the Report of the Cambridge Royal Commissioners, p. 36, presented to both Houses of Parliament, by command of her Majesty, 1852.

were transmitted by the Vice-chancellor to the Cambridge University Royal Commission.

In reply to the observations of the Town Council of Cambridge, that the powers, exercised by the Proctors and Pro-proctors, of search for common women, and of punishing them by imprisonment, etc., "tend to place all the unfortunate women of the class referred to, on a level with the very lowest," the academical Syndics remark, that "the University is not chargeable with this imputation. It pays attention to difference of condition and demeanour, and makes arrangements accordingly; and it is also the obvious duty of the chaplain who is in attendance upon the persons imprisoned, and who is provided and paid by the University, to attend to such differences in his treatment of them, and in his endeavours to reform them. Moreover, it is well known, that the fear of imprisonment operates, in a very great degree, to deter those of better condition from walking the streets."

Various medieval oaths, which originated in a charter of 52 Henry III., were quoted by the Town Council of Cambridge in their memorial, as still annually administered before the Vice-chancellor and Proctors to some members of the municipal Body, and these oaths are so utterly unsuited to the altered circumstances and improved state of the local Cambridge police at the present day, that they merely serve to revive the distasteful recollection of the ancient dominant control of the University over the town of Cambridge.

Among the oaths still administered to the borough authorities, the following form is expected to be sworn to, by two inhabitants of every parish, relating to the search for suspected persons:—

"You shall swear, [if called upon,] every fortnight, to

make diligent and faithful search for all suspected persons lying within your parish, and to present every such, so tarrying for three nights, to the Vice-chancellor and the Mayor. So help you God in Jesus Christ."

Of late years, the memorialists state, that the words, "if called upon," have been usually, but not uniformly, introduced into the foregoing oath. Parties summoned by the Mayor to take this oath, frequently decline to attend.

No adequate reason, in the opinion of the Cambridge Town Council, exists at the present day for such an oath; and they consider that the exacting it tends much to impair the solemnity with which an oath ought ever to be regarded, and engenders or sanctions a notion that the town authorities are dependent on the University. The Town Council refer on this subject to the following observation of a writer of the early part of the last century on Cambridge: "The town seems to be subordinate to the University, for their Mayor, every year, when he is elected, takes an oath to observe and conserve the privileges of the University."—*Macky's Journey through England*, 5th edit. vol. i. p. 158.

Among the proofs which still remain of the subordination of the Town of Cambridge to the University, one of the most remarkable is, the absolute power exercised by the Vice-chancellor of the University over theatrical performances in the town and neighbourhood. An authority is also said to be claimed by the Vice-chancellor, of prohibiting all other entertainments within the town of Cambridge, to which he has not given his express sanction. The Town Council remark, that "instances have occurred in which such sanction has been apparently withheld capriciously. A few years ago, Mr. John

Braham, the celebrated vocalist, was desirous of giving a concert here, but the Vice-chancellor withheld his assent, and the design was abandoned."

"We believe," observe the Town Council, that "no valid reason exists, why theatrical and other entertainments of the like nature should be subject to other control here than elsewhere."*

* Report of the Cambridge University Royal Commission. Evidence, p. 38. Relations between the University and the Town.

UNIVERSITY REPRESENTATION.

YOUTHS, in ancient times, were accustomed to enter at an early age in the Universities of Oxford and Cambridge, and to remain for many consecutive years in those seats of learning. The changes in study occasioned by the introduction of Greek learning, the Reformation, and the compulsory disuse of the scholastic system, in the sixteenth century, diminished the necessity for long periods of academical apprenticeship, and the age for taking the first or Bachelor's degree in Arts gradually approached to twenty-one years.

Under the circumstances of early entrance into the Universities, a governing body, limited by the degree of Master of Arts, and other higher degrees, had been established, and in 1300, when the Chancellor and Universities of Oxford and Cambridge were directed, by a writ of King Edward I., to send representatives to Parliament, selected from among their more discreet members, and those most skilled in written law, the Masters of Arts and other higher graduates formed a suitable constituency to return a few lawyers, in order to assist the King in the examination of his title to Scotland.

In 1604, Letters Patent were granted by King James I., to the Chancellor, Masters, and Scholars of the Universities of Oxford and Cambridge, respectively, to elect two of the more discreet and sufficient members of each University, to be burgesses in the English Parliament; and in 1613, a similar privilege was conferred on the Provost, Fellows, and Scholars of Trinity College, Dublin, to return two members, elected from their own body, to sit in the Irish Parliament.

Under the Commonwealth no writs were issued for the return of members, either to the ancient English Universities or to Trinity College, Dublin. At the time of the union of Great Britain and Ireland, in 1800, the representation of Trinity College, Dublin, was restricted to one member, and in 1832 the franchise in that seat of learning was extended to the Masters of Arts and other higher graduates of the University of Dublin, and two members were appointed for the constituency, including, with the older graduates of the University, the Fellows and Scholars of the College who were twenty-one years of age.

Permanent residence in Trinity College, Dublin, does not appear to have been intended for the Fellows of that institution by Lord Burghley, their first Chancellor, as the Royal Charter of foundation, in 1592, directs the Fellowships to be vacated seven years after the degree of Master of Arts had been taken, so as to provide rewards for other candidates, who were to succeed to the vacant emoluments.

In the University of Cambridge, an important alteration took place in 1608, when the heads of houses decided that academical residence was not requisite after the degree of Bachelor of Arts, in the following words :—

"Those who for their learning and manners, are according to statute admitted Bachelors in Arts, are not so strictly tied to a local commorancy and study within the University or Town of Cambridge, but that being at the end of nine terms able, by their accustomed exercises and other examination, to approve themselves worthy to be Masters of Arts, may justly be admitted to that degree."

New Cambridge regulations of the past year render unnecessary even the appearance in Cambridge of a candidate for the degree of Master of Arts, which is conferred, as a matter of course, after the payment of the usual fees, on the Bachelor of Arts who has attained the academical standing of three years of interval from his first degree.

In the University of Oxford, one Term of residence after the B.A. degree is required for the M.A. degree, and after the usual interval of three years, further residence is dispensed with, in each individual case, by a letter from the Chancellor of the University, which is given as a matter of course.

So completely is the dispensation a form, that a stock of such letters is believed to be deposited, in blank, with the Registrar of the University, to be filled up as required.

Very few graduates continue their residence in either University, of Oxford or Cambridge, after their M.A. degree, unless they are on the foundation of a College. In May, 1841, a census of Cambridge academical residents was taken, at the request of the author of this work, which was followed, in May, 1842, by a similar census of Oxford academical residents, and which led to the following results :—

At Cambridge there were 15, and at Oxford 39 Masters of Arts, and other higher graduates, resident, who were not on any College foundation, whilst 145

Masters of Arts, and other higher graduates, belonging to the foundation of the different Colleges respectively, were resident at Cambridge, and 191 similarly resident on the College foundations in Oxford.

Among the Bachelors of Arts, and other graduates below the M.A. degree, there were 22 Fellows of Colleges, and 92, including Scholars, resident at Cambridge. At Oxford, among the resident Bachelors of Arts, and other graduates below the M.A. degree, were 38 Fellows, 39 Scholars, 22 Chaplains, and 3 Clerks on the College foundations, and 59 graduates who were not on any College foundation.

The enumeration of resident undergraduates included, at Cambridge, 75 Scholars and 1120 other Students; whilst at Oxford the corresponding list comprised 29 undergraduate Fellows, 154 Scholars, and 1039 other Students.

Of the Masters of Arts, and other higher graduates, who constitute the resident members of the Senate at Cambridge, about three-fourths are Clergymen, and one-eighth probably intend to take Orders, so that not more than one-eighth of the resident constituency remain permanently laymen: a similar proportion may probably be found in the Oxford residents. College Tutors, both at Oxford and Cambridge, are usually selected by the Heads of Colleges from among the graduate Fellows who are in Orders, and private Tutors are generally chosen by the Students themselves, from among the more successful of the graduates, who have attained a reputation in the art of preparing candidates for the University and College examinations.

For the degree of Master of Arts, at Oxford, which gives the right of the electoral franchise, subscription is required to the Thirty-Nine Articles, and to the three articles of the Thirty-Sixth Canon of the Church of England. At Cambridge, where the Senate possesses the power of returning the two University representatives to Parliament, no person is admitted into that body, unless he has declared himself to be a member of the Church of England.

The six Parliamentary representatives of the ancient Universities possess the same privileges with other members of Parliament in legislating for the whole British nation, whilst the present exclusive University franchise limits the right of voting in the Universities of Oxford and Cambridge to Churchmen.

On referring to the Letters Patent of 1604, granting the right of representation to the Universities of Oxford and Cambridge, Colleges and Collegiate property will be seen to have been especially regarded in those Royal Charters.

Each University is described as "consisting" of a certain number of Colleges, Halls, and Hostels, of good learning, founded partly by illustrious ancestors of royalty, the kings and queens of this kingdom, and partly by archbishops, lords, grandees, nobles, bishops, and other distinguished, pious, and devout persons; and endowed with noble and ample rents, revenues, possessions, privileges, and other property, to the honour of God, and the support and promotion of piety, virtue, scholarship, and learning.

For the government of the Colleges, Halls, and Hostels, and their members, local statutes had been made, and many Acts of Parliament had been passed, respecting the property and administration of these institutions.

Burgesses in Parliament were therefore granted to

each of the Universities of Oxford and Cambridge, for the common advantage of the whole State, of the Universities respectively, and of every College, Hall, and Hostel therein situated, so as to enable the Parliament to become acquainted with the condition of these ancient seats of learning, as well as of their Colleges, Halls, and Hostels, and to prevent prejudice or injury from arriving to any of these institutions through the want of proper knowledge and information.*

In 1852, the Oxford Royal Commissioners thus report on the modern state of that venerable seat of learning, which corresponds with the union of Colleges in the University, alluded to in the Letters Patent of 1604.

"The Colleges have now become the University, and have absorbed all the functions of that institution, both educational and literary. Its students must be all members of one of these societies."

The following summary of the members of the Oxford Convocation who possess the electoral franchise, and of the remaining members of the University, shows the relative numbers in January, 1858:—

	Members of Convocation.	Members on the Books.
University College	150	285
Balliol College	197	345
Merton College	105	170
Exeter College	291	501
Oriel College	208	387
Queen's College	167	251
New College	108	186

* An English translation of these Cambridge Letters Patent of 1604, is contained in the Collection of Statutes of the University and Colleges of Cambridge, by James Heywood, p. 355. The Oxford Letters Patent of 1604 are published in Peckwell's Election Cases, vol. i. p. 48.

	Members of Convocation.	Members on the Books.
Lincoln College	120	195
All Souls' College	92	114
Magdalen College	162	220
Brasenose College	281	424
Corpus College	99	158
Christ Church	464	807
Trinity College	177	304
St. John's College	216	339
Jesus College	83	154
Wadham College	168	310
Pembroke College	103	219
Worcester College	192	359
St. Mary Hall	53	75
Magdalen Hall	131	254
New Inn Hall	20	34
St. Alban Hall	11	21
St. Edmund Hall	45	70
Litton's Hall	1	7
	3644	6189*

A detailed summary of the members of the Senate of the University of Cambridge and of the undergraduates is subjoined from the Cambridge Calendar for 1858:—

	Members of the Senate.	Under-Graduates.	Members on the boards.
Trinity College	1598	473	2451
St. John's College	904	292	1467
Caius College	256	125	494
Emmanuel College	215	93	380
Christ's College	202	95	369
Corpus Christi College	181	62	284
Queen's College	163	43	263
Jesus College	148	39	234
Trinity Hall	81	68	231
St. Peter's College	163	33	225

* See the Oxford University Calendar for 1858.

	Members of the Senate.	Under-Graduates.	Members on the boards.
Clare College	147	42	218
St. Catharine's College	144	31	216
Magdalen College	130	51	213
Sidney College	75	21	138
King's College	101	15	137
Pembroke College	86	29	136
Downing College	41	6	60
Commorantes in Villâ	21	0	0
	4656	1518	7516

From the latter table, it appears that there are 6174 members of the Senate and undergraduates belonging to the University of Cambridge, and as the total number of members of the University is 7516, there will be 1342 Bachelors of Arts, Law, Medicine, and Music, who have graduated at Cambridge, and have preserved their names on the books of the respective Colleges. A similar number of probably about 1300 Bachelors of Arts, Law, Medicine, and Music, are still unenfranchised in the University of Oxford, and a considerable class of graduates will, in like manner, have taken their degrees in Trinity College, Dublin, and have not as yet been allowed to exercise the electoral suffrage.

College interests are especially represented in the University of Dublin, where the chartered scholars of the College who are twenty-one years of age, possess the right of suffrage. A sacramental test limits the possessors of chartered scholarships to members of the Church of England, but the Board of the College has recently added several non-foundation scholarships, which are open to candidates of all religious denominations; and the whole of the College scholarships are bestowed according to merit in the respective classes of the candidates, who are entered to compete either for chartered or for non-foundation scholarships in the same examination.

The subjects appointed for Scholarships in Science in Trinity College, Dublin, are thus enumerated:—

> Pure Mathematics—(Geometry, Algebra, Differential and Integral Calculus).
> Mechanics.
> Astronomy.
> Experimental Physics.
> Logic and Metaphysics.

For Classical Scholarships in Trinity College, Dublin, the following subjects are included:—

> Composition in Greek Verse and Latin Prose, as well as in Latin Verse and Greek Prose.
> Questions in Grammar and Philology.
> *Ancient* History, and Aristotelian Logic.
> Passages from Classical Authors of some difficulty for translation.
> *Vivâ voce* Examination in Classics and in Aristotelian Logic.

Success, either in the scientific or classical examination for a Scholarship, may be regarded as more than equivalent to an ordinary degree; but the non-foundation Scholars should receive additional privileges, and the electoral franchise ought to be alike conferred on the holders of either description of Scholarship, as soon as they attain the age of twenty-one.

No beneficial effect seems to arise from an exclusive system, at the present day, in increasing the number of Students who obtain Divinity certificates in Trinity College, Dublin; indeed, the number of candidates from that institution, for Holy Orders, were, from 1844 to 1848, almost continuously diminishing, as will appear in the following table:—

Number of Students entered in the University of Dublin.	Number of Candidates for the B.A. degree.	Number of Candidates who passed the examination for the B.A. degree.	Number of Candidates rejected at the examination for the B.A. degree.	Number of Students who obtained Divinity certificates.
1844	366	281	266	15	124
1845	368	254	237	17	128
1846	371	267	251	16	116
1847	333	261	241	20	96
1848	327	254	242	12	93 *

In the University of Oxford, the Thirty-Nine Articles of the Church of England form a part of the Examination for the degree of Bachelor of Arts, in all cases where the candidate has not expressly declared that he is outside the Anglican Church,—"*extra ecclesiam Anglicanam,*"—when some other subject of Examination is provided for him in place of that of divinity.

The Rev. Professor Walker, after long-continued experience as a University Examiner, thus expressed his opinion to the Oxford Royal Commission of 1852, on the failures in the B.A. Degree Examination at Oxford:—

"Failures are perhaps most common in Divinity. Those who are rejected on other grounds are almost always deficient in several points. Latin writing is a great stumbling-block, but candidates are seldom rejected for defect in this point only. If decent Latin writing should be insisted upon, the number of failures would be more than quadrupled.

"The following table exhibits the numbers of those

* Appendix K. to Oxford University Royal Commission Report, p. 72.

who were candidates for an ordinary degree during the years in which I have held the office of Examiner, and in the next columns are the numbers of those who passed, failed, and withdrew their names. In the years 1831 and 1832, the whole number of candidates is shown; in the other years only half. Two schools were open for the examination of passmen, and my records extend only to the school in which I was present:—

	Candidates.	Passed.	Failed.	Withdrew.	No. per 100 Passed.
Easter, 1831 ..	...	...	...	...	...
Michaelmas, 1831.	123	87	19	26	71
Easter, 1832 ..	162	118	26	18	73
Michaelmas, 1832.	...	...	...	...	...
Easter, 1835 ..	...	...	...	...	...
Michaelmas, 1835.	58	41	11	6	71
Easter, 1836 ..	85	69	11	5	81
Michaelmas, 1836.	68	52	11	5	76
Easter, 1841 ..	71	45	12	14	63
Michaelmas, 1841.	76	47	17	12	62
Easter, 1842 ..	82	54	18	10	66
Michaelmas, 1842.	75	49	16	10	65
Easter, 1846 ..	71	49	18	4	69
Michaelmas, 1846.	79	57	10	12	72
Easter, 1847 ..	70	55	9	6	79
Michaelmas, 1847.	70	49	13	8	70
Easter, 1849 ..	87	65	11	9	76
Michaelmas, 1849.	81	61	14	8	74
Easter, 1850 ..	72	48	20	4	67
Michaelmas, 1850.	76	57	7	12	75

"In the above table blanks are left where my records are imperfect, and in the last column decimals are omitted, and the nearest integer given.

"It appears that the average per cent. of the candidates for an ordinary degree who pass, is, on the seventeen Examinations of the above table, rather above seventy-one."*

So much uncertainty and annoyance must arise to the candidates themselves, from the extraordinary proportion of nearly thirty per cent. who do not pass the Degree Examination, that the total omission of the Thirty-Nine Articles from the subjects proposed for the B.A. degree at Oxford would be of advantage to the students, and would be more satisfactory with reference to the electoral franchise, which ought not to depend on the success of a student in repeating by heart, and endeavouring to prove, a series of disputed points of ecclesiastical doctrine.

A new kind of University franchise was established by Parliament, in 1858, for the local government of the Scotch Universities, by the constitution of a General Council in each of those Northern seats of learning, comprising the Chancellor, the Members, six or eight in number, of an executive governing body termed the University Court, the Professors, the Masters of Arts of the University, and the Doctors of Medicine of the University, who had, as Matriculated Students, given regular attendance on classes in any of the faculties in the University, during four complete sessions. The Scotch academical franchise for the General Council was further extended to all persons who had attained the age of twenty-one years, and who had, as Matriculated Students of the University, given regular attendance on the course of study in the University for four complete sessions, including two sessions in the faculty of Arts, or such regular attendance for three complete sessions in the University, and regular attendance for one such complete session in any other Scotch University.

* Evidence of the Rev. Professor Walker, in Oxford University Royal Commission Report.

The attendance of the Students, for at least two of the four Sessions last enumerated, is required to be on a course of study in the faculty of Arts: no person is allowed to be a Member of the General Council while he is a Student enrolled in any class of the University, nor until he has attained the age of twenty-one and has registered his name in a book to be kept for Matriculated Students in each University.

All questions affecting the well-being and prosperity of the University may be taken into consideration by the General Council, and representations may be made from time to time by that body on such questions to the University Court, who are to consider the same, and to forward the result of their deliberations to the Council.

The University Court, or Executive Committee, in Edinburgh, consists of the following Members:—

> An Assessor to be nominated by the Chancellor.
> The Principal of the University.
> An Assessor to be nominated by the *Senatus Academicus*.
> The Lord Provost, for the time being, of the City of Edinburgh.
> An Assessor to be nominated by the Lord Provost, Magistrates, and Town Council of Edinburgh.
> An Assessor to be elected by the General Council of the University.
> A Rector to be nominated by the Matriculated Students.
> An Assessor to be nominated by the Rector.

The Rector and the Assessor nominated by him are to continue in office for three years; the other Assessors continue in office for four years; and five Members of the University Court are to form a quorum.

To the General Council, the duty of effecting improvements in internal academical arrangements is entrusted, as well as the regulation of the fees of Professors, and the control * of the administration of all the pecuniary concerns of the University and of any College therein.

In the department of Medical Education, Parliament has, by the Medical Act of 1858, constituted a General Representative Medical Council, including branches for England, Scotland, and Ireland.

Representatives from the most important Medical Institutions of the United Kingdom are chosen, under this Act, to sit on the General Council, one person being selected by each of the following bodies:—

The Royal College of Physicians.
The Royal College of Surgeons of England.
The Apothecaries' Society of London.
The University of Oxford.
The University of Cambridge.
The University of Durham.
The University of London.
The College of Physicians of Edinburgh.
The College of Surgeons of Edinburgh.
The Faculty of Physicians and Surgeons of Glasgow.

One person is chosen from time to time by the University of Edinburgh and the two Universities of Aberdeen collectively.

One person is also chosen, from time to time, by the University of Glasgow and the University of St. Andrew's collectively.

One person is chosen from time to time by each of the following bodies:—

The King and Queen's College of Physicians in Ireland.
The Royal College of Surgeons in Ireland.

* 21st & 22nd Vict. c. 83. 1858.

The Apothecaries' Hall of Ireland.
The University of Dublin.
The Queen's University in Ireland.

And six persons are nominated by her Majesty, with the advice of her Privy Council, four of whom are appointed for England, one for Scotland, and one for Ireland, together with a President, who is elected by the General Council.

Members of the General Council are chosen and nominated for a term not exceeding five years, and are capable of re-appointment.

To this Parliament of Medical Science, large powers are entrusted, and considerable public advantage may be expected from the improvements which they will introduce into the system of Examinations for qualified Practitioners of Medicine,* as well as into the general rules of the Medical profession. Considerations of health may also be beneficially regarded with reference to competitive Examinations now so much in vogue, and more accurate knowledge and attention are required respecting the mental strain imposed on youth in the tasks and Examinations which constitute so large a portion of the business of public instruction.

The Rev. Henry Fearon, B.D.,† observes on school exercises, that "it is a great temptation to a schoolmaster who may be overworked or indolently inclined, to have recourse to long repetition tasks, because it economizes his own time. It keeps a class actively employed, and costs him a very little time to hear what it has cost them a very long time, comparatively, to learn. This is a very

* 21st & 22nd Vict. c. 90, entitled "The Medical Act."
† Mental Vigour; its Attainment impeded by Errors in Education. By the Rev. Henry Fearon, B.D. Rivingtons.

different thing from labouring with boys, and patiently solving their difficulties."

In the school in which he was educated, Mr. Fearon observes, that it was the custom once a year, that boys in the middle and lower classes should repeat all the Latin and Greek poetry they had learned in the year, with such addition to it of fresh matter as each boy could accomplish. "So much," he continues, "did our place in the school depend on success in this, and so severe was the rivalry, that although we were then only about fourteen years of age, the usual quantity for the boys to repeat was from six to eight thousand lines, which we did in eight different lessons, and it took about a week to hear us. One boy, in my year, construed and repeated the enormous quantity of fourteen thousand lines of Homer, Horace, and Virgil; I heard him say it; the master dodged him about very much, but he scarcely ever missed a single word. One wonders in what chamber of the brain it could possibly have been stowed away."

"Now," remarks Mr. Fearon, "I do not think that this excessive strain on the mnemonic faculty is calculated to strengthen it; nor do I believe, that this or any other faculty ought to be so severely pressed. I have a lively recollection of the long-sustained exertion it required; how, week after week, we rose early and late took rest, in our anxiety to outstrip others, upon which our station in the school, and I may say the *bread* of many of us, depended. This custom is, I hope, now, though not given up, modified. Boys ought to be rather repressed than encouraged in such a trial. Do not send them out into the world with minds overweighted, and with things which, after all, are, in such an excess, not needed. Education, as a rule, ought to be directed more to what elicits thought, than what merely encourages memory."

With reference to Examinations at the Universities, we agree with Mr. Fearon, in his belief that the *absolute* labour undergone, at the present day, by the most successful Students is incomparably greater than it was in the last century. Thus, in striving for classical honours at the ancient Universities, the Student is expected to be minutely and critically acquainted with the ancient languages of Greece and Rome; to possess a facility of composing both in Latin and Greek prose or poetry; to be familiar with the details of the Greek theatre; to have mastered difficulties in the historical works of the Greeks and Romans; and to have studied the most complicated portions of ancient logic, and of Grecian choruses.

We remember the case of a lamented Cambridge friend and contemporary, who was Senior Wrangler in 1833, and whose health suffered much from over-exertion in high mathematical reading. After an evening of abstruse scientific study, a little novel reading became essential to him, as a relaxation, to compose and calm the mind before retiring to rest, and for a few days previous to his Degree Examination, he visited the country-seat of a relative, for the refreshment of air and exercise in a rural district.

A long Continental tour did not suffice to renovate his system after the fatigue of the intellectual race in which he had been the distinguished winner; and, to the grief of his acquaintance, an early death terminated his worldly career, which had commenced under such brilliant Academical auspices.

More recently we have seen a successful candidate in the Indian Civil Service Examination, evidently much exhausted from the severe mental excitement of the intellectual strain to which he had been at that time subjected, and probably not on that account the better qualified to undergo the future hardships, and encounter the lassitude which Englishmen must suffer from the sultry clime of Hindostan.

An alphabetical arrangement of the names of the successful Students in the highest classes is adopted at Oxford for the Degree Examination, and is recommended by Mr. Fearon for the University of Cambridge, so that the Senior Wrangler may in future be merged indistinguishably among six or eight others in a first class. Considerate regard would thus be shown to the health of distinguished students, and excessive competition would be diminished.

Academical distinction affords no longer the same probable road, as in former times, to the highest Legal or Clerical advancement. Judges and Bishops are not at the present day generally selected on account of their early University honours.

According to an able article in the 'Times,' referred to by Mr. Fearon,* "the old type of the academically distinguished Judge is now hardly to be found; self-taught and energetic genius" has invaded the field of legal promotion, and "the course of University study has become too laborious and exhausting for young intellects." Exclusive religious tests, and the maintenance of an antiquated system of learning have seriously impaired the usefulness of the endowed Universities of England and Ireland; the progress of civilization demands alike the revision of the remaining tests, and a modification of

* Mental Vigour, by the Rev. H. Fearon, p. 34.

the course of study imposed on undergraduates in those venerable corporations.

At the present day, the public interest felt in a Reform Bill affords a fair opportunity of reconsidering the various restrictions which limit the elective franchise in the Universities of Oxford, Cambridge, and Dublin, and of improving the system of English University representation.

High pecuniary fees for the registration of University electors, and for keeping their names on the College boards, may be mentioned as especially injurious to the increase of the number of Academical voters, either at Oxford or Cambridge.

According to the Oxford University Calendar of 1858, the University fee, on taking the degree of Master of Arts, is £12; an additional fee for the same degree would be required in the case of compounders, who possess a moderate annual income in land or other property.

Any Master of Arts, coming from another University, and wishing to become incorporated in the University of Oxford, is allowed the right to vote, after an accredited residence of 42 days and the payment of £15, accompanied by the subscription to the Thirty-Nine Articles, as well as to the Three Articles of the Thirty-sixth Canon of the Church of England; his privileges as an elector commence after an interval of 180 days from the time of presentation for his Degree.

Every member of the University of Oxford pays £1. 6s. annually, that his name may be kept on the boards as a voter, and in lieu of this annual payment, any member who has graduated, may at his option, compound for all such University dues on the following scale, viz.:—

	£.	s.	d.
If he have not exceeded his 25th year .	22	15	0
,, ,, 30th year .	21	15	0

			£.	s.	d.
If he have not exceeded his	35th year	.	20	12	6
,,	,,	40th year	.	19	8	6
,,	,,	45th year	.	18	0	0
,,	,,	50th year	.	16	7	6
,,	,,	55th year	.	14	15	0
,,	,,	60th year	.	13	1	6
,,	,,	70th year	.	9	6	6

The degree of B.A. is usually taken at twenty-one years of age, and consequently that of M.A. would be taken at twenty-four years of age, so that the ordinary fees for obtaining for life the right of voting for a Parliamentary representative may amount, in the University of Oxford, to £12+£22. 15s., or nearly £35.

At Cambridge, the fees for the registration of electors vary slightly from those of the sister University. College fees for the M.A. degree, amount in Trinity College, Cambridge, to £8. 13s. 6d.; in St. John's College, to £6; and these charges differ more or less in the remaining Colleges. The ordinary University fee for a Master of Arts is £13. 0s. 6d.; an incorporated M.A. pays £12. 11s.; and compounders who possess an estate, income, or Church living, of the value of £26. 13s. 4d. a year, pay over and above the usual fees, the sum of £8. 6s. 4d. In all the Colleges of Cambridge, there is an annual fee, usually amounting to about £1 a year, for keeping the name of the Master of Arts on the boards: and the composition for this annual payment, within the first ten years, is £25. For those graduates whose names have continued on the boards as M.B., LL.B., M.A., or any superior degree for ten years, the composition is £20; and when the names of the graduates have been for twenty years on the boards, that payment is reduced to £15.

Under ordinary circumstances, the expenses of becoming an elector for life in the University of Cambridge would amount to £13. 0s. 6d.+£25, or about £38;—and in either University of Oxford or Cambridge, the accumulated charges and fees of the M.A. degree amount occasionally to the sum of £50.

In the case of the University of Dublin, Masters of Arts were first admitted to vote under the Reform Act of 1832, and an annual fee of £1 was directed to be paid to Trinity College, Dublin, for every person whose name should be continued on the books of that University, for the purpose of entitling him to vote at the election of Members to serve in Parliament for the University.

Ten years afterwards, this Act was amended by the 5 & 6 Vict. c. 74, in respect of the right of voting in the University of Dublin, and a composition of £5 to Trinity College was directed instead of the annual payment of £1, upon the removal of the name of the voter from the College books to those of the University.

Under this Act of 1842, the Provost, Fellows, and Scholars, for the time being, whose names are on the books of the foundation of Trinity College, retain the suffrage without any payment at all, and the composition, on their part, does not become due, until they relinquish their College emoluments, and thus formally remove their names from the College books.

The Registrar of Trinity College, Dublin, was directed by the same Act to make out every year an alphabetical list of the electors entitled to vote at the election of Members of Parliament for the University, to print copies of this list for reference, and to publish a copy annually in the University Calendar.

In the case of the Author of the present work, an

excellent arrangement for compounding for College dues was adopted, in 1840, by the authorities of Trinity College, Cambridge, of which notice was sent to him in the following friendly note from the Rev. Charles Perry, at that time College Tutor, and now Bishop of Melbourne, in Australia :—

"*Trinity College, February* 15, 1840.

"MY DEAR HEYWOOD,—I have availed myself, on your behalf, of the permission afforded you by the College, to compound for all future annual dues, and by a single payment of £15, to become a Member of our Society for life. I trust that you will approve of my conduct in this respect. . . . .

"Believe me, my dear Heywood,
"Very sincerely yours,
"CHARLES PERRY."

The caution-money paid on admission at each College in Cambridge is, for a

Nobleman	£50.
Fellow-Commoner	£25.
Pensioner	£15.
Sizor	£10.

In every case the caution-money remains in the hands of the College Tutor, and is not returned until a person takes his name off the boards. When a Member of a College wishes to remain for life associated with the institution in which he has been educated, the transfer of his caution-money, amounting to £15, in each instance, for the majority of the undergraduates, who are pensioners, appears to be a ready mode of compounding for future College payments, at the least possible expense, as the requisite sum is already in the hands of the College Tutor, and would be transferred by him to the Bursar, or Treasurer of the College, in lieu of all future demands from the College, as soon as the Tutor received the sanction of the party interested in the matter, to make this payment to the College.

Suitable arrangements for the preparation, publication, and correction of the Lists of Voters for the Universities of Oxford and Cambridge, will form essential portions of a well matured Reform Bill. Regulations may be introduced for the appointment of a revising barrister to examine the University lists of electors, which appointment may be annually made, as in the case of boroughs, by the senior judge, for the time being, in the commission of assize for each of the counties of Oxford and Cambridge, and provisions may be arranged that the usual fee of five guineas a day shall be payable to such revising barrister for his attendance.

The three Universities of Oxford, Cambridge, and Dublin, according to their original charters for returning representatives, and subsequent custom, are regarded as boroughs, and, with proper modifications, the plans for the boroughs, in arranging, revising, and correcting the Lists of Voters, may be adapted to the case of the Universities.

In 1858, the number of the Oxford University electors was 3644; at the same time, there were 4656 electors enrolled in the University of Cambridge. The Calendars of these two ancient seats of learning do not contain the addresses of the non-resident voters belonging to either University, and in the case of a contested election, the permission of the respective Colleges in Oxford and Cambridge would be requisite, in order to obtain from the College books the addresses of the electors, so far as they are preserved in those records.

Blackstone is of opinion, that the representation of the Universities of Oxford and Cambridge in Parliament was intended "to serve for those Students who, though useful members of the community, were neither concerned in the landed nor the trading interests, and to protect in the legislature the rights of the republic of letters."*

In order to realize this beautiful theory of the learned judge with reference to the University of Oxford, of which Blackstone was a member, fresh legislation is requisite, so as to allow Candidates who are desirous of entrance into that republic of letters, to matriculate, and to take the degree of Bachelor of Arts at Oxford, without any declaration or certificate respecting religious opinion.

A singular line of policy has been adopted by the University of Oxford in consequence of the Oxford Act of 1854. The University has passed a statute directing that the Examinations in Theology at the B.A. degree are to be optional for those Members of the University on whose behalf the Head of the College to which they belong has signed a certificate, stating that they are not members of the Church of England; but no provision has been made for Churchmen who do not agree with the Thirty-Nine Articles, and who will, as members of the Church of England, still be expected to submit to the University Examinations in Theology, at the B.A. degree, and be subject to the arbitrary will of a Head of a College, whether they are to be admitted on, or not, the College books.

In 1855, Sir Culling Eardley, Bart., requested the Provost of Oriel College, Oxford, to re-admit him as a Member of his College, with a view to his proceeding to the degree of Bachelor of Arts. The honourable Baronet

* Stephen's Commentaries, partly founded on Blackstone, vol. ii. p. 384.

had been educated at Oriel College, and had passed his Examination for the B.A. degree in 1827, but without graduating. Fourteen years afterwards, in 1844, a bill had been sent to him for College battels, or provisions, relating to a series of years when he had not resided at Oxford, and as in 1844, he could not conscientiously subscribe to the Thirty-Nine Articles, and did not anticipate that Parliament would abolish that subscription, he removed his name from the books of his College.

The passing of the Oxford University Act of 1854, obviously afforded facilities for graduation without any religious test, but the Provost of Oriel referred Sir Culling Eardley to the local University statute already mentioned, which practically empowered him, as the Head of a College, to inform himself as to what any person was, who sought to be admitted or re-admitted into that College.

"If," remarked the Provost * to Sir Culling Eardley, "you are a member of the Church of England, then you must perceive that you do not come within the terms of the statute, and I am not at liberty to re-admit you into this College; but if you are *extra Ecclesiam Anglicanam*, then I am at liberty, and I left the determination to yourself. One of the two you must be, and not both at once.

"Having put this clearly before you, I cannot but understand, of course, that your seeking re-admission at my hands implies that you are *extra Ecclesiam Anglicanam*, in which capacity alone I can receive you."

In reply, Sir Culling Eardley wrote as follows to the Provost of Oriel, on the 15th of June, 1855 :—

* Correspondence with the Rev. Dr. Hawkins, Provost of Oriel College, Oxford, p. 33.

"If you have quite made up your mind, that you cannot admit me to Oriel, except I will acknowledge myself to be *extra Ecclesiam Anglicanam*, I must submit to your decision. I cannot conscientiously make that acknowledgment. I cannot admit the principle, that a layman, born and brought up in the Church of England, loses his quality of membership, because he exercises his right, or rather fulfils his duty of private judgment. I cannot allow myself to be precluded in a parish, where the preaching is not to my opinion Scriptural, from frequenting or even building another place of worship, or to be tied down to the whole of the phraseology of the Thirty-Nine Articles, which are properly binding on the Clergy, but cannot be considered as a test for the laity.

"I suppose, as I said at an earlier period of our correspondence, that to have acted on these feelings, technically constitutes me a Nonconformist, that is, in my case, a nonconforming member of the Church of England."

Sir Culling Eardley, in a subsequent letter, thus explained to the Provost of Oriel, his reasons for refusing to acknowledge himself as out of the Church of England:—

"I object to admitting that I am 'out of the Church,' for this simple reason, that by the law of the land (as I understand) I am not so. And I think you (the Provost of Oriel) must see that, once admitting your principle, every the slightest deviation from Church order will put a person out of the Church. Who is to be the judge of the degree of nonconformity which renders a person excommunicated *de facto?*"

On the 13th of August, 1855, Lord Monteagle presented to the House of Lords a petition from Sir Culling Eardley, in which the honourable Baronet expressed his desire, "that the laity of England who wish to enter

Oxford, and who happen not to concur with the whole of the Thirty-Nine Articles, nor always to worship in the Established Church, may not be compelled to admit that they are *extra Ecclesiam Anglicanam."*

Lord Cranworth, at that time Lord Chancellor, observed with reference to this petition, that the Oxford University Act of 1854 would be a dead letter, "if all those who entertained conscientious doubts as to the propriety of some of the doctrines to be deduced from the Articles, were to be excluded from the University. He had heard with much pain of the obstacles which had been thrown in the way of the petitioner, and thought it was like compelling a man to wear a cockade in his hat, when the object of the law was to abolish the use of cockades altogether."

Lord Campbell had no difficulty in saying, "the refusal of the Provost was contrary to the letter, to the spirit, and to the policy of the Act of Parliament. He (the Provost of Oriel) had no right to say the applicant was without the Anglican Church, because at one period of his life he had expressed doubts as to some of the Thirty-Nine Articles. Their Lordships were aware, that one of the Articles declared that judicial oaths might be taken, and were consistent with Scripture. Some members of the Church of England applied to be relieved from taking them, and on that occasion, that most distinguished prelate the Bishop of London (Dr. Blomfield) said a man might be *bonâ fide* and truly a member of the Church of England, and yet dissent from some of the Thirty-Nine Articles. In his opinion, the Provost was in every way mistaken." *

* Hansard's Parliamentary Debates, 3rd series, vol. cxxxix. p. 2141. August 13th, 1855.

From the foregoing account of the policy adopted by the University of Oxford, which has been exemplified in the refusal of the Provost of Oriel to allow a former undergraduate who had passed the examination for the B.A. degree, to be re-admitted into his own College, it is manifest that further legislation is requisite to amend the state of the University and its Colleges, with reference to the religious tests for offices connected with the degrees of that seat of learning.

No adequate security can be obtained for the Head of a House being really disposed to admit persons who do not agree in the Thirty-Nine Articles of the Church of England, into the College over which he presides, as long as a subscription to these Articles is insisted on by law from the Head of a House previous to his admission into office.

Subscription to the Thirty-Nine Articles was directed by the Act of Uniformity of 1662, for all Heads of Colleges at each of the ancient English Universities, as well as at the public schools of Westminster, Winchester, and Eton, together with a declaration of unfeigned assent and consent unto, and approbation of the Thirty-Nine Articles and the book of Common Prayer, and an agreement to use all the prayers, rites, and ceremonies, forms, and orders prescribed in that Liturgy.

By the same Act of Parliament of 1662, the Heads and Fellows of Colleges, and the University Professors at Oxford and Cambridge, are required to subscribe a declaration of conformity to the book of Common Prayer of the Church of England.

Nearly all the Heads of Houses at Oxford and Cambridge are in Holy Orders; a large majority of the resident constituency, who elect the Council or governing body of the University, are clergymen of the Established Church; the Tutors of Colleges are almost invariably members of the clerical body; and as the degree of Master of Arts is more usually taken by clergymen than by laymen, the elective franchise in the ancient English Universities, which is limited to the Masters of Arts and other higher graduates, is principally held by voters who are in Holy Orders.

At Cambridge, no person is allowed to vote for the representatives of the University, until he has subscribed himself a Member of the Church of England; at Oxford the same subscription is required for the elective franchise as for Holy Orders, including an acknowledgment of the Thirty-Nine Articles, and of the three Articles of the Thirty-Sixth Canon of the Book of Ecclesiastical Canons of the year 1603.

In the reign of Edward VI., the Forty-Two Articles drawn up by Archbishop Cranmer, under the 3 & 4 Edw. VI., c. 11, were neither submitted to the Convocation of the Clergy, nor confirmed by any Act of Parliament,* but were published by Royal Authority, sent to all the Bishops in their respective dioceses, and forwarded to the Universities of Oxford and Cambridge.

One of the points of accusation brought against Cranmer, under Queen Mary, was that "he had published or caused to be published these articles." The Archbishop allowed that they had been published by his advice.

Four years after the accession of Queen Elizabeth, in 1562, Archbishop Parker undertook the revision of Cranmer's Forty-Two Articles. According to the copies of the Articles of 1552 and 1562, in Dr. Lamb's edition of

* Dr. Lamb's Historical Account of the Thirty-Nine Articles, p. 4. London: Rivingtons. 1829.

the alterations, eight of the older Articles were omitted by Parker,—the tenth, sixteenth, nineteenth, thirty-fifth, and the four last from the thirty-ninth to the forty-second inclusive.

Archbishop Parker altered various others, and added five new Articles for the edition of 1562,—the fifth, twelfth, twenty-ninth, thirtieth, and thirty-sixth: these were considered and agreed to by the Bishops under Queen Elizabeth, and represented their opinions.

During the Commonwealth, subscriptions to the Thirty-Nine Articles were not permitted, and under Oliver Cromwell in 1656–7 the Knights, Citizens, and Burgesses assembled in Parliament took into their most serious consideration the state of the three nations of England, Scotland, and Ireland, and thus petitioned the Lord Protector for a confession of faith to be agreed upon in Parliament, to which his Highness gave his consent.

The Parliament declared their "most just and necessary desires" to his Highness, that "the true Protestant Christian religion, as it is contained in the Holy Scriptures of the Old and New Testament, and no other, be held forth and asserted for the public profession of these nations, and that a confession of faith to be agreed by his Highness and the Parliament, according to the rule and warrant of the Scriptures, be asserted, held forth, and recommended to the people of these nations, that none may be suffered or permitted, by opprobrious words or writing, maliciously or contemptuously to revile or reproach the confession of faith to be agreed upon as aforesaid; and such who profess faith in God the Father, and in Jesus Christ his eternal Son, the true God, and in the Holy Spirit, God co-equal with the Father and the Son, one God blessed for ever, and do acknowledge the Holy Scriptures of the Old and New Testament to be the revealed will and word of God, and shall in other things differ in doctrine, worship, or discipline from the public profession held forth, endeavours shall be used to convince them by sound doctrine and the example of a good conversation; but that they may not be compelled thereto by penalties, nor restrained from their profession, but protected from all injury and molestation in the profession of the faith and exercise of their religion, while they abuse not this liberty to the civil injury of others or the disturbance of the public peace; so that this liberty be not extended to Popery or Prelacy, or to the countenancing such who publish horrible blasphemies, or practise or hold forth licentiousness or profaneness under the profession of Christ.

"And that those ministers or public preachers who shall agree with the public profession aforesaid in matters of faith, although in their judgment and practice they differ in matters of worship and discipline, shall not only have protection in the way of their churches and worship respectively, but be esteemed fit and capable, notwithstanding such difference (being otherwise duly qualified and duly approved), of any trust, promotion, or employment whatsoever in these nations, that any ministers who agree in doctrine, worship, and discipline with the public profession aforesaid are capable of."*

Parker's Articles were again adopted, after the restoration of episcopacy, but the gradual influence of more enlightened sentiments subsequently became manifest when John Wesley reduced the number of Articles for

* Scobell's Collection of Acts and Ordinances made in Parliament, 1640–1656, p. 381.

the ministers of the Wesleyan Methodist denomination, from thirty-nine to twenty-five, and also altered the Articles which he retained in such manner as he deemed expedient.

Wesley had the courage, in the Liturgy which he proposed, to give up the use of the Nicene and Athanasian Creeds, and the Church of England catechism; he also rejected, according to Archbishop Magee, among the Articles, the third, the eighth, the greater part of the ninth, the thirteenth, fifteenth, seventeenth, eighteenth, twentieth, twenty-first, twenty-third, twenty-sixth, much of the twenty-seventh, twenty-ninth, thirty-third, and three others of the less important ones at the end.*

Wesleyan Methodists are thus plainly excluded from obtaining any high Collegiate office in either of the Universities of Oxford and Cambridge, for which subscription to the Thirty-Nine Articles may be requisite; and the members of other religious denominations, who differ more widely from the doctrines or discipline of the Established Church, are, in like manner, prevented from attaining those important academical positions, which may be considered as the most lucrative prizes of Student life in the ancient Universities of England.

Among the British seats of learning at the present day, the University of London is distinguished by the open character of its exhibitions, prizes, and degrees. The degree of Bachelor of Laws may be obtained in the Metropolitan University, on examination, by any candidate, after the lapse of a year from the degree of B.A., taken either in the University of London, or in any other University of the United Kingdom. An examination for honours is held after the LL.B. degree examination, and

* Archbishop Magee's Works, vol. i. p. 106. London: 1842.

if, in the opinion of the Examiners, any candidate possesses sufficient merit, the candidate who distinguishes himself the most in the principles of Legislation, receives fifty pounds per annum for three years, with the title of "University Law Scholar." In 1858, this Scholarship was awarded, after the required examination, to a member of Merton College, Oxford.

Similar liberality has been manifested by the University of London in granting the degree of Doctor of Laws, on examination, after the expiration of two academical years from the time of a candidate obtaining the degree of LL.B., either in the University of London, or in any other University from which the Metropolitan University is or may be authorized to receive certificates.

If, in the opinion of the Examiners for the LL.D. degree, sufficient merit be evinced, the candidate who distinguishes himself the most, at the examination for the degree of Doctor of Laws, receives a gold medal of the value of twenty pounds.

Among the gold medalists for the LL.D. degree, in the University of London, are the names of a member of St. Mary Hall, Oxford, and two members of Jesus College, Cambridge, in addition to other names connected with University College, London.

For the degree of Master of Arts, in the University of London, any candidate of twenty years of age may be admitted to the examination, after the expiration of a year from the time of his obtaining the degree of B.A., either in that University, or in one of the Universities of Oxford, Cambridge, Dublin, or Durham.

The position of the University of London, and the recent movements of that academic body for obtaining the right of representation in Parliament, have been recently referred to by Earl Granville, K.G., Chancellor of the University, in the following portions of his address to the assembled Members of the University and their friends, at Burlington House, Piccadilly, on the 11th of May, 1859, previous to degrees being conferred and medals distributed in the faculties of Law, Medicine, and Arts.

After the Chancellor had described the establishment of the University of London in consequence of an Address of the House of Commons to the Crown declaring the expediency of founding some institution which should have the power of conferring degrees upon that large proportion of British subjects whose religious opinions prevented their admission to the full benefits of the then existing Universities, his Lordship thus continued his address to the members of the University:—
"The University of London was endowed with power to confer degrees, and it was established with the distinct promise that it should be placed in all respects upon the same footing as the sister Universities. University College and King's College were at the same time admitted to the privilege of sending pupils for degrees, and subsequently numerous Colleges of the most distinguished class had been affiliated to the University under the sanction of the Secretary of State. It was hardly necessary to remind them how the University had progressed (cheers); how, although occasionally perhaps somewhat more slowly than they could have wished, its members had gradually greatly increased; how, with regard to its degrees in Arts, men who had obtained them had engaged most successfully in those open competitions which were now giving so useful a stimulus to education throughout the country,—while,

with regard to its mathematical degrees, it was scarcely necessary to remind any one connected with the University of the names of Routh, of the two Savages, of Slessen, and of Brown, who had gained the highest honours, having carried off three Senior Wranglerships, two second Wranglerships, and Smith's Prize, at the University of Cambridge. (Cheers.) With regard to the important and noble profession of Medicine, the success had, if possible, been still more marked. It was now admitted as an undoubted fact that the University of London offered the best School of Medicine in this country, and he believed it was equal, if not much superior to any other School of Medicine in the world. (Cheers.) This fact had been affirmed before a Committee of the House of Commons; it had never been denied; and it was to a certain degree easily accounted for by the comprehensiveness and strictness of the Medical examinations, together with the immense advantages enjoyed by the larger proportion of Medical Students belonging to the University of London in the extensive hospitals which abounded in this great city. These examinations, he was happy to say, had now been rendered still more useful and efficient by an arrangement which had been cordially and warmly entered into by all the great hospitals in London, for allowing the practical part of the Medical Examinations to be conducted successively in their establishments. (Hear, hear.) The position of the Medical Graduates of this University was shown, not only by the general estimation in which they were held, but by the rapid manner in which they gained important public appointments, and by the confidence reposed in them in private practice. (Cheers.) The principal topic of his address last year referred to the changes which had been wrought in the University by the recent charter which had been granted to it. One of the most important of these changes was the throwing open of the examination to all persons, irrespective of their education, in the affiliated Colleges. He was quite aware that that step did not meet with entire approval. Some objection had been raised to it on the ground that persons who had enjoyed the advantage of a Collegiate discipline would be enabled to obtain degrees by 'cramming.' They had endeavoured to meet that objection by multiplying the examinations; and this very multiplication having been objected to, and justly, on the score of the expense which it involved, they had instituted local examinations, for which pressing applications had been made, and which would certainly increase the number of those who applied for degrees. He was perfectly free to admit that it must still remain in doubt whether this change would injuriously affect existing Colleges, or whether it would prove advantageous by exciting that competition which in all the affairs of life was found to produce some good. It was quite clear, however, that the number of those applying for degrees would be increased. Whether this increase would add, as he hoped, to the distinction of the University, or whether it would, in some degree, lower the grade of the Students, was a question upon which he himself entertained a strong opinion, but which was still open to discussion, and which could only be decided by the lapse of time and by experience. The other great change introduced by the Charter, and to which he believed no one present could make any objection, was the incorporation of the University, and giving it the same *status* as the older Universities by the establishment of a Convocation. (Loud cheers.) There was no change which he hailed more heartily, or from which he anticipated more advantage."

With reference to the regulations of the Senate of the University of London respecting degrees, Lord Granville observed, that "the original framers of the regulations for degrees, rightly had regard to real utility in the course of education they prescribed; and they judged that real utility was best consulted by rendering that course as comprehensive as possible, at the same time avoiding superficiality, which was equally to be deprecated in any system of education. Upon this principle the Senate had endeavoured to continue to act. One of their objects, as he had already stated, had been to multiply the examinations, such multiplication enabling a more even distribution of the subjects. They had given what they considered due place to mental and moral philosophy, and they had attached the importance they thought it deserved to the study of our own mother tongue—to the language of Milton, of Shakspeare, of Bacon, of Chatham, of Pitt, of Fox, and of some illustrious men who were then present (cheers), by including it as a subject for honours, and by providing an exhibition for the candidate who most distinguished himself in a branch of knowledge which was certainly so important to every Englishman. (Hear, hear.) The Senate had also directed their attention to another subject which was one of the most important that had engaged, for some time past at least, the attention of any University. He alluded to the question of a degree for Science. (Hear, hear.) They had been accused of being, as a nation, not scientific but too practical, and with that sort of false pride with which they often welcomed accusations against themselves, they had accepted the charge. When they considered that to Englishmen was owing the great spread of inductive science throughout Europe, when they remembered that it was an Englishman who deprived the thunderbolt of its terrors; that it was an Englishman who deprived that loathsome disease the small-pox of its virulent and loathsome power; that Englishmen had perfected and put into application that invention which had enabled them to flash information from town to town, and from country to country, as swiftly as the wind, he thought it was rather 'soft' of them to admit so readily that they had no claim to be regarded as a scientific nation. (Laughter and cheers.) At the same time he believed that Science did not hold such an estimation in the public mind as to lead to the education in Science which was so much to be desired. During the last year, two memorials had been presented to the Senate by most distinguished men of science in this country, urging the University of London to fill up the void which existed in this respect, and pointing out to them that scientific eminence was not sufficiently recognized by the degrees which they granted, or by the honours which they conferred. The Senate immediately appointed a Committee to consider the question. That Committee examined sixteen of the gentlemen who signed the memorial; the Registrar of the University also afforded some very valuable evidence; and he recommended the perusal of the first Report of the Committee, containing this body of evidence to those who were interested in the progress of Science. The Committee reported that they saw no great difficulty—although, of course, the subject required mature consideration—in conferring such degree or degrees as would encourage scientific education, and enable a candidate for distinction in Science to place himself in the same position as a B.A. or as an M.A. He need hardly remind them how very superior were the degrees of the University of London in Arts as compared with other Universities, because no single degree was given without a thoroughly searching examination, while in other Universities some of the higher degrees were granted merely as a matter of form. The Senate confirmed the Report of the Committee, which had met again, and had drawn up the scheme of a *curriculum* for the degrees of Bachelor of Science and Doctor of Science. With regard to the Bachelor's degree, they wished it to be open to all those who could show they had a general knowledge of existing Science. They wished that the Doctor's degree should only be given to men who displayed not only a general knowledge of Science, but such an intimate and special acquaintance with one subject as to justify the belief and expectation that by an industrious application of their talents they would be able to add to the general stock of human knowledge. This scheme had not yet been considered by the Senate. Some modifications might be introduced, but he believed they would before long be able to set an example which he could not doubt other institutions would follow, by establishing Scientific degrees. Especial pains would, of course, be necessary in the appointment of Examiners; but he hoped this step would give an impetus to Science and to Scientific education in general which had hitherto been wanting, and which must be hailed with satisfaction in a country which owed its power, its wealth, and its national position to the application of Science beyond, perhaps, any other country in the world."

Preliminary steps for proposing the University of

London as a constituency to be represented in Parliament, were thus described by the Chancellor of the University:—

"They had now, as members of their Senate, some of the most distinguished men in Parliament, who had never failed them in their need, and who probably never would fail them; but it must be remembered that from their very distinction these gentlemen had other interests to represent, and that they could not give such entire attention to the interests of the University of London as would be insured if this, like the other Universities, were represented in the House of Commons. (Cheers.) Neither Convocation nor the Senate had, he hoped, neglected their duty on this point. They had presented memorials to the Government, which had been very cordially received. Sir J. Graham had presented a petition on the subject in the House of Commons. He (the Chancellor) had presented a similar petition in the House of Lords, and, although he had advisedly abstained from making any observations on the prayer of the petition, he observed with pleasure that that prayer was heartily cheered by men perfectly independent of the University— as, for instance, the Lord Chief Justice of England—and he entertained great hope that their claim would be conceded. It was quite true that the present Government had not included such a proposal in their Reform Bill, but he might be allowed to anticipate that their next Reform Bill would remedy the omission. (Laughter and cheers.) They had evinced great courtesy in answering the applications which had been made to them at different times, and he hoped that either spontaneously or under the influence of a little pressure from without they would be induced to propose that the University should be represented in Parliament. If, however, in the vicissitudes of human affairs any change were to take place in the government of the country, it was only reasonable to suppose that among the members of the new Cabinet some one person would at least be found who would press upon his colleagues the claims of the University to Parliamentary representation." (Cheers.)

The memorial of the Senate to the Government, alluded to in the foregoing address, had been forwarded by the Chancellor to the Earl of Derby on the 24th of March, 1859, and in acknowledging the receipt of this document, the Prime Minister promised to submit the memorial to his colleagues, that it might receive their fullest consideration. Its form was to the following effect:—

"*To the Right Hon. the Earl of Derby, First Lord of the Treasury.*

"In urging upon her Majesty's Government the claim of the University of London to be represented in Parliament, the Senate do not feel it necessary to enter into any discussion of the abstract principles upon which Representative Government may be supposed to be based. They do not seek that any new element should, for the sake of the University, be introduced into the Representative system. In this country University Representation is an established fact. The Senate are prepared to show that the University of London sufficiently fulfils the conditions under which the right of representation is now enjoyed by the Universities of Oxford, Cambridge, and Dublin.

"Upon this point the claim of the University, already advanced by its Graduates, has received the sanction of two successive Governments. On the 10th of May, 1852, during the former administration of Lord Derby, a deputation from the Graduates of the University waited upon his Lordship at Downing Street, and received the assurance that, in the opinion of the then Government, there was no claim of the kind which could come in competition with that of the University of London. On the same day the Chancellor of the Exchequer (Mr. Disraeli), addressing the House of Commons on a motion for leave to bring in a bill for creating other Constituencies in lieu of St. Albans and Sudbury, is reported, in Hansard's Debates, to have made express reference to the University of London; and, while postponing the desired concession on the ground of the then 'immature constitution and imperfect development' of the University, to have expressed the opinion of the Government that 'the principle upon which the claim was urged was a principle entitled to respect and approbation; that there was nothing fantastic or unfitting in the claim; but that it was in perfect unison with principles which were already acted upon in the House in the case of Oxford, of Cambridge, and of Dublin.'

"In 1853, Lord Derby's Government having retired, the claim was brought under the consideration of Lord Aberdeen by a numerous deputation of Members of the Senate, Graduates, and Officers of the principal London Hospitals, and of about thirty Colleges and Theological Seminaries of various denominations, connected with the University. His Lordship's reply was as follows:—

"'I have no hesitation in acknowledging the very strong claims you have urged for the favourable consideration by the Government of the object you have in view; and I readily admit, that the constituency which would be afforded by the University of London is such a one as it would be most agreeable to the Government to organize. You will not, I suppose, expect me to give you a final answer today; but I assure you that, so far from throwing cold water on the subject—a course which was deprecated by one of the deputation—I do, in the most sincere and warmest manner, assure you that the matter will be taken under the most serious consideration of the Government. I beg you to believe that I am not by any means making use of mere words of course, but I assure you that such will positively be the case.'

"The result was that, in 1854, a Bill for amending the Representation, introduced into the House of Commons by Lord John Russell on the part of the Government, contained clauses giving a Member to the University of London.

"It had been represented by the Deputation to Lord Aberdeen, that the objections interposed by Mr. Disraeli were in actual process of removal. It can now be stated that they have no longer any existence.

"At the time when these objections were made, the University consisted solely, in point of law, of the Senate —a body of thirty-eight Fellows who were appointed by the Crown for the purpose of drawing up proper Curricula of study in Arts, Laws, and Medicine, and conferring Degrees on such Collegiate Candidates as should appear by examination to answer the requirements of these Curricula. Its Graduates scarcely reached 700 in number, and were not legally incorporated in the University.

"Since that time a New Charter has been granted, under which every Graduate becomes, immediately upon taking his Degree, a member of the Corporation. Upon taking the higher degree or attaining a few years' standing in the lower, and paying a small fee, he becomes a Member of Convocation. This body has the right of submitting to the Crown lists out of which one-fourth of the Senate is chosen, and of declaring its opinion on all University matters. The powers also of the University itself are enlarged. It may now create and confer Degrees in Science generally, as well as in Arts, Laws, and Medicine; and, except in Medicine, it may admit to its Examinations Candidates who have not pursued their studies in a College. Convocation has already organized itself, expressed opinions on University matters, and submitted lists out of which vacancies in the Senate have been filled up. The new Curricula for Degrees in Arts have been completed, and applications for Provincial Examinations have been complied with. The necessary Curricula for Degrees in Science are nearly matured.

"For several years past, the number of Graduates has been increasing at the rate of nearly one hundred per annum; and those who have attained Convocation-standing will, in a few months, exceed 1000 in number. It is obvious, therefore, that the objections of immature constitution and imperfect development, however well-founded in 1852, have no application at the present moment.

"When the University was founded, University College and King's College alone were authorized to send Candidates to its Examinations. But the fact is now, that all the important Schools of Medicine, and Roman Catholic, Nonconformist, and Secular Colleges, Provincial as well as Metropolitan, have become connected with the University.

"The claim now urged for the admission of the University of London to Representation in Parliament is nothing more than was generally understood to be contemplated when the University was founded: an understanding which was expressed in the following terms by the Chancellor of the Exchequer (Mr. Spring Rice, now Lord Monteagle) while the arrangements for the University Charter were still pending:—

"'It should be always kept in mind, that what is 'sought on the present occasion is an equality in all re-'spects with the ancient Universities, freed from those 'exclusions and religious distinctions which abridge the 'usefulness of Oxford and Cambridge.'

"In no case in which this principle of equality with the ancient Universities has been brought under the notice of the Government, has it been departed from.

"In 1837 the Legislature recognized this principle, by placing London Graduates on the same footing with those of Oxford and Cambridge in respect of their being admitted as Attorneys and Solicitors (stat. 1 Vict. c. 56, consolidated by Lord Langdale's Act, 6 & 7 Vict. c. 73). In 1852 the Inns of Court, by common regulation, adopted it in their calls to the Bar.

"In 1849 the Home Secretary (Sir G. Grey), when receiving deputations on the subject, acknowledged it as a valid objection to a Medical Bill, that it failed to place the London Medical Graduates in the same professional status with those of Oxford and Cambridge: and in 1854 a Bill for according this status passed the Legislature. The Medical Act of 1858 extends the professional privileges of Graduates of all the Universities alike, and confers upon the University of London equally with the other Universities the right of naming a Representative on the Medical Council.

"So with regard to exemptions. The Grammar School Act (3 & 4 Vict. c. 77), the Militia Act (15 & 16 Vict. c. 60), and the Charitable Trusts Act (16 & 17 Vict. c. 137), all contain clauses by which the Universities of Oxford, Cambridge, and London are equally exempted from their operation.

"The Senate observe that, under the provisions of the Parliamentary Representation Bill, now laid before Parliament, four seats remain undisposed of; and having before them this unbroken succession of instances in confirmation of the principle of their claim, and the strong sanction accorded by former Administrations to the claim itself, they concur with Convocation in pressing earnestly upon the consideration of her Majesty's Government the propriety of providing on this occasion for the due Representation in Parliament of the University of London."

This Memorial to the Earl of Derby with Petitions to both Houses of Parliament were agreed to, both by the Senate and the Convocation of Graduates of the University of London. The arguments and prayer of both Petitions were to a similar effect, and were varied only to suit the forms of each House of Parliament. Earl Granville presented the Petition addressed to the House of Lords, and Sir James Graham took charge of that intended for the House of Commons. Shortly afterwards occurred the dissolution of Parliament, and a change of government followed the meeting of the new Parliament. The Petitions were thus worded :—

"The Humble Petition of the University of London
"Showeth,
"That the Universities of Oxford, Cambridge, and

Dublin are represented in Parliament; but the University of London is not as yet so represented.

"That the University of London was created by his late Majesty King William IV., for the 'purpose of holding forth to all classes and denominations of her Majesty's faithful subjects, without any distinction whatever, an encouragement for pursuing a regular and liberal course of education.'

"That by virtue of the Charter granted by his Majesty, and of subsequent Charters granted by her Most Gracious Majesty, the University comprises the Senate, consisting of the Chancellor, Vice-Chancellor, and thirty-six Fellows nominated by the Crown, in whom is vested the Executive of the University; and a Convocation, of which all Graduates of a certain standing become members upon payment of a small fee, and which is empowered (*inter alia*) to submit to the Crown lists of persons from which one-fourth of the Senate is chosen.

"That the University is empowered to grant Degrees in Arts, Laws, Medicine, and Science generally; and that all the more important Schools of Medicine, and Nonconformist, Roman Catholic, and Secular Colleges, both in London and in the Provinces, have for several years been connected with the University, for the purpose of entitling their Students to be examined for its Degrees.

"That the Graduates who have attained the standing of Members of Convocation will, before the close of the present year 1859, exceed 1000 in number, and are increasing at the rate of nearly 100 annually.

"That the foundation of the University was settled upon an express compact that it should be equal in all respects with the ancient Universities, and that this understanding has been acted upon in all instances in which it has been brought to the notice of the Legislature.

"That under several Acts of Parliament, and by the concurrent regulations of various Public Corporations in that behalf, the fact of Graduation in the University of London has for some time formed part of the title to practise in the learned professions of Law and Medicine, equally with Graduation in any of the ancient Universities.

"That the Grammar School, the Militia, and the Charitable Trusts Acts, passed in the reign of her present Majesty, contain respectively provisions placing the University of London in the same position in regard to the said Acts with the Universities of Oxford, Cambridge, and Dublin.

"That the Charter creating the Convocation of the University was also granted in pursuance of the same understanding, for partially according to the Graduates the right enjoyed by those of Oxford and Cambridge in respect of their Universities, of sharing in the management of its internal affairs.

"That measures for amending the Representation of the United Kingdom having been, or being likely to be, introduced into your [Right] Honourable House, the present is a fitting opportunity for providing for the Representation in Parliament of the University of London.

"And your Petitioners humbly pray that in any measure for the amendment of the Representation of England which may pass your [Right] Honourable House, provision may be made for conferring the right of being represented in the House of Commons upon the University.

"And your Petitioners will ever pray."

(Seal of the University of London.)

On the 1st of January, 1859, there were 38 Fellows and 1195 Graduates of the University of London, the Graduates being distributed into the three following faculties of Medicine, Law, and Arts :—

      153 Doctors of Medicine.
      156 Bachelors of Medicine.
        9 Doctors of Law.
       75 Bachelors of Law.
       83 Masters of Arts.
      719 Bachelors of Arts.
     ————
    1195 Graduates.

Dr. Foster, in his account of the University of London as a Parliamentary constituency, published some years ago, thus described the occupations and places of residence of the Graduates, as far as they had been then ascertained :—

"The Medical Graduates are occupied in their professional practice. Of the other faculties, it is computed that about one-fifth are engaged in the religious ministries of their respective denominations, as Clergymen of the Established Church, and Roman Catholic Priests, or Dissenting Ministers. Nearly another fifth hold tutorial or professional posts in the affiliated Colleges, or in other institutions. Some are bankers or merchants; and nearly one-half are members of the legal profession, and in a large proportion of instances, at the Bar. In the London hospitals, the most important positions are undoubtedly filled by men of older standing in the profession than the London Graduates have as yet attained; but vacancies are already beginning, as a general rule, to be filled by them. At least half of the entire number of Medical Graduates hold posts of responsibility in the London and country hospitals.

"It may be added, with respect to residence, that it has been ascertained, that a proportion of between one-third and one-half of the Graduates are permanently resident within twenty miles of the Post Office. A large proportion of the remainder are found to be collected around the chief provincial centres of population."

Scientific interest in the University of London, will be increased by an arrangement for granting Degrees in Science, which may, in time, create a faculty of Science, as a new characteristic of that University.

According to a scheme of Examinations for Degrees in Science, recently prepared by a Committee of the Senate of the University of London, the matriculation of Scientific Students will consist of the same subjects, and be regulated in the same manner, as in the case of other Undergraduates of the University, and Candidates will not be approved by the Examiners for matriculation, unless they show a competent knowledge in—

1. Classics.
2. The English Language, English History, and Modern Geography.
3. Mathematics and Natural Philosophy.
4. Chemistry.
5. Either the French or the German Language.

At subsequent periods after matriculation, special Examinations in Science will be held, commencing with the Examination of Candidates in the following subjects: viz.:—

Arithmetic, Algebra, as far as Quadratic Equations; and the nature and use of Logarithms.
Geometry, including the relations of similar figures.
The Eleventh Book of Euclid to Prop. 21.

The Equation to the straight line, and the Equation to the Circle referred to rectangular co-ordinates.

The Equations to the Conic sections referred to rectangular co-ordinates.

Plane Trigonometry, as far as to enable the Candidate to solve all the cases of Plane Triangles, with simple propositions on Sines, co-Sines, and Tangents, and the expression for the area of a Triangle in terms of its sides.

Mechanical and Natural Philosophy treated by simple Geometrical Methods.

Heat.

Electricity.

Magnetism.

Elementary Substances and their combinations in Chemistry.

Botany and Vegetable Physiology, Zoology, and Animal Physiology.

Later Examinations in Science will also be held.

Subjects required for the Degree of Bachelor of Arts in the University of London, have been already described in this work, page 25.

For the Degree of Bachelor of Laws in the University of London, the Examination includes :—

Stephen's Blackstone, the three portions of Dumont's edition of Bentham's Morals and Legislation, which contain the Principles of Legislation, the Principles of a Civil Code, and the Principles of a Criminal Code.

For the Degree of Bachelor of Medicine, Candidates are required—

1. To have been engaged during four years in their professional studies at one or more of the Institutions or Schools recognised by the University of London.
2. To have spent one year at least of the four in one or more of the recognised Institutions or Schools in the United Kingdom.
3. To pass two Examinations.

No Candidate is admitted to the first Examination in Medicine unless he have produced Certificates—

1. Of having completed his nineteenth year.
2. Of having taken a Degree in Arts, or of having passed the Matriculation Examination of the University of London.
3. Of having obtained some instruction in the various subjects in which he will be examined.

Candidates are examined in the following subjects:—

Morning, 10 *to* 1.

Monday...Anatomy and Physiology, by printed papers.
Tuesday...Chemistry, by printed papers.
Wednesday, 10 *to* 12...Botany, by printed papers.

Afternoon, 3 *to* 6.

Monday...Anatomy and Physiology, by printed papers.
Tuesday...Materia Medica and Pharmacy, by printed papers.

To commence on Friday, at 10.

Chemistry, by *Vivâ Voce* and Experiment; and Materia Medica and Pharmacy, by *Vivâ Voce*, and Demonstration from Specimens.

To commence on Tuesday in the following week, at 10.

Anatomy and Physiology by *Vivâ Voce*, Demonstration from Preparations, and Dissection.

On Wednesday Morning in the week following the commencement of the Examination, the Examiners arrange in two divisions, each in alphabetical order, such of the Candidates as have passed.

Candidates for the second Examination in Medicine are required to produce fresh Certificates of instruction, and also a Certificate of Moral Character from a Teacher in the last School or Institution at which he has studied, as far as the Teacher's opportunity of knowledge has extended.

The Candidates are required to translate passages of the Latin Pharmacopœia into English, and of the English Pharmacopœia into Latin.

The Examination is conducted in the following subjects:—

FIRST WEEK. *By printed papers.*

Morning, 10 *to* 1.

Monday ......Physiology.
Tuesday ......Surgery.
Wednesday...Midwifery.

Afternoon, 3 *to* 6.

Monday ......General Pathology, General Therapeutics, Hygiene.
Tuesday ......Medicine.
Wednesday...Forensic Medicine.

Friday.

The Candidates to report on the Cases of actual Patients.

SECOND WEEK.

By Vivâ Voce *Interrogation and Demonstration from Preparations, with Translations from the Pharmacopœias.*
To commence on Monday Morning. at 10.

At the conclusion of these Examinations, the names of the successful Candidates are arranged in two divisions, each in alphabetical order; and the Degree of Bachelor of Medicine is conferred on each of the Students thus honourably enrolled in the books of the University.

Bachelors of Arts, Law, Medicine, and possibly Science, will constitute the more numerous portion of the Electoral body of the University of London, and the franchise may be considered as a reward for the care and attention which they have bestowed in preparing themselves for Academical Examinations.

Valuable assistance to University studies is afforded at the present day, by the preliminary examinations conducted in different parts of England, under the care of Graduates of Oxford or Cambridge, and which serve to test the efficiency of Education in Local Grammar Schools, with respect to the requirements of modern times in different branches of learning.

As a specimen of the regulations adopted in each of the ancient English Universities, for the Examination of Students who are not Members of the University, we may quote the following arrangement laid down in 1858 by the University of Cambridge :—

Students must be under eighteen years of age on the day when the Examination begins.

Part 1. Preliminary.

Every Student will be required to satisfy the Examiners in

1. Reading aloud a passage from some standard English poet.
2. Writing from dictation.
3. Analysis of English sentences and parsing.
4. Writing a short English composition.
5. The principles and practice of Arithmetic.
6. Geography.

Every Student will be required to answer questions on the subject and to draw from memory an outline map of some country in Europe, showing the boundary lines, the chief ranges of mountains, the chief rivers, and the chief towns.

7. The outlines of English History; that is, the succession of Sovereigns, the chief events, and some account of the leading men in each reign.

Part II.

The Examination will comprise the subjects mentioned in the following eight sections; and every Student will be required to satisfy the Examiners in three at least of the sections marked A, B, C, D, E, F; or in two of them, and in one of the sections marked G, H; but no one will be examined in more than five. Section A must be taken by every Student, unless his parents or guardians object to his Examination in that section.

Section A.

Religious knowledge:
The Examination will consist of questions in

1. The Historical Scriptures of the Old Testament to the death of Solomon.
   The Gospel of St. Luke and the Acts of the Apostles: credit will be given for a knowledge of the original Greek.
2. The Morning and Evening Services in the Book of Common Prayer: and the Apostles' Creed.
3. Paley's 'Horæ Paulinæ.'

Every Student, who is examined in this section, will be required to satisfy the Examiners in the subject marked 1, and in one at least of the subjects marked 2 and 3.

Section B.

1. English History, from the battle of Bosworth Field to the Restoration; and the outlines of English Literature during the same period.
2. Shakespeare's 'Julius Cæsar,' (Craik's edition).
3. The outlines of Political Economy and English Law.

The Examination will not extend beyond the *subjects* treated of in the first book of Smith's 'Wealth of Nations,' and the first volume of Blackstone's 'Commentaries.'

4. Physical, Political, and Commercial Geography.

A fair knowledge of one of these four divisions will enable a Student to pass in this section.

SECTION C.

1. Latin:

Passages will be given from Livy, Book XXI., and Horace, Odes,' Book III., for translation into English, with questions on the historical and geographical allusions, and on Grammar:
Also passages for translation from some other Latin authors:
And a passage of English for translation into Latin.

2. Greek:

Passages will be given from the 'Olynthiacs' of Demosthenes, and the 'Alcestis' of Euripides, for translation into English, with questions on the historical and geographical allusions, and on Grammar:
Also passages for translation from some other Greek authors.

3. French:

Passages will be given from La Bruyère's 'Characters,' and Molière's 'Misanthrope,' for translation into English, with questions on Grammar:
Also passages from some other French authors for translation into English:
And a passage of English for translation into French.

4. German:

Passages will be given from Schiller's 'History of the Revolt of the Netherlands,' and Goethe's 'Hermann and Dorothea,' for translation into English, with questions on the historical and geographical allusions, and on Grammar:
Also passages from some other German authors for translation into English:
And a passage of English for translation into German.

A fair knowledge of one of these four languages will enable a Student to pass in this section.

Section D.

Every Student, who is examined in this section, will be required to satisfy the Examiners in

Euclid, Books I., II., III., IV., VI., and XI. to Prop. 21, inclusive.
Arithmetic and Algebra.

Questions will also be set in the following subjects :—

Plane Trigonometry, including Land-surveying.
The simpler properties of the Conic Sections.
The elementary parts of Statics, including the equilibrium of forces acting in one plane, the laws of friction, the conditions of stable and unstable equilibrium, and the principle of virtual velocities.
The elementary parts of Dynamics, namely, the doctrines of uniform and uniformly accelerated motion, of projectiles and collision.
The elements of Mechanism.
The elementary parts of Hydrostatics, namely, the pressure of elastic and inelastic fluids, specific gravities, floating bodies, and the construction and use of the more simple instruments and machines.
The elementary parts of Optics, namely, the laws of reflection and refraction of rays at plane and spherical surfaces (not including aberrations), lenses, the phenomena of vision, the eye, microscopes, and telescopes.
The elementary parts of Astronomy, so far as they are necessary for the explanation of the more simple phenomena, together with descriptions of the essential instruments of an Observatory ; and Nautical Astronomy.

Section E.

1. Chemistry.

Questions will be set on the facts and general principles of Chemical Science.

There will also be a practical Examination in the elements of Analysis.

2. The experimental laws and elementary principles of Heat, Magnetism, and Electricity.

3. The elementary principles of Physical Optics according to the Undulatory Theory, and Acoustics, with descriptions of the fundamental experiments.

A fair knowledge of Inorganic Chemistry, or of one of the divisions 2 and 3, will enable a Student to pass in this section.

Section F.

1. Comparative Anatomy and Animal Physiology:

The Examination will be confined to the active and passive organs of locomotion.

2. Botany, and the elements of Vegetable Physiology.
3. Physical Geography and Geology:

Explanations of Geological terms will be required, and simple questions set respecting stratified and unstratified rocks, the modes of their formation, and organic remains.

A fair knowledge of one of these three divisions, including a practical acquaintance with specimens, will enable a Student to pass in this section.

Section G.

Drawing from the Flat, from Models, from Memory, and in Perspective; and Drawing of Plans, Sections, and Elevations.

Design in Pen and ink, and in colour

A fair degree of skill in free-hand drawing will be required in order that a Student may pass in this section.

Questions also will be set on the history and principles of the arts of Design.

SECTION H.

The Grammar of Music.
The history and principles of Musical Composition.
A knowledge of the elements of Thorough Bass will be required, in order that a Student may pass in this section.

Similar plans for the annual Examination of Candidates, who are not members of a University, are pursued under the sanction of the University of Oxford. Encouragement is thus afforded to the maintenance of an improved system of instruction in Grammar Schools, as well as to the selection of clever youths to be entered as Students in the Universities of Oxford and Cambridge.

Intellectual exertion is also promoted in a similar manner by the Matriculation Examinations of the University of London. New Students matriculate, and the attention of youth in Colleges and under private tuition is directed to the special subjects proposed for these Examinations.

Whilst, however, general Academic Examinations receive so large a measure of attention, some change is required in the religious tests and Examinations for Holy Orders in the Church of England, which affect the majority of the electors in each of the ancient English Universities, and influence parishes and endowed schools throughout the southern part of Britain.

The present forms of subscription for ordination in the Established Church date from the sixteenth, and the commencement of the seventeenth centuries.

Every Clergyman is, by the Act of the 13th Elizabeth, chapter 12, required to subscribe to all the articles of religion, which concern the confession of the true Christian faith, and the doctrine of sacraments. In obedience to the 36th Canon passed by the Convocation of the Clergy in 1603, he must farther subscribe to three articles, comprising:—

1. The spiritual and temporal supremacy of the sovereign;
2. The reception of the Book of Common Prayer, as containing in it nothing contrary to the Word of God; and,
3. The acknowledgment of the Thirty-nine Articles, as agreeable to the Word of God.

The Act of Uniformity of 1662 imposes an additional declaration of "unfeigned assent and consent to all and everything contained and prescribed in and by" the Book of Common Prayer.

Examinations are periodically held under the superintendence of chaplains of Bishops, to ascertain the amount of knowledge possessed by Candidates for ordination; the subjects of Examination comprise the Old and New Testament History, the Liturgy, and Articles of the Church of England, the general history of the Christian church, with the ecclesiastical events specially connected with England, and natural and revealed religion. Papers are set to Candidates for Deacons' Orders, in which passages in Greek and Latin are to be translated into English; a passage in English is also given to be translated into Latin, and another English passage is placed before the Candidates, which may be translated either into Greek or Hebrew. A paper on the Greek Testament forms a part of the Ordination Examination, both for Deacons and Priests, and an Essay in English is requested from the Candidates for Deacons' Orders, on a text set by the Examiner.

A collection of ordination questions "as given at the

recent Examinations for Holy Orders of Priests and Deacons," was published at Cambridge in 1854,* and it is remarkable how small a space questions on moral science occupy in this little Manual, and how questions are occasionally introduced which the enlightened opinion of scientific inquirers at the present day would not acknowledge as referring to physical truth.

One of the Examination Papers on the subject of Old Testament History, begins with the following question :—

"State the order of creation, and what were the kind of days?"†

An answer to this question may be given as follows, from the narrative of the first cosmogony in the order of the successive days, by Professor von Bohlen :—

"Primitive chaos is described as surrounded with darkness, and as brought into complete form by the Divine Being in the work of six days. First, light is created and separated from darkness, thereby forming day and night; then the vault of heaven is made, dividing the waters under it from those above it; after this, the land is separated from the sea, and plants are produced on the land; next, the sun, moon, and stars are placed as lights in the vault of heaven, to give light to the earth, and to divide time; then follows the creation of birds and of fish, and lastly the creation of land animals, and of man himself, to whom dominion over the whole is given. At the conclusion of the work of creation, the Deity hallows the seventh day, and sets it apart as a day of rest."‡

---

* Cambridge: Hall & Son. London: Whittaker & Co.; and G. Bell.
† Collection of Ordination Questions, p. 9.
‡ Introduction to the Book of Genesis, from the German of Professor von Bohlen, edited by James Heywood, F.R.S. Vol. ii. p. 1.

The evening, Professor von Bohlen remarks, is first mentioned in the account of each day, "because not only darkness preceded light, but also the Hebrews, like the Egyptians, Greeks, Persians, Gauls, Germans, and other nations, began the day, in civil matters, with the evening."* "Thus was it evening and morning, the first day."

"Upon the very face of the document," observes Dr. Pye Smith, "it is manifest, that in the first chapter of Genesis the word day is used in its ordinary sense."†

Candidates for the priesthood in the Church of England are asked to prove from Scripture, that under the terms "heaven and earth" are comprehended all things.‡

No Hebrew word expresses the modern idea of the universe; their phrase, "the high and the low," meant the heavens and the earth, which are spoken of in Deut. xxxii. 1, and Isaiah i. 2. In Psalm cxlviii. 13, the glory of Jehovah is described as "above the earth and heaven."§

According to Von Bohlen, the firmament, described in Genesis i. 6, 7, as a partition between the waters above and below the firmament, was conceived by the Hebrews to be a solid vault, in which the stars were studded like nails, and which rested on mountains, on the rim of the earth's disk.‖ Thus in Job xxxvii. 18,

---

* Von Bohlen's Genesis, vol. ii. p. 11.
† On the Relation between the Holy Scriptures and some parts of Geological Science, by J. Pye Smith, D.D., F.G.S., p. 209.
‡ Collection of Ordination Questions, p. 51.
§ Prof. Tuch on Genesis, referred to in Von Bohlen's Genesis, vol. ii. p. 7.
‖ Von Bohlen's Genesis, vol. ii. p. 12.

the Deity is said to have spread out the "sky, which is strong, and as a molten looking-glass." In Exodus xxiv. 10, the body of heaven is likened in its clearness to a paved work of sapphire stone; and in Ezekiel i. 22, the firmament is compared to the colour of crystal, and is stretched over the heads of the winged creatures seen in the vision of the prophet.

From Genesis vii. 11, it appears, that there were windows in heaven, which were opened for the fall of rain; the "waters above the heavens" are mentioned in Psalm cxlviii. 4: these were the upper waters separated by the firmament, or partition, from the sea.

Of air, or any other elastic fluid, the Hebrews had no idea. According to Dr. Pye Smith, the Hebrew writers "supposed, that at a moderate distance above the flight of birds, there was a solid concave hemisphere, a kind of dome, transparent, in which the stars were fixed as lamps; and containing openings, to be used or closed, as was necessary. This vault was understood as supporting a kind of celestial ocean, called "the waters above the firmament," and "the waters above the heavens," which formed a grand reservoir, containing water to be discharged at proper times in rain.*

Among various questions on the Book of Common Prayer set to Candidates for Holy Orders, one on Trinity Sunday requires the Candidate to state what renders the first chapter of Genesis an appropriate lesson for the service of that day? †

Without doubt, the plural form of Elohim (Gods) for the name of the Deity, in Genesis, chap. i., and the

* Dr. Pye Smith on the Holy Scriptures and Geological Science, p. 272.
† Collection of Ordination Questions, p. 5.

plural phrase, "let us make," Genesis i. 26, were intended by the Examiner to be mentioned in the answer to this question; but on referring to Genesis iii. 22, we meet with the expression, "one of us," manifesting a distinction of similar beings. Von Bohlen does not regard the phrase, "let us make," as a plural of majesty. He refers to Isaiah vi. 8, where Jehovah addresses the Seraphim in a direct manner, "Who will go for us?" as well as to other passages, such as, 2 Sam. xvi. 20, where Absalom says to Ahithophel, "What shall we do?" 2 Sam. xxiv. 14, where David says to Gad, of himself and others, "let us fall." So Bildad understands Job and his friends, who speak in a direct manner, "Lay down now, put me in a surety with thee; who is he that will strike hands with me?" (Job xvii. 3,) in opposition to the party of Bildad, who observe, in reply, "How long will it be ere ye make an end of words? mark, and afterwards we will speak." Job xviii. 2.

"The one only God," according to Von Bohlen, "could not speak in such a manner as that even the pronouns received the plural,* and Gnostic sects freely inferred from the passage in Genesis i. 26, 'Let us make,' the existence of several divine beings, one of whom worked upon matter, as the Demiurgos, or architect."

Original sin forms a frequent subject of questions for Candidates for Ordination, who are expected to "define and prove 'original sin,' and illustrate by analogy its effects upon Adam's posterity." They are asked, "What is the account of the Pelagians with reference to the effect produced on mankind by the fall of Adam," and are requested to "recite the Scriptures, by which Pelagianism is refuted."

* Von Bohlen's Genesis, vol. ii. p. 17.

The concupiscible part of the soul, as the seat of the affections and lusts, was considered by scholastic disputants to be inseparable from matter, whilst the intellect alone was the immortal spiritual principle. Bishop Hampden, who has paid much attention to scholastic philosophy, describes the flesh, or concupiscible part of our nature, as having been, in the language of the schools, vitiated by the sin of the first man, and that by this sin, according to the schoolmen, our nature having been changed for the worse, not only became sinful, but even propagated sinners. The evil was described as a vitiation of the original flesh, transmitted like hereditary diseases, which show themselves in the body. Bishop Hampden is of opinion, that "the positive manner in which Augustine declared the transmission of the material element of corruption from Adam to the whole race of mankind, laid the groundwork of the scholastic discussions on the subject."*

Pelagius contended, according to Bishop Hampden, that the first sin had been hurtful to the human race, not by propagation, but by example, because all who had afterwards sinned had imitated him, the first sinner. In the opposing theories of Pelagius and Augustine, Bishop Hampden observes, that we may perceive something like the contrast in ancient philosophy, between the Pythagorean "similitude" and the Platonic "participation:" the orthodox account for the universality of evil by "participation" of the common nature; the Pelagians, by the principle of "similitude," or imitation.†

"The notion of Augustine corresponded with the Platonic notion of good and evil, as abstract, *à priori*

* Bampton Lectures on Scholastic Philosophy, 1837, p. 225.
† Bampton Lectures, *ut supra*, p. 223.

grounds of right and wrong in human conduct; as what constituted, by the participation of them, in each instance, the actual good and evil of the world."

On the other hand, " the notion of the Pelagians was in accordance with that of Aristotle, who held that we were endued with capacities of virtue and vice, but that virtue and vice, moral good and moral evil, were only the results of acting, of exercising those capacities well or ill."*

According to Professor Jowett, the earliest trace of a connection between sin and death, and the sins and death of mankind with the sin of Adam, is found in the Apocryphal Book of Wisdom, ii. 23, 24: "God created man to be immortal, and made him to be an image of his own eternity. Nevertheless, through envy of the devil came death into the world." "It was," remarks Professor Jowett, "a farther refinement of some of the Jewish teachers, that when Adam sinned, the whole world sinned. Human nature, or philosophy, sometimes rose up against such inventions, but, on the whole, it seems to have been admitted that the doctrine of Augustine had been in substance generally agreed to by the rabbis, and that there is no trace of the Jewish teachers having derived it from the writings of St. Paul."†

The controversy respecting original sin may now be regarded as a portion of ecclesiastical history. In this point of view, it has been referred to in June, 1859, by the Theological Examiners of Manchester New College, London, in the following questions set to the Members of that College:—

---

* Bampton Lectures, p. 224.
† Epistles of St. Paul, edited by Professor Jowett, vol. ii. p. 165.

"Explain the origin and progress of the Pelagian controversy. Show how the different characters and early experiences of Augustine and Pelagius may in part have determined the side which they adopted in this controversy. State the chief points of the question at issue between them."

Questions on the early condition of human beings according to the opening chapters of Genesis, with the general language of the Old Testament, and the teaching of Jesus Christ on man's condition and capacity, were thus proposed in the same examination:—

"What are the two views of man's creation and earliest condition contained in the opening chapters of Genesis? How are they distinguished? Is it possible to reconcile them? What is remarkable with respect to one of these views? Where do we find the first distinct allusion to it? By whom is it first made use of for a theological purpose? What do the Scriptures of the Old Testament generally and the teachings of Jesus Christ affirm of man's condition and capacity as a *fact?*"

In the Theological Examination of the University of Cambridge, October, 1858, the following questions occur, respecting the Article of the Church of England on original sin:—

"What do you understand by 'original sin?' Support your statement by proof from the Old and New Testaments. Point out the evil consequences as regards (1) doctrine, and (2) practice, to which Pelagian teaching upon this subject is likely to lead. Distinguish between *reatus peccati* and *morbus peccati.*"

"Give the Latin for 'original sin,' 'following of Adam,' 'regenerate,' 'is very far gone from original righteousness,' 'them that believe and are baptized.'

From what source was the ninth Article probably derived?"*

The paper on the Articles of religion in the Cambridge University Theological Examination of May, 1859, thus alludes to the doctrine of original sin:—

"Art. IX. *De Peccato originali*.—What is the subject of this Article, and against whom was it specially directed? In what respect are the positions of this Article at variance with the Decrees of the Council of Trent, and with what confessions of faith do they most nearly agree? Prove that original sin is not derived from imitation, but inherited by birth; and state the difference of opinion between the Calvinists and Arminians as to the extent of the corruption in our nature produced by the fall. What do you conceive to be the true and scriptural opinion?"†

German researches on the Paradisiacal narrative in Genesis afford a new and more satisfactory explanation respecting this mythical subject, and it may therefore be interesting to refer to views which attract considerable attention in Germany, and are supported both by philosophical and theological authority.

Professor von Bohlen is of opinion that the Paradisiacal narrative of the first sentiment of shame by human beings portrays an advancement in civilization beyond the mere animal state in which they were created.

Man's disobedience to the command of Jehovah appears to have been intended by the narrator, in order to elevate the mortal beings whom he described; indeed, observes Von Bohlen, there is so little allusion to a fall

---

* Cambridge Examination Papers, p. 15. London: Bell & Daldy. 1859.

† Cambridge Examination Papers, p. 237. 1859.

through sin, that the object of the writer seems rather to have been the elevation of the human race towards the Deity.

Professor Tuch remarks that "the Paradisiacal myth has been generally more profoundly understood by philosophers than by theologians. Kant and Schiller have employed the Scriptural document in elucidating physiological inquiries on the progressive development of mankind; both of these philosophers correctly remark, that the myth does not represent a debasement or sinking down from original perfection to imperfection, not a victory of sensuality over reason, but, on the contrary, it manifests the advancement of man from a state of natural rudeness to freedom and civilization. The historical individuality of Adam is no longer maintained; he becomes the general representative of humanity. On the other hand, no sufficient explanation has been given, or rather it has been left unexplained, how this advance to freedom, which is here described, can include the idea of a fall through sin; indeed, Von Bohlen wholly denies that the notion of a fall through sin is here taught; according to his view, the myth only represents the elevation of man toward God. This more correct and satisfactory explanation of the mythical narrative has been first given by the philosophy of the present age."*

Professor von Bohlen observes, that "whoever desires practically to instruct his fellow-countrymen, must discard the dreams of the dark ages respecting the introduction of hereditary sin as the consequence of man's tasting the tree of knowledge, a doctrine which is alike dishonouring to God and man, and he must direct his

* Tuch's Commentary on Genesis. pp. 54–61. quoted in the English edition of Von Bohlen's Genesis, vol. ii. pp. 78, 79.

attention to the refined features of the narrative, such as marriage with one wife, conjugal love, the natural inclination of man to social intercourse, and his earnest desire to obtain knowledge."*

From the pages of the Bible itself, Professor von Bohlen quotes the following passages to elucidate the meaning of a "knowledge of good and evil." In Deuteronomy i. 39, we read that young children and little ones have no knowledge of good and evil. An understanding heart is spoken of in 1 Kings iii. 9, as the means of discerning between good and evil, and butter and honey are mentioned in Isaiah vii. 15, as giving the power to refuse evil and choose what is good. The exercise of the senses in full age is described in Hebrews v. 14, as the way to discern both good and evil.

In 2 Samuel xix. 35, the old Barzillai, enfeebled at eighty years of age, asks how, in the weakness of his bodily senses, he can discern between good and evil?†

After having quoted the foregoing passages, Von Bohlen explains the knowledge of good and evil to mean the attainment of a manly intellect, and he regards the account of the possibility of the tree of life being subsequently tasted, as in accordance with the ideas of Oriental nations, who sought to attain long life by potions. The tree of eternal happiness in the Mahometan paradise, according to D'Herbelot, is termed the "Tooba tree," and Thomas Moore thus describes the privilege of the Peri, on being admitted into the garden of Eden:—

> "My feast is now of the Tooba tree,
> Whose scent is the breath of eternity."‡

---

* Von Bohlen's Genesis, vol. ii. p. 61.   † *Ibid*, vol. ii. p. 39.
‡ Lalla Rookh, Paradise and the Peri.

Among modern writers, who have dwelt on the early ignorance and progressive elevation of human nature, we may refer to the Rev. Theodore Parker, by whom the development of the whole human race is compared to the intellectual progress of a single human being in the following manner:—

"We all see," observes Mr. Parker, "the unity of life in the individual: his gradual growth from merely sentient and passive babyhood, up to thoughtful, self-directing manhood. I have tried," continues that eloquent writer, "to show there was a similar unity of life in the human race, pointing out the analogous progressive development of mankind, from the state of ignorance, poverty, and utter nakedness of soul and sense, the necessary primitive conditions of the race, up to the present civilization of the leading nations.

"The primitive is a wild man, who generally grows up to civilization. To me, the notorious facts of human history, the condition of language, art, industry, and the footprints of man left all over the torrid and temperate lands, admit of no other interpretation.

"Of course, it must have required many a thousand years for Divine Providence to bring this child from his mute, naked, ignorant poverty, up to the many-voiced, many-coloured civilization of these times; and as in the strata of mountain and plain, on the shores of the sea, and under 'the bottom of the monstrous world,' the geologist finds proof of time immense, wherein this material Cosmos assumed its present form, so in ruins of cities, in the weapons of iron, bronze, or stone, found in Scandinavian swamps, on the sub-aquatic enclosures of the Swiss lakes, in the remains of Egyptian industry, which the holy Nile, 'mother of blessings,' now spiritual to us as once material to those whose flesh she fed, has covered with many folds of earth and kept for us, and still more in the history of art, science, war, industry, and the structure of language itself, a slow-growing plant, do I find proof of time immense, wherein man, this spiritual Cosmos, has been assuming his present condition, individual, domestic, social, and national, and accumulating that wealth of things and thoughts which is the mark of civilization.

"I have tried to show by history the progressive development of industry and wealth,—of mind and knowledge,—of conscience and justice,—of the affections and philanthropy,—of the soul and true religion. The many forms of the family, the community, state, and church, I look on as so many 'experiments in living,' all useful, each perhaps in its time and place as indispensable as the various geological changes.

"But this progressive development does not end with us; we have seen only the beginning; the future triumphs of the race must be vastly greater than all accomplished yet.

"In the primal instincts and automatic desires of man, I have found a prophecy, that what he wants is possible, and shall one day be actual. It is a glorious future on earth which I have set before your eyes and hopes, thereby stimulating both your patience to bear now what is inevitable, and your thought and toil to secure a future triumph to be had on no other terms. What good is not with us is before, to be attained by toil and thought and religious life."*

A kindred doctrine of human development has been

* Theodore Parker's Experience as a Minister, p. 82. Boston: U.S. 1859.

quoted by Mr. John Stuart Mill, from a German work on the Sphere and Duties of Government, by Wilhelm von Humboldt, in which the eminent Prussian politician expresses his opinion, that "the end of man, or that which is prescribed by the eternal or immutable dictates of reason, and not suggested by vague and transient desires, is the highest and most harmonious development of his powers to a complete and consistent whole;" that therefore the object towards which every human being must ceaselessly direct his efforts, and on which especially those who design to influence their fellow-men must ever keep their eyes, is the individuality of power and development;" that for this there are two requisites, "freedom, and a variety of situations;" and that from the union of these arise "individual vigour and manifold diversity," which combine themselves in "originality."*

No class of human beings have a more important sphere for influencing their fellow-men than the parochial clergy of the English Established Church, if the religious tests to which they are subjected, and the examinations which they must pass in order to enter on their sacred profession, could be revised and modified so as to allow them a larger amount of mental and individual freedom, and to render them better acquainted with matters likely to be useful in their respective parishes.

Each of the British Houses of Parliament possesses representatives of the clergy of the Established Church, a privilege which is not accorded to any other religious denomination. The House of Lords undertakes especially the care of ecclesiastical interests, which has been shown by their insertion of tithes in a bill relating to the parliamentary powers of new tracts of land reclaimed

* Mill on Liberty, p. 103. London. 1859.

from the ocean. Peers for life are appointed by the Crown from among the Protestant episcopalian clergy to watch over the especial rights of the Anglican Church. In the House of Commons, where a clergyman of the Establishment is not allowed to sit, the three Universities of Oxford, Cambridge, and Dublin, each return two representatives; and as the constituencies of those ancient academic bodies contain a majority of clerical electors, the six University seats may be regarded as under the control of the Protestant episcopalian clergy.

Every parochial Sunday-school, and a large number of parochial and district day and infant schools throughout the kingdom own an allegiance to the local clergy, who are often accustomed actively to superintend their organization and to assist in their practical working.

Of late years, the liberal grants of the Committee of Council on Education in aid of denominational schools have greatly increased religious party-spirit, and threaten to deepen those lines of demarcation which subsist between different sects.

On the 22nd of July, 1859, the Right Honourable Robert Lowe, Vice-President of the Committee of Council on Education thus alluded, in the House of Commons, to the change which had recently taken place in the wording of denominational differences in the trust-deeds of schools receiving grants from Government:—

"At the beginning of the Committee of Council system," he said, "the trust-deeds of schools were often very loosely worded; but as soon as it was known that it was intended to assist the voluntary efforts of the different denominations, then the deeds began to be drawn with great care, and the denominational differences of the founders were brought out in the sharpest possible manner. It was very much to be regretted that public money should have been expended in endowing schools, most of which were founded on very exclusive principles. He could not but think that the suggestion of the honourable Member for Belfast with respect to another matter would be well applied to this, and that before a grant was made to any denominational Church, the founders should be required to introduce some sort of conscience clauses into its trust-deed, so that children might not be compelled to learn the formularies of the sect to which the school belonged if its parents objected. (Hear, hear.) That was in effect already done in many instances. There were clergymen of the Church of England who were better than their bond, and were willing to open their schools; but there were many others who read the formularies of their religion as a test to drive away children of Dissenters, unless they were willing to submit at once to the religious teaching of their schools. (Hear, hear.) Another evil in the system was the arrangement which the different sects had made with the Council, that their schools should each be inspected by an inspector of the same religion. The result was, that of the fifty-nine inspectors, the services of at least one-third might be dispensed with if a different rule prevailed."

A large part of the exclusiveness complained of, both in the management of denominational, and especially Church of England schools, and in the limitation of the inspectorships for what are called National schools to members of the Established Church, arises from the ecclesiastical restrictions to which the clergy of the Church of England have been in early life accustomed in endowed schools and in the Colleges of Oxford or Cambridge, and which they therefore desire to perpetuate in schools entrusted to their care.

If mental freedom may be allowed in the course of study and ecclesiastical services of the ancient monastic Colleges near the Cam and the Isis, and an improved system may influence education at the schools of Eton, Westminster, and Winchester, as well as in other endowed schools, the students brought up in those ancient seminaries will in future be more ready than their predecessors to co-operate in liberal views of enlightened public instruction.

Alterations in the law with respect to educational charities will also lead to beneficial changes in the ancient establishments for instruction, which were founded either before or about the period of the Reformation.

At the present day, legal constructions of the Court of Chancery, according to Sir R. Bethell, assume that all educational charities founded before the Reformation must of necessity be confined exclusively to members of the Church of England. A second presumption of the same Court insists that all schools founded after the Reformation, and before the passing of the Act of Toleration, must be administered for the exclusive benefit of members of the Church of England.

Another artificial rule of the Court of Chancery decides, that where an educational charity is established without anything being said about religious instruction, or that the nature of the religious instruction is not defined, the Court presumes that religious instruction must be intended, and that it can only be given, according to the form of which alone the Court is cognizant, viz. in conformity with the principles and doctrines of the Church of England.

It is also assumed, that if a school be founded with a direction in the trust deed that the schoolmaster shall be a clergyman in holy orders, the Court of Chancery will make no regulation concerning religious instruction, which will be left entirely to the master.

Sir Richard Bethell enumerated to the House of Commons in 1859, these rules of the Court of Chancery, and in alluding to the decision of Vice-Chancellor Wood, respecting the Chelmsford Grammar School case, mentioned to the House that it had then been laid down, "that religious instruction being a necessary part of education in a grammar school, and there being reason to believe that such instruction was originally intended to be according to the doctrines and principles of the Church of England, the Court could not sanction the insertion of any clause in the scheme, exempting those scholars whose parents conscientiously objected thereto, from receiving such instruction."

"To take these foundations," observed Sir Richard Bethell, "and attribute to them a character arising only from the intolerance of the times, is not a wise rule of administration, not conducive to the real interests of the Church, and opposed to all true principles of public policy and the dictates of Christian charity."

Mr. Dillwyn, M.P., who had the charge of the Bill in the House of Commons, respecting endowed schools, described a special grievance arising from a decision, in 1858, of the Lords Justices Sir George Turner and Sir James Knight Bruce, in the case of the Ilminster Grammar School.

Certain inhabitants of the parish of Ilminster, in the reign of Edward VI., had founded this grammar school for the benefit of the poor generally, who were, in the terms of the endowment, to receive instruction "in godly learning and knowledge," under a master who was to be "an honest and discreet person."

The trustees were to be "honest men of the parish of Ilminster," and for 150 years the school had been well administered by trustees coming within that designation, and who had invariably been Churchmen and Dissenters, in varying proportions, but the Churchmen preponderating. About two or three years ago, a new light appeared in the parish in the person of a fresh Vicar, who objected to the presence of Dissenters in the trust.

Subsequently, when the trustees had dwindled down to three Dissenters, it became necessary to reconstruct the trust, and the Master of the Rolls judiciously appointed twelve Churchmen and three additional Dissenters, thus making the Churchmen two-thirds, and the Dissenters one-third of the whole number. The Vicar, objecting to the presence of the six Dissenters, appealed to the Lords Justices, and the names of the Dissenters were struck out of the trust on this appeal.

The Endowed Schools Bill has been intended to amend the law relating to endowed schools,—and to afford facilities, in the case of grammar schools with open trusts, of admitting duly qualified persons of any denomination, not merely to trusteeships, but to offices within those institutions.

A Committee of the House of Commons was appointed in the summer of 1859, to consider the bill on endowed schools, and the result of its deliberations has had the practical effect of explaining how a conscience clause may be framed for the scheme of a charitable endowment to be regulated by a Judge of the Court of Chancery sitting in chambers.

The conscience clause in the instance of Church of England instruction forming part of the course of education, in an endowed grammar school with an open trust deed, is recommended by the Committee to be thus worded:—

"No boy shall be required to learn the Catechism, Articles, or Liturgy of the Church of England, or to attend the celebration of divine worship according to the ritual of the Church of England, in case his parent or parents, or the person or persons standing to him *in loco parentis*, shall express to the trustees in writing his or their objections, on conscientious grounds, to the boy's doing so."*

Various alterations were introduced by the Select Committee into the Endowed Schools Bill, which proved so little acceptable to its promoters, that legislation on endowed schools has been postponed to a future session.

When the opening of offices in endowed grammar schools is again submitted to parliamentary consideration, the suitable preparation of candidates for masterships in such schools ought also to be noticed, with a view to the improvement of those institutions.

A Master of Arts of Oxford or Cambridge in the fifteenth century was expected to be a Regent, or teacher for several years, in the University, and the qualification of the degree of Master of Arts for the principal officers in endowed schools, was intended, no doubt, to ensure teachers for the schools who had already practised the business of teaching either at Oxford or Cambridge.

* Endowed Schools Bill, as amended by the Select Committee of the House of Commons. Schedule, p. 3, 1859.

No such guarantee exists at the present day in the degree of Master of Arts, which is conferred at Cambridge on Bachelors of Arts of three years' standing, without any examination, and even without the necessity of any academical residence or study after the degree of Bachelor of Arts.

To clergymen of the Church of England the M.A. degree affords the privilege of wearing a silk hood over the surplice, as well as the M.A. gown, and to Fellows of Colleges it occasionally increases the share of College dividends arising from the endowments.

Special instruction in the art of teaching is needed for the office of master in a grammar school, that the information which has been obtained by the teacher may be imparted to the scholars in the most efficient and impressive manner.

The Committee of Council on Education have already encouraged normal schools for the education of elementary school teachers; and if the University authorities cannot arrange for the special instruction of grammar school teachers, some extension may be made of the plans of existing normal schools, so as to include lectures for teachers, to prepare them for the instruction of youth of the middle and upper classes.

Her Majesty's Inspector of Schools, Mr. Matthew Arnold, M.A., reported on the Borough Road Training Institution of the British and Foreign School Society, in 1858, that "increased attention was evidently paid to the inculcation of correct methods of teaching; faults of exposition, faults in questioning, into which inexperienced teachers are liable to fall, were brought into clear light and sedulously examined."

Among the remarks of Mr. Fitch, M.A., Principal of the

Normal School, upon a criticism lesson, addressed to candidates for teacherships, Mr. Arnold heard him caution the students "to avoid vagueness in their comments upon the lesson under discussion. Do not," said the Principal, "accustom yourselves to say that such and such a thing in the lesson is good or bad, without alleging precise grounds for your opinion." In his own *résumé* of the lesson, Mr. Fitch illustrated his meaning by giving instances of faults in the criticism lesson, in every one of which he fortified, by clear, definite reasons, the course which he pursued. Again, in a lecture on school management, the Inspector heard him insisting, with great good sense and clearness, on certain signal faults in teaching, on the want of arrangement in lessons, and the attempt to crowd too much matter into single lessons; on the want of management by which scholars are allowed to answer by a single technical word, without paraphrase or explanation, or by which the willing are allowed to give all the answers, and the unwilling left without notice."

Mr. Arnold further remarked, "how Mr. Smith, the mathematical tutor, practically exemplified in his own teaching, the best methods of giving instruction in arithmetic, by his clear explanation of the principles of the rules of decimal arithmetic, on which he was lecturing; by the way in which he continually treated them by the rules of vulgar fractions; and then when he had been through two or three sums on the black board, set a sum for the students to work themselves, and went round to examine their slates." *

If some system of special instruction for teachers had

* Report for 1858–9 of the Committee of Council on Education, p. 342.

been in vogue for offices connected with tuition in English schools, the analysis in 1858 of the Oxford local examinations of school-boys, would not have resulted in nearly two-thirds of the total number being unsuccessful, and in many of the failures relating to the spelling of English words, and the first four rules of arithmetic.*

No Colleges would probably benefit more from the extension of special plans of training for teachers than Eton and King's College, Cambridge, the statutes of which are, at present, under the control of the Cambridge University Commission.

Fashion and aristocratic prestige have so increased the number of boys receiving education at Eton, as almost to surpass the powers of a small staff, principally composed of King's College Graduates, for the adequate supervision of 800 boys. The preparation of Eton schoolmasters, to whom many of the future leaders of British affairs may be, in their youth, entrusted, is in fact a subject of national importance. Hence revised statutes by the Cambridge University Commission for the improvement of the two Colleges of King's and Eton, will necessarily merit the attention of Parliament.

An extension of the academical franchise at Oxford and Cambridge to Bachelors of Arts, will confer the privilege of the University suffrage in those ancient seats of learning without a subscription test, and will aid in modifying the spirit of Collegiate exclusiveness, and in disseminating principles of religious equality among the Graduates, some of whom may be elected to responsible public offices either in Church or State, whilst others may be chosen to succeed to the management

* Of 1150 candidates at the Oxford local examination in 1858, 429 passed, and 721 were unsuccessful.

of Colleges and endowed grammar schools, in which educational superintendence will be requisite for youth of different religious denominations.

A happier day for English society may be expected to dawn, when a general spirit of mental freedom has been established in the ancient seats of learning, and political rights are no longer withheld from Graduates on account of conscientious religious convictions.

In the House of Commons, Members who are returned by the Universities of Oxford and Cambridge possess the same power with all other representatives of the people, over the lives, liberties, and property of British subjects of all denominations, and it is therefore just and fair that the mode of admission to the electoral lists in the ancient English Universities should be as open and free from religious test as in the registers of other borough constituencies.

The political bias of the Universities of Oxford and Cambridge will probably continue to a large extent under the influence of the clergy of the Church of England; but the introduction of the University of London, as a new Parliamentary constituency, will form a valuable portion of the expected Reform Bill, and the equalization of electoral rights in the various English Universities returning Members to Parliament, by extending the franchise to Bachelors of Arts of three years' standing, will prove advantageous to the cause of English education, as well as to the fair representation of English academical interests in Parliament.

OPENING AND IMPROVEMENT OF CAMBRIDGE COLLEGE HEADSHIPS, FELLOWSHIPS, AND SCHOLARSHIPS.

LOCAL revision at Cambridge of academical statutes was allowed by the Cambridge University Act of July, 1856, until the 1st of January, 1858, when the eight Commissioners appointed under the Act entered on their business of framing statutes, with a view to the promotion of useful learning and religious education in the Colleges and the University, as well as to the advancement of the main designs of the founders and donors, so far as such designs had been consistent with the purposes of useful learning and religious education in the different academical institutions of Cambridge and Eton.

When the Cambridge University Act passed, the Commissioners included the Right Rev. Dr. Lonsdale, Bishop of Lichfield, D.D. of King's College, Cambridge; the Right Rev. Dr. Graham, Bishop of Chester and formerly Master of Christ's College, Cambridge; the Right Hon. Lord Stanley, M.P.; the Right Hon. M. T. Baines, M.P.; the Vice-Chancellor Sir Page Wood, Knt.; the Right Hon. Sir Lawrence Peel, Knt.; the Very Rev. Dr. Peacock, Dean of Ely, and formerly Fellow and Tutor of Trinity College, Cambridge, and the Rev. Dr. Vaughan, Head Master of Harrow School.

Drafts of proposed new statutes were forwarded by the Commissioners, in 1858, to the authorities of Trinity and St. John's Colleges, and the principles of legislation embodied in these ordinances were understood to be intended as a guide to the formation of statutes by the Commissioners, for the smaller Colleges.

Considerable opposition soon manifested itself at Cambridge against the new regulations; copies of the draft statutes were reprinted and circulated among the Masters and Fellows of all the Colleges, and on the 26th of October, 1858, resolutions adverse to several proposals of the Commissioners were agreed to in Cambridge, at a meeting of the governing bodies of Colleges.

The Dean of Ely, Dr. Peacock, one of the most experienced Commissioners of the University, was at this time in declining health, and in November, 1858, he died, as it has been said, "in the effort to serve and improve the University, which he had loved so long and so well."*

Shortly after the appointment of the Cambridge Commission, in 1856, the Bishop of Lichfield had tendered his resignation as a Commissioner, and the vacancy thus created, as well as that arising from the death of the Dean of Ely, were filled up by the nomination, under the Crown, of the Lord Justice Sir George Turner, Knt., and Mr. Horatio Waddington, Under-secretary of the Home Department, as Commissioners.

Large concessions were made by the Commissioners to the agitation of the governing bodies of Colleges;

* Funeral Sermon on the Very Rev. G. Peacock, D.D., Dean of Ely, by the Rev. Professor Thompson, p. 15.

and the altered statutes have consequently obtained the acquiescence of the College authorities. An important provision for the conscientious scruples of Students who are not members of the Church of England does not appear in the later statutes, and the subject of College chapel attendance is practically left to the regulation of the Master and Senior Fellows of Trinity and St. John's Colleges respectively, in the case of the Under-graduates of those institutions.

Compulsory ordination for the Master of Trinity College, which was not inserted in the draft statutes, had a place in the revised copy of those regulations, so that a lay Graduate, however eminent, cannot be selected for that great Crown appointment.

Instead of the Fellowships of Trinity College being open to the competition of all the Members of the University who have obtained the degree of B.A., LL.B., or M.B., and whose standing, after such degree, does not exceed three years, as suggested in the draft statutes, the candidates are all to be Bachelors either in Arts, Law, or Medicine, belonging to the *College*, or the Fellows may be selected, "if the Master and Seniors should at any time think fit, from all members of the University, of similar degrees or standing."

A modification of this arrangement has been adopted in St. John's College, with reference to the Commissioners' proposals, and the Fellows are allowed to be chosen from among members of that College, or of the University of Cambridge, who have attained the degree of Bachelor of Arts, Bachelor of Laws, or Bachelor of Medicine, so that the enlargement of the field of competition from the College to the University is not left to the option of the Master and Senior Fellows.

In an earlier portion of this work (p. 74) will be found conditions of a limited tenure of Fellowships suggested in the draft statutes of the Cambridge Commissioners, which were intended to supersede various ancient rules for compulsory ordination and compulsory celibacy in the monastic institutions of Cambridge; but the proposal of limiting the general duration of a Fellowship to ten years after the M.A. degree, was stoutly combated at the meeting of the governing bodies of Colleges, in October, 1858, and the Commissioners now relinquish the valuable improvement of a limited tenure for a Fellowship, and pay but little regard to the influential and numerously signed Memorial* on the Fellowship restriction upon marriage, which, in 1857, had been presented to them.

A considerable majority of the Masters and Fellows of Colleges in October, 1858, voted, as might have been expected, in favour of a resolution, "That any tax upon the distributable income of Colleges, for University purposes, as proposed by the Cambridge University Commissioners, would be highly objectionable."

The proposal to St. John's College for a five per cent. income-tax on the distributable income of the College, to be paid to the University chest, and applied to purposes for the benefit of the University at large, has been met by a direct negative on the part of the Master and Senior Fellows; and two-thirds of the governing body of St. John's College have declared, by writing under their hands, that in their opinion such a statute would be prejudicial to their College as a place of learning and education. Further progress of voluntary College taxation is consequently checked. The Commissioners have re-

* See, *supra*, in this Work, p. 76.

ported what has occurred to the Secretary of State for the Home Department, and Sir George C. Lewis, Bart., M.P., has, in compliance with their request, laid the Report before both Houses of Parliament, which has been printed by order of the House of Commons.

Statutes framed by the Cambridge University Commissioners for the government of Trinity College and St. John's College, have also been laid before Parliament, and on the 11th of July, 1859, were ordered by the House of Commons to be printed.

Either House of Parliament may address the Crown against any of these statutes, within forty days from the time of their presentation, and the notice, within that period, of a motion for an address to the Crown, has been regarded as sufficient to delay the ratification of statutes.

Mr. Pollard Urquhart, M.P., on the 3rd of August, 1859, gave notice of his intention next session, to move an humble address to the Crown, praying that her Majesty will be graciously pleased to withhold her consent from certain portions of the statutes of Trinity College and St. John's College, Cambridge, relating to the compulsory ordination of the College Masters, the compulsory celibacy of all the Senior Fellows, and the delegation to the Master and Seniors exclusively, of rules respecting the attendance of Undergraduates, who are not members of the Church of England, at the College chapel; and that her Majesty will be graciously pleased to give such directions as to her may seem fit, to refer the above-mentioned statutes to the consideration of the Cambridge University Commissioners.

When the four Commissioners of Edward VI., Thomas Goodrich, Bishop of Ely, Sir John Cheke, William Meye, Dean of St. Paul's, and Dr. Wendye, physician to the

King, prepared the foundation statutes of Trinity College, Cambridge, no clause of compulsory ordination was inserted for the Master of the College. He was to "excel all others in learning, religion, uprightness of life, prudence, justice, faith, and affection towards the College, in order that his authority and dignity might shine forth by his illustrious virtues, and that he might be set forth as an example to others; and that consequently due honour might be paid to him."*

Under the visitation of Cardinal Pole, in the reign of Queen Mary, the statutes of Trinity College were remodelled, and the regulations of the Marian authorities served as a basis for the code prepared by the direction of Queen Elizabeth's Commission, including Matthew Parker, Archbishop of Canterbury, Sir William Cecil, Knt., Sir Anthony Cook, Knt., W. Bill, D.D., Walter Haddon, LL.D. and Master of Requests, W. Meye, LL.D., Dean of St. Paul's, R. Horne, D.D., Dean of Durham, James Pilkington, B.D., Master of St. John's College, and Thomas Wendye, physician to the Queen.

By the statutes of these Commissioners, the Master of Trinity College was directed to be of the true Catholic and orthodox faith, in priest's orders, and admitted to the degree of a Doctor, or at the least to that of a Bachelor in Theology.

It must be borne in mind that Trinity College has in modern times become a secularized ecclesiastical foundation; but in the sixteenth century, according to the statutes enforced by Elizabeth, every Fellow of Trinity College was obliged to swear—

"I will make Theology the end of my studies, and when the time prescribed in these statutes shall arrive

* Statutes of Edward VI. for Trinity College, Cambridge, chap. ii.

(seven years after the degree of Master of Arts), I will either take holy orders or quit the College."

This clause is left out in the declaration of the new statutes which takes the place of the ancient Fellowship oath. The omission has been acquiesced in by the College, and, in fact, the new rule is only in accordance with modern practice, by which lawyers and other laymen have constantly held Trinity College Fellowships for the period of seven years after the M.A. degree, without any idea of taking orders.

In the draft statutes for Trinity College, the Commissioners proposed to the College, that the Master should be "a member of the Church of England."

Under the statutes of Archbishop Parker and his colleagues in the reign of Queen Elizabeth, the endowment of Trinity College, Cambridge, was in great part devoted to the training of Scholars and Fellows for degrees in Theology, and with such an object mainly in view, the Master of the College may have sympathized in the preparation of Graduates of Theology, by being himself either a Bachelor or a Doctor of that branch of learning.

In modern times, however, degrees in Theology are rarely taken by the Fellows of Trinity College, and the Cambridge Commissioners propose that the Master of Trinity College, for the future, may be either a Master of Arts, or a Master of Laws, or a Doctor of Medicine, or he may have taken some higher degree in the University, so that a Theological degree is perfectly optional.

This opening of secular degrees as a qualification for the Trinity College Mastership has been proposed subsequently to the Cambridge University Act of 1856, from which the Commissioners derive their powers, and is not therefore subject to the restriction imposed by that Act, for limiting offices to members of the Church of England, in cases where any degree in Arts, Law, Medicine, or Music, "has *heretofore* constituted one of the qualifications."

A test of Church membership necessarily limits the choice of the Crown for the Mastership of Trinity College, and it will be desirable, that not only compulsory ordination, but also Church membership, should be omitted in the new College statutes, from the qualifications for the Trinity College Mastership, and that a Master of Arts, or Laws, or Doctor of Medicine, or higher Graduate of any British or Irish University, should be declared eligible for that important and national office.

A revision is much needed of the New Trinity College statute, on the power of removal of Fellows, by which open secession on the part of a Fellow of Trinity College from the Church of England is to render him liable to lose his Fellowship. In this regulation it seems to be assumed, that a Fellow must, at the time of his election, have been a member of the Church of England, which is not the case, as the Act of Uniformity test for Fellowships merely requires a declaration of conformity to the Liturgy, and as a Fellowship is not an office, the Church of England clause of the Cambridge University Act relating to offices does not legally affect the class of College Fellows.

Any Mastership or Fellowship test of conformity to the Liturgy is injurious to the College, as it impedes a useful abbreviation of the chapel services, which might be carried into effect if religious tests were removed from the governing bodies of Colleges.

Not only Fellows and Masters of Colleges, but University Professors, both in Oxford and Cambridge, and Masters of Eton, Winchester, and Westminster schools, are all subject to a declaration of Liturgical conformity, under the Act of Uniformity of 1662; which further directs Masters of Colleges to subscribe the Thirty-Nine Articles, and to declare their unfeigned assent and consent to and approbation of both the Thirty-Nine Articles and the book of Common Prayer.

A shorter religious service would be of great value in the College chapels of Oxford and Cambridge, but the Master of each College is compelled by the Act of Uniformity to subscribe a declaration approving of the use of all the prayers, rites, and ceremonies, forms and orders, prescribed and contained in the Book of Common Prayer.

Once at least in every quarter of a year, unless prevented by some lawful impediment, the Head of a College is ordered, by the Act of Uniformity, openly and publicly to read the Morning Prayer and service of the Liturgy of the Church of England in the College chapel, on pain of losing his Collegiate Headship.

Another ecclesiastical test, from the early Trinity College statutes of the sixteenth century, is retained in ordinances of the Commissioners of 1856, directing the Master and Fellows to make a declaration that they will "embrace, with all their souls, the true religion of Christ; that they will prefer the authority of Scripture to the judgment of men; that they will seek for a rule of life and for the substance of faith from the Word of God; that they will account other matters which are not proved from the Word of God as human; that they will consider the Royal authority as supreme among men, and by no means subject to the jurisdiction of foreign bishops;

that they will refute, with all their hearts and souls, opinions contrary to the Word of God; and that when religion is concerned, they will prefer what is true to what is customary, and what is written to what is not written."

A variation in this test may be noticed between the declaration prescribed by Bishop Goodrich and that of Archbishop Parker, which consists in the omission of the word "unnecessary," with reference to human matters not proved by the Word of God. In the statutes of Trinity College, under Edward VI., matters not proved from the Word of God were declared to be "human and unnecessary." Under Elizabeth, the Trinity College Commissioners contented themselves with directing that matters not proved from the Word of God were to be regarded as "human."*

In the Goodrich code of statutes for Trinity College, all the Fellows, with the exception of four, were expected to undertake, as the end of their pursuits, the study and profession of the Scriptures. Under Parker's Trinity College statutes, the excepted number was reduced to two.

The Examination for Fellowships under the rules of Edward VI.'s Commissioners, was intended to be in the knowledge of languages, and in other branches of learning.

Ecclesiastical forms under Queen Elizabeth probably approached somewhat more nearly to the customs of the Roman Catholic Church than under Edward VI., as the qualification of skill in singing was introduced into the chapter on the election of Fellows ordained by Archbishop Parker for Trinity College.

* "Cætera, quæ ex verbo Dei non probantur, pro humanis habitura."

Those Candidates for Fellowships who were skilled in singing, provided they had sufficient qualifications in other respects, were to be preferred before the Candidates who were unskilled in singing.

An Examination for four days was directed in the Parker statutes of Trinity College, as follows:—

The Master and Senior Fellows are to examine the Candidates for Fellowships, on four successive days:

Day.
1. Logic and Mathematics.
2. Natural and Moral Philosophy.
3. Knowledge of Languages, History, the Poets, and the whole range of Polite Literature.
4. Exercises in Writing on some subject, in Composing Verses, and in Singing.

In our own time, the Trinity College Examination for Fellowships includes a passage in Latin verse to be translated into English prose; a portion of English verse, such as the following extract from the 'Merchant of Venice,' to be translated into Greek Iambic verse:—

> "The quality of mercy is not strain'd;
> It droppeth, as the gentle rain from heaven
> Upon the place beneath: it is twice bless'd;
> It blesseth him that gives, and him that takes:
> 'Tis mightiest in the mightiest; it becomes
> The throned monarch better than his crown:
> His sceptre shows the force of temporal power,
> The attribute to awe and majesty,
> Wherein doth sit the dread and fear of kings;
> But mercy is above this sceptred sway,
> It is enthroned in the hearts of kings,
> It is an attribute to God himself;
> And earthly power doth then show likest God's,
> When mercy seasons justice."

Then follow three passages from Greek prose, to be translated into English prose, accompanied with historical and critical questions.

Another paper comprises a copy of English verses, to be rendered into Latin hexameters and pentameters, as well as a portion of English prose to be translated into Latin prose. Next follow passages from the Greek tragedies of Sophocles, Æschylus, and Euripides, to be translated into English prose.

An English prose extract is given to be translated into Greek prose, and a piece of Latin prose to be translated into Greek prose.

Two mathematical papers are set, including various questions in pure mathematics, and numerous exercises in the higher departments of physical science.

Logic, metaphysics, and moral philosophy form together the subjects of a special paper, in which a knowledge is expected of the opinions and reasoning, both of ancient and modern philosophers, and questions are asked on the moral government of mankind, and on mental philosophy, such as the following :—

"Show the moral uses of the duration of human life being uncertain."

"Show (1) that man is strictly under God's government in this life; and (2) that this is a moral government."

"State the circumstances in the dispensation of punishments in this life, which are analogous to the doctrines of religion concerning punishments in a future existence."

"Show (1) that the present life is fitted to be a state of discipline in the virtue of resignation."

"And (2) show further, the probability from analogy,

that there may be uses for this temper of mind even in a future state where there is no affliction."*

" In what does personal identity consist, according to Locke, Butler, Reid, and Dr. Brown?"

" Give, from the light of nature, a proof of the soul's immortality."

" Prove, by the analogy of nature, that the doctrine of rewards and punishments is not incredible."†

Polite literature, in the sixteenth century, meant the ancient languages and classical works of Greece and Rome. The Trinity College Fellowship Examination, after the lapse of three centuries, does not, in literary subjects, now go beyond Greek and Latin works, and composition is expected both in Latin and Greek prose and verse, which necessitates the devotion of years of previous study to this antiquated branch of education, and excludes all Candidates from any reasonable chance of success, who have not acquired the art of transferring both the poetry and prose of English writers into the dead languages of ancient Rome and Greece.

For the purposes of modern life in the nineteenth century, the result of a recent examination for the Indian Civil Service, in July, 1859, shows the position of members of Trinity College, Cambridge, in the following classification of the successful Candidates, forty in number, who were arranged in the order of merit, with their places of education :—

	Age.	Place of Education.
1.	20 ...	Trinity College, Dublin.
2.	20 ...	Queen's College, Belfast.

* Cambridge Classical Examinations, 1831. Trinity Fellowships, p. 190.
† *Ibid.*, p. 209.

	Age.	Place of Education.
3.	21	Edinburgh University.
4.	20	Trinity College, Dublin.
5.	21	Trinity College, Dublin.
6.	21	Merton College, Oxford.
7.	22	St. John's College, Oxford.
8.	20	Edinburgh University.
9.	22	Sidney Sussex College, Cambridge.
10.	21	Brasenose College, Oxford.
11.	21	*Trinity College, Cambridge.* (1.)
12.	22	Trinity College, Dublin.
13.	21	Wadham College, Oxford.
14.	21	Trinity College, Dublin.
15.	22	Trinity College, Dublin.
16.	22	Oriel and Queen's Colleges, Oxford.
17.	22	Queen's College, Belfast.
18.	20	Private Tuition.
19. {	22	New College, Oxford.
	22	Merton College, Oxford.
21.	22	Magdalene College, Cambridge.
22.	22	Trinity College, Dublin.
23.	21	Queen's College, Cork.
24.	20	Edinburgh University.
25.	22	Trinity Hall, Cambridge.
26.	21	*Trinity College, Cambridge.* (2.)
27.	22	Christ Church, Oxford.
28.	20	Exeter College, Oxford.
29. {	21	St. John's College, Cambridge.
	19	University and King's Colleges, Aberdeen.
31.	21	Queen's College, Oxford.
32.	19	Victoria College, Jersey.
33.	22	St. John's College, Cambridge.
34.	22	King's College, London.
35.	21	Brasenose College, Oxford.
36.	20	Pembroke College, Oxford.
37.	20	St. John's College, Cambridge.
38.	19	Marischal College, Aberdeen.
39.	21	*Trinity College, Cambridge.* (3.)
40.	18	King's College, London.

Of these forty selected Candidates, only three had received their education in Trinity College, Cambridge.

If preparation for such an important public examination had been specially regarded in the College, the number of successful candidates for Indian Civil Service appointments would probably have been larger from Trinity College, Cambridge, and it is manifest from the following enumeration of subjects and marks obtained by the three members of that institution who were admitted, that the range of the subjects read by College students is more modern and comprehensive than those required in the College Fellowship Examination:—

Result of the Indian Civil Service Examination, 1859, for three Members of Trinity College, Cambridge.

	(1.)	(2.)	(3.)
English Composition	270	164	214
English Literature	558	432	454
Language and Literature of Greece	233	150	226
Ditto ditto Rome	290	282	173
Ditto ditto France	—	125	160
Ditto ditto Germany	—	—	135
Mathematics	521	425	284
Natural Science	—	263	79
Moral Science	—	72	—
Arabic	319	—	—
Total number of Marks	2191	1913	1725

New seminaries are rising up, in different parts of the country, to prepare young men for the various departments of Government Competitive Examinations. One of the most successful of these new training schools has been established at Tonbridge Castle, Kent, under the care of Mr. Fleming, four of whose pupils obtained respectively the following credits, or marks, in the Competitive Examination for the Cadetships of the Royal Military Academy, Woolwich, in July, 1859:—

Subjects of Examination.	Tonbridge Castle Pupils admitted to Cadetships.			
	1.	2.	3.	4.
French	475	645	570	555
Pure Mathematics . . .	1010	1165	1020	920
Mixed Mathematics . . .	345	348	435	555
English	495	497	429	500
Classics: Latin . . .	615	—	455	—
Greek . . .	374	—	223	—
Experimental Sciences . .	380	580	175	270
Drawing: Geometrical .	Qualified.	260	Qualified.	167
	3694	3495	3307	2967

Some changes have been made during the last two years, in the subjects of examination, as well as in the number of marks for the admission of cadets to the Royal Military Academy, Woolwich. A summary of the requirements of 1857 has been given in the present work (page 11): subsequent changes comprise the omission of moral science, and the insertion of the Hindustani language, among the examination subjects. An increase of 250 marks has been allowed for the ancient Greek language, as well as for modern German; and *vivâ voce* examinations have been introduced, both for French and German.

The following table comprises the subjects of examination in July, 1859, for the admission of gentlemen cadets to the Royal Military Academy, Woolwich:—

                                                                          Marks.   Marks.

1. Mathematics, Pure 2000
———————— Mixed, including Statistics,
      Dynamics, and Hydrostatics . . 1500 ... 3500

		Marks.	Marks.
2.	English Language, Literature, Composition, History, and Geography		. 1250
3.	Classics: Language, Literature, Geography, and History of Ancient Rome	1000	
	Ditto of Ancient Greece	1000	... 2000
4.	Language, Literature, Geography, and History of France, with *vivâ voce* as well as written examination		. 1000
5.	Ditto of Germany, with *vivâ voce* as well as written examination		. 1000
6.	Hindustani Language		. 1000
7.	Experimental Sciences, *i. e.* Chemistry, Heat, Electricity, including Magnetism		. 1000
8.	Natural Sciences, Mineralogy, and Geology		. 1000
9.	Drawing, *i. e.* Elementary Geometrical Drawing, including the use of Drawing Instruments, and either Mechanical, Architectural, Engineering, or Landscape Drawing		. 1000

No Candidate is allowed to be examined in more than five subjects, of which one must be mathematics, and no one who does not obtain at least 1000 marks in mathematics, of which 700 at least must be in pure mathematics, and at least 300 in mixed mathematics, is eligible for an appointment. A close and searching examination is conducted in pure mathematics, including arithmetic, algebra, plane geometry, logarithms, and plane trigonometry.

From the other subjects of examination, each Candidate may select any, not exceeding four in number, in which he desires to be examined; but no one is allowed to count the marks gained in any such subject, unless these marks shall at least amount to one-sixth of the total number of marks allotted to that subject.

No Candidate is admitted into the Royal Military

Academy, unless he obtain an aggregate of at least 2500 marks.

Notice is given to the Candidates, that, although a very small qualifying test has been imposed in respect to French and drawing, a qualification is required to be obtained by the cadets at the Royal Military Academy, in either French, German, or Hindustani, and in drawing, without which no one can obtain a commission in the Royal Artillery or Royal Engineers.

These Artillery Examinations manifest the desire of Government to encourage useful education. French and German are now regarded as more important than either Latin or Greek, and the time has arrived, when the Legislature should insist on the introduction of modern literary subjects into some examinations for College Scholarships and Fellowships at Cambridge and Oxford.

Hints for an improvement of Scholarship Examinations have been given by the Cambridge Commissioners in the new Trinity College statutes, where permission is granted to the Master and Senior Fellows, if they should think fit, to give a preference in adjudging one or more Scholarships to excellence in one or more of the learned or Oriental languages, or in special departments of mathematics or of physical science, or of any other branch of the University studies.

A similar allotment of one or more Fellowships to special departments of learning would tend to enlarge the system of public instruction connected with Trinity College. Absolute power is at present left exclusively in the hands of the Master and Senior Fellows, to determine the intellectual qualifications of the Candidates for Fellowships, and their proficiency in any branch or

branches of University studies, but no provision is made
for introducing modern literature into examinations, so as
to keep pace with the advancing requirements of society.

The subjects of Oxford and Cambridge Scholarship
and Fellowship Examinations direct, in a large measure, the course of study in English endowed grammar-schools. A parent who intends his son for the clerical profession in the Church of England, feels desirous that the
youth should master at school the art of writing Latin
and Greek verses, on account of such exercises being
generally set in Oxford or Cambridge Examinations for
Scholarships and Fellowships. Classical proficiency is
absolutely requisite in Trinity College Cambridge, for
success in the Scholarship and Fellowship Examinations.

Grammar-school instruction does not, under these circumstances, include adequate arrangements for modern
studies, and a large amount of ignorance prevails among
English schoolboys, respecting the history and grammar
of their own nation, mathematics, physical science, and
modern languages.

Examples of the deficiencies of schools in modern
subjects are shown in the Report of the Syndicate, appointed by the Cambridge Senate, to regulate the first
examination of students not members of the University. The examination took place in December, 1858,
and included junior students under sixteen years of age,
and senior students under eighteen years of age.

Regulations for the senior students have been already
given in this work, page 218. Very nearly two-thirds
of the total number of candidates succeeded in satisfying
the Examiners, and received Certificates accordingly.*

* The Cambridge University Local Examination of December, 1858,

Of the preliminary part of the examination, the Syndics report, that the parsing of English sentences appeared to show, that in many schools boys were not taught English grammar directly, but were left to apply the rules of construction which they had learnt only from the Latin. And in this application many failed entirely.

The Examiners report, that in English history the performance of Candidates was unsatisfactory, especially among the juniors. The subject set in the preliminary department, both to the junior and senior students comprised the outlines of English history since the Conquest; that is, the succession of sovereigns, the chief events, and some account of the leading men in each reign. "Forty-six of the junior Candidates failed to pass, but this number of failures did not measure the full extent of the general deficiency. The questions were of a very elementary character, and the Candidates had received notice of the range of reading within which their knowledge would be tested. But their answers, even when accurate, showed a general uniformity of expression, which seemed to imply that meagre handbooks had been placed before the students to be got up, and that little attempt had been made by their instructors to excite the interest of their pupils by questionings or remarks of their own. The answers of the senior Candidates were on the average superior to those of the junior, though there were fewer cases in proportion to their number, of decidedly high merit."*

was held in the following eight local centres:—London, Birmingham, Brighton, Bristol, Cambridge, Grantham, Liverpool, and Norwich; a total number of 386 candidates were examined, of whom 240 passed, and 146 failed.

* First Annual Report of the Syndicate, Cambridge, 1859, page 6.

"English history," observe the Syndics, "contains much that boys may learn and appreciate beyond the dates and names of the principal events and persons, and much that they will find full of interest, if they have some guidance from a teacher. And it is this guidance of which the papers betrayed the greatest want. Out of 248 juniors and 64 seniors, about six of each class answered really well; less than a third answered fairly.

"On the whole, the classical papers appear to have been better answered than the rest; and in some instances, the spirit and accuracy displayed in the translations showed that a sound and rational method of instruction had been adopted by the teacher, and that the student had been accustomed to refer his work to a high standard of excellence.

"In mathematics, the answers to the questions proposed, showed, in general, imperfect preparation on the part of the Candidates."

The simplest questions in geology and physical geography were answered in a very unsatisfactory manner. In the former subject, a considerable portion of such knowledge as was exhibited, appeared to have been obtained from sources which are now entirely obsolete. It would be very useful to direct the attention of the student to the better kind of elementary works on this subject. A singular want of all accurate knowledge of physical geography was manifested.

Systematic monthly or quarterly examinations in schools are recommended by the Examiners, as likely to "promote greater accuracy of acquirement, and the facility and perspicuity of expression, which were so much wanting in the late examination."

In French, the senior students had read the books

specified beforehand with considerable care, and showed a better practical knowledge of the idioms and genius of the language than the junior students. The translations were generally fairly done, but the answers to the grammatical questions were very poor. The teaching of German did not seem as yet to have been sufficiently directed to the plain elementary principles of the language.

A more general cultivation of modern languages would result from the appropriation of several College Scholarships to French and German, and the introduction of modern literature into the annual College Examinations, which greatly influence the studies of young men at the ancient Univesities.

Trinity College, Cambridge, encourages too much the exclusive attention of public schools to classical studies, by having hitherto declined to confer a College Scholarship on any Student who had not proved himself to be a proficient in Latin and Greek.

When the late Professor White was at Trinity College, Cambridge, so high a standard of Latin and Greek Scholarship was insisted upon, that his thorough knowledge of mathematics did not enable him to obtain a place among the scholars. He was, however, distinguished as a mathematical private tutor at Cambridge, and became subsequently one of the Professors of Mathematics in University College, London.

Some little innovation on the ancient exclusively classical system has been recently carried into effect, under the Oxford University Commission, in several Oxonian Colleges, of which the following examples may be given :—

Among the Christ Church statutes of 1858, a provision has been inserted, "that in elections to one in every three open junior Studentships, the subjects of competitive examination shall be alternately Mathematics and Physical Science." No person is admissible as a Candidate for any open junior Studentship at Christ Church, who has completed the eighth term of academical residence, or two years at Oxford, from the date of his matriculation, or who has not produced a certificate of baptism, and testimonials of his moral character satisfactory to the Dean of Christ Church.

Twenty exhibitions have been recently instituted in Magdalen College, Oxford, of the annual value of £75 each, inclusive of all allowances, whether for rooms, commons, tuition, or otherwise, and tenable for five years from the day of election. The subjects of examination for one exhibition, at least, in each year, are to be alternately either Mathematics or Physical Science, with a provision, that no person shall be admitted to such an examination, unless he shall have proved that he is sufficiently instructed in other subjects to matriculate as a member of the College.

The exhibitioners of Magdalen College, Oxford, are intended to be "deserving persons," ascertained to be in need of support at the University.

Demyships at Magdalen College correspond to Scholarships in other Colleges, and in the election to one Demyship at least in each year, the subject of examination is to be Mathematics, and in the election to one at least, Physical Science.

The system of Examinations for Magdalen College Fellowships is directed always to be such, as to render Fellowships accessible, from time to time, to excellence in every branch of knowledge for the time being recognized in the schools of the University. A special provision has been enacted in the statutes of Magdalen College, that the Examination for every fifth Fellowship shall be alternately in subjects recognized in the school of mathematics, and in that of physical science.

At Balliol College, Oxford, no Student is admitted who cannot translate from English into Latin.

Classical studies predominate at Balliol College, but the new statutes direct that the system of Examinations for Fellowships is to be such, as to render Fellowships accessible from time to time to excellence in every branch of knowledge for the time being recognized in the schools of the University. Every Fellow of Balliol College who marries, is thereupon to vacate his Fellowship, unless he shall be a professor, or public lecturer in the University, when he may be retained in his Fellowship, by a majority of the votes of the Master and all the Fellows.

According to Professor Jowett, M.A., of Balliol College, the total number of Fellowships in Oxford is about 540. The annual value of each is extremely different at different Colleges. An average may perhaps be struck at £200 a year, including commons, rooms, and other allowances, which gives a total on the whole number, of £108,000 per annum for Oxford Fellowships.*

Balliol College was characterized by the Oxford Royal Commissioners of inquiry, in 1852, as peculiarly free from all restrictions which might prevent the election of the best candidates to its Headship, Fellowships, Scholarships, and even to its Visitorship. "The result of this has been, that Balliol, which is one of the smallest Col-

* Evidence of the Rev. Professor Jowett, M.A., to the Oxford University Royal Commission, p. 34.

leges in Oxford, as regards its foundation, is certainly at present the most distinguished."*

A provision is inserted in the Ordinances of the Oxford University Commissioners, under the Act 17 & 18 Vict. c. 21, for Balliol College, that no person shall be eligible for a Fellowship in that College, who shall not have taken the degree of Bachelor of Arts in some University of Great Britain or Ireland, or passed all the Examinations required by the University of Oxford for the degree of Bachelor of Arts.

It is to be regretted, that the new statutes of Trinity and St. John's Colleges, Cambridge, do not contain any similar opening of their Fellowships to Bachelors of Arts of any University either of Great Britain or Ireland. Balliol College has the merit of being in advance of the largest and most important Colleges of Cambridge, respecting the openness of its Fellowships, and indeed the new statutes of St. John's College, Cambridge, contain the following evidence of a retrograde policy:—

"Every Fellow previous to his admission shall declare that he is *bonâ fide* a member of the Church of England."

Such a declaration is, in fact, the introduction of a new religious test for Fellowships, and we are not aware that any College precedent can be adduced for such an exclusive regulation, except the chapter on the qualifications of Fellows, in the new statutes of Exeter College, Oxford, which limits the candidates who are eligible for Fellowships in that College, to "members of the Church of England, or of some Church in communion with it."

The removal of all declarations of religious opinion or belief from College Scholarships, and from the degrees of B.A. and M.A. at Cambridge, by the University

* Report of the Oxford University Royal Commission, 1852, p. 191.

Act of 1856, renders the introduction of a new Church of England test between these two degrees an encroachment on the religious liberty conceded by the Cambridge Act.

Public opinion in this country fully supports the removal of tests which has taken place in the ancient exclusive systems of Oxford and Cambridge, and the House of Commons is not likely to sanction any new religious tests.

On the 22nd of June, 1854, the Oxford Matriculation test was abolished by a majority of 252 to 161 in the House of Commons, and a week afterwards the degree of Bachelor at Oxford, in Arts, Law, Medicine, and Music was opened by a still more decided Parliamentary majority. A restrictive clause was subsequently added by the House of Lords, introducing the old Oxford degree test of subscription to the Thirty-Nine Articles and the three Articles of the Thirty-Sixth Canon in the case of offices, for which the degree of Bachelor in any of the secular faculties had been previously a qualification; to this addition the House of Commons submitted.

When the Cambridge University Bill was under the consideration of the House of Commons, in 1856, the opening of the Cambridge Academical Senate without religious test was carried by a majority of eighty-five to sixty; but the clause conferring this boon was lost in the House of Lords, by a majority of seventy-three to twenty-six.

If we take a survey of the general state of the inhabitants of this country, we find by the computations of Mr. Horace Mann, that of the total population, in 1851, of 17,927,609 persons for England and Wales, 58 per cent., or 10,398,013 persons would have been at liberty

T

to have attended public worship at one period on th[e] census Sunday in that year, the 30th of March. Th[e] total number of members of all denominations wh[o] were present at any of the most numerously attende[d] religious services on the census Sunday in 1851, wa[s] 6,356,222, so that 4,041,791 persons were not presen[t] at any such religious service.

The relative numbers of persons who were present a[t] the most numerously attended religious services on th[e] census Sunday, were thus classified according to deno[-]minations:—

 2,971,258 Church of England.
 3,110,782 Protestant Dissenters.
  249,389 Roman Catholics.
   24,793 Members of other Denominations.

 6,356,222 Total number of all denominations presen[t] at the most numerously attended religious ser[-]vices on the census Sunday in 1851.

From this table it is manifest that the number of Pro[-]testant Dissenters, who attend public worship on Sunday is greater than the number of members of the Church o[f] England, who are present on the same day in the edifice of the Establishment.

Some reform in the Liturgy and services of the Esta[-]blished Church, appears therefore to be required for th[e] adaptation of the most venerable and imposing eccle[-]siastical structures of England to the religious wants o[f] the masses of the community. The Church of Englan[d] has ceased to attract a majority, even of Protestant[s] within her precincts, and College foundations at Oxfor[d] or Cambridge, if exclusively restricted to members o[f] the Anglican Church, will no longer merit the name o[f] *national* institutions.

Among the most practical plans suggested for encouraging a more wide-spread unity of opinion in doctrine and worship, may be mentioned the following hint, attributed to Dr. Watson, Bishop of Llandaff, in 1790 :—

"A Commission should be issued, empowering an equal number of laymen and churchmen to revise the Liturgy, and to propose to the consideration of Parliament such alterations in it as they should think fit; having respect, in the execution of their office, to what was done by the Commissioners in 1689, to what has since been offered from the press in various publications, and to what has been adopted in the Liturgy of the Episcopalian Church in America." *

The Convention of the Protestant Episcopal Church of five States in the great North American republic met at Wilmington, Delaware, in 1786, and consisted of clerical and lay deputies. On the question of admitting the creed commonly called the Athanasian Creed into the Liturgy of the Protestant Episcopal Church for the United States of America, the Convention divided, and the Ayes and Noes were taken as follows :—

New York (Nay).

Rev. Dr. Provost, Rector of Trinity Church, afterwards Bishop of New York	No.
Hon. James Duane	No.
Mr. Rutherford	No.

New Jersey (Divided).

Rev. Uzale Ogden, Rector of Christ Church, Sussex	No.

---

* Considerations on the Expediency of revising the Liturgy and Articles of the Church of England, by a consistent Protestant (supposed to be the Bishop of Llandaff, Dr. Watson), 1790, p. 98.

The alterations in the Book of Common Prayer, prepared by Royal Commissioners in 1689, were printed by Parliament in 1854.

Rev. Mr. Frazer . . . . . . No.
Mr. Cox . . . . No.
Mr. Wallace . . . . . . Ay.
Mr. Waddel . . . . . . Ay.

Pennsylvania (Nay).

Rev. Dr. White, Rector of Christ Church and St. Peter's, Philadelphia, afterwards Bishop of Pennsylvania, President of the Convention . . No.
Rev. Dr. Magan, Rector of St. Paul's, Philadelphia No.
Rev. R. Blackwell, M.A. . . . . . No.
Mr. Hopkinson . . . . . . No.
Mr. Powell . . . . No.
Mr. Gilpin . . . . No.

Delaware (Divided).

Rev. Dr. Wharton, Rector of Emmanuel Church, Newcastle . . . . No.
Rev. Mr. Thorne . . . . . . Ay.
Mr. Sykes . . . . . . No.
Mr. Grantham . . . No.

South Carolina (Nay).

Rev. Mr. Smith . . . . No.
Mr. Rutledge . . . . . . No.

And so it was determined in the negative.

A copy of this decision, and of the other proceedings of the Convention, was transmitted to the standing committees of the Protestant Episcopal Church in the States of Maryland and Virginia, with the affectionate hope that their brethren of those States would approve and adopt their proceedings. A letter was also agreed upon to the Archbishops of Canterbury and York, in which the Convention informed their Graces that they had done what they could to comply with the fatherly wishes and advice of the two English Archbishops, "consistently with their own local circumstances, and the peace and unity of their own Church." *

The absent members of the Convention and the two Archbishops acquiesced in the changes thus arranged; and a similar desire of promoting peace and unity would probably characterize a Commission appointed to revise College Chapel services at the present time, but the introduction of an additional religious test for Fellowships in St. John's College, Cambridge, manifests a different spirit, which is not sanctioned by the Cambridge University Act of 1856.

Subscription to a declaration of *bonâ fide* Church membership is required by the 19th and 20th Vict. cap. 88, as a qualification for the holding of any *office*, either in the University of Cambridge or elsewhere, which has been heretofore always held by a member of the united Church of England and Ireland, and for which a Cambridge secular degree, such as that of Bachelor of Arts, has heretofore constituted one of the qualifications.

Fellowships for Bachelors of Arts are, however, not *offices*, and this clause does not consequently apply to the junior class of College Fellows.

St. John's College, Cambridge, had a definition of "offices" settled under the Parliamentary regulations of 1643–44. The Earl of Manchester was at that time empowered by Parliament to appoint a Committee to sit at Cambridge; and by virtue of his directions that Com-

---

* Journals of the American Convention, appointed to frame an Ecclesiastical Constitution and prepare a Liturgy for the Episcopal Churches in the United States; published in 'Observations upon the Liturgy,' by William Knox, Esq., a layman of the Church of England, and late Under-secretary of State, p. 210. Debrett. London: 1789.

mittee required the Master, President, and Fellows of
John's College, to forbear from admitting any person in
any office within their College, until such person had tak
the National League and Covenant.

On the 24th of January, 1644–45, a fuller declarati
of the intentions of the Committee was sent to t
College, by which the Committee declared, that "
the word 'office,' they understood any place of spec
trust, viz. the Bursar, Dean, the Steward, and Sacri
or of especial command, the President, Seniors, and t
Deputies." *

About ten years ago, a revised copy of the Johni
statutes was sanctioned by the Crown, in which
Church of England test was introduced for Fellowships
The more recent preparation of such a test can therefc
only be regarded as an attempt to interfere with t
legitimate working of the Cambridge Act of 1856, whi
certainly allows competition for Fellowships, without a
new religious test.

Interest will be felt in observing that among the d
clarations contained in the new Johnian statutes laid b
fore Parliament, the early idea of the sixteenth century
repeated, of accounting matters not proved from the Bib
to be "unnecessary."

We have already seen in this work, p. 257, that t
Trinity College Commissioners, after the accession
Queen Elizabeth, did not use the word "unnecessary
in the corresponding clause of a Trinity Fellowship oat

* Cambridge University Transactions during the Puritan Cont
versies, collected by James Heywood, F.R.S., and Thomas Wrig
F.S.A. London: Bohn. Vol. ii. p. 463.

† Statutes of St. John's College, confirmed by the Crown in 1
12th year of the reign of Queen Victoria. Cambridge Univers
Documents. Longmans. 1852. Page 248.

and there must have been some oversight in proposing to oblige newly-elected Fellows of St. John's College to declare, at the present day, that they account "matters not proved from the Word of God to be unnecessary."

"It is obvious," remarks the Rev. John James Tayler, "that inquiry cannot stop, but scientific research must be freely prosecuted, and scientific results be fearlessly adopted. If an historical religion be shut out from the quickening influence of all those branches of knowledge with which it is so intimately connected, and which are living and growing around it,—if it insists on maintaining the old points of view, fixed at a time when the horizon of learning was far more contracted than now, while comparative philology, ethnology, and mythology are assuming new dimensions as sciences, and displaying in a new light the mutual relations of the languages and races, the religions and civilizations of the earth,—it must soon disappear from the world of reality, and become a mummy entombed in the chambers of the past." *

College income both at Oxford and Cambridge is largely expended in the encouragement of academical learning. Under the new statutes of Trinity College, Cambridge, a dividend, which of late years has been usually valued at £250, is made the basis of the calculation for the emoluments to be received by different members on the foundation, and the following salaries will, by this arrangement, be granted from the income of Trinity College, besides allowances, in various cases, of commons and rooms.

* Address at the opening of the Session of Manchester New College, London, October, 1859, by the Rev. J. J. Tayler, B.A., Principal. Christian Reformer, No. 179. Whitfield. London.

To every Scholar, a sum equal to one-tenth of the dividend, which, reckoned at £250, will leave an annual money payment of £25 to each scholar.

To every Fellow, being a Bachelor of Arts, Laws, or Medicine, a sum equal to four-fifths of the dividend, or £200.

To every Fellow, being a Master of Arts, Master of Laws, Doctor of Medicine, or of some superior degree, and not being one of the Seniors, one dividend, or £250.

To each of the Chaplains and the Librarian, a sum equal to two-fifths of the dividend, or £100.

To each Senior Fellow, one dividend, and a sum equal to three-fifths of a dividend in addition, or £400 in all.

To the Master, a sum equal to six times the amount of the dividend, or £1,500, in addition to a fixed money-payment of £1,000 a year, and the repairs and furniture of the Master's Lodge.

In addition to their dividends, the Fellows, if in residence, and the Chaplains and Librarian, are entitled to rooms and commons.

Minor Scholars, elected from among persons who have not as yet commenced academical residence, are each of them to be entitled to such annual payment, not exceeding £40, as the Master and Seniors shall determine.

Each of the Sizars is to receive such a sum from the funds of the College as, together with any customary payment to him as a Sizar, shall amount, on the whole, to not less than £20 per annum.

To each of the three Regius Professors of Divinity, Hebrew, and Greek, respectively, an annual stipend shall be paid of £40, with commons and rooms in the College free of charge.

The total annual charge of the twenty-four poor men,

or Bedesmen, from the income of the College, is about £125.

Scholars and Sizars are entitled, in addition to their allowances from the College income, to have rooms and commons, unless a pecuniary equivalent for either or both be assigned to them by the Master and Seniors.

According to the new constitution of Trinity College, the Foundation consists of the Master, at least sixty Fellows, at least seventy-two Scholars, at least sixteen Sizars, four Chaplains, a Librarian, three Professors of Divinity, Hebrew, and Greek, respectively, and twenty-four poor men.

Provision is made for a future increase of value in the College property, and when each Fellow receives an average income of £300 a year, exclusive of rooms and commons, but inclusive of all other allowances, the Master and Seniors may determine that the number of Fellowships shall be increased, or part of the surplus may be set apart, and applied, by the Master and Seniors, either in increasing the number or emoluments of the Scholarships within the College, or for such other College purposes as may be considered most advantageous to the College, as a place of education, religion, and learning.

College tuition affords a considerable source of income to various resident Fellows of Trinity College. The annual payments to the College tutors, of £10 from each Student, amount in all to about £5,000 a year, and Fellows in Holy Orders have been hitherto usually preferred for the office of College tutors.

Private tutors form a numerous and important class in academical society at Cambridge. A student at first frequently selects his private tutor by the advice of older friends, but when, from any circumstances, a change is deemed desirable, undergraduates themselves possess a large amount of power in the choice of a private tutor, and graduates whose pupils have already obtained high academical honours are usually selected by ambitious students.

More than three times the sum paid annually to the whole body of public tutors and University professors was considered by the late Dean of Ely, in 1841, to be expended in private tuition at Cambridge. Examinations, in fact, place the whole University in the hands of private tutors. Numerous, young, and keenly alive to their own interests, private tutors may influence the elections of the University council, and as representatives of the existing system, they cannot be expected to come forward in defence of new branches of public instruction, in which they have not been themselves educated.

According to the calculations of the late Dean of Ely, there is an average number of about 1,300 students resident in the University of Cambridge: £14 a term is the usual fee paid for private tuition, and £20 a term is given to a Fellow of Trinity College, who is a private tutor; £10 is generally paid for private tuition in the Christmas vacation, and £30 for the long vacation.

"It is not an unfrequent practice," observes Dr. Peacock,* "for a student to engage a classical and a mathematical tutor on alternate days, and sometimes even on the same; the system extends to students of all classes, industrious or idle, rich or poor; and so very general has the practice become, that it would not be an extravagant estimate to fix the *average* annual expenditure of every student at the University for private tuition at £40."

* Observations on Cambridge University Statutes, by George Peacock, D.D., Dean of Ely, p. 153.

Assuming then the average number of resident students at 1,300, the amount annually paid by Cambridge undergraduates for private tuition would be £52,000; and if the average number of the resident students of Trinity College be assumed at 350, the sum expended every year by undergraduates of that college alone, would be about £14,000.

The Rev. J. Cooper, Fellow and public tutor of Trinity College, remarks in his evidence to the Cambridge Royal Commission,* in 1852, that " the assistance of a private tutor is necessary, when, as is too often the case, the work of preparation for the University examinations has been deferred to the last few months of residence."

An entrance-examination is required at Trinity College, with a view to test, in some measure, the school acquirements of new students, who usually assemble in that College, between the 12th and 15th of October, and who are expected to pass in a satisfactory manner, an examination in the following subjects before they commence academical residence :—

>Cicero, ' De Amicitiâ,' and ' De Senectute.'
>The First Book of the Æneid.
>The First Book of Xenophon's ' Memorabilia.'
>The First Book of the Iliad.
>The Gospel of St. Luke.
>Arithmetic, including Fractions and Decimals.
>Algebra, as far as Simple Equations.
>Euclid, books 1 and 2.

Dr. Whewell, the Master of Trinity College, regards the College-entrance examination as principally useful in turning the attention of the tutors upon those students

---

* Evidence presented to the Cambridge University Royal Commission, p. 153.

who are the worst prepared, but still who may be allowed to pass. The learned Master was not desirous, in 1850, to recommend an initial University examination to the Cambridge Royal Commissioners. In his opinion, "a single examination given once for all is a very bad test, either of knowledge or of training. If the requirements are made high, many very fit students will be rejected by accident; if they are made low, the examination will be futile. So far as it affects the system of the schools, it will do them harm, as every attempt to make a long course of study bear on a single examination must do."*

In the University of Durham no one is admitted to residence, as a student in Arts, Civil Law, or Medicine, unless he has passed an examination in the Rudiments of the Christian religion, the Greek and Latin languages, Arithmetic, and the Elements of Mathematics.

Students who present themselves for entrance into the University of Dublin are required to answer in any two Greek, and any two Latin, classical authors, of their own choosing, together with Latin and English composition.

The General Council of Medical Education are of opinion, that all students intended for the medical or surgical profession should pass an examination in general knowledge, such as will be equal, at least, to that required by national educational bodies.

Hence, before students commence their career of medical or surgical instruction, they will be expected to produce testimonials of general knowledge and mental training, which will certify success in one or other of the following examinations.

* Evidence on a Matriculation Examination, by the Rev. Dr. Whewell, Master of Trinity College, to the Cambridge University Royal Commission, p. 207.

Oxford University: local examinations, senior and junior.
Cambridge University: local examinations, senior and junior.
University of London: Matriculation examination, which is held simultaneously in different localities.
University of Durham: local senior examination.
Dublin University: entrance examination.
Oxford responsions, or moderations.
Cambridge previous examination.

A degree examination in Arts of any University of the United Kingdom or the Colonies, or of such other Universities as may be specially recognized from time to time by the Medical Council is also admitted as a qualification, as well as an examination by any other University of the United Kingdom equivalent to the local examinations of Oxford and Cambridge.

Under these new rules of the Medical Council, the earliest period for entrance on professional studies may probably be found in Oxford University local examination for junior candidates whose age does not exceed fifteen years.

Five days were given to this examination, from the 14th to the 20th of June, 1859, and the subjects were arranged in the following order:—

Tuesday, 9 to 12: Elementary Arithmetic. 2 to 3·30 P.M.: Modern Geography. 3·30 to 5 P.M.: An English composition on one of the following subjects,—Iron and its uses; chief points of interest in any one county of the United Kingdom; brief sketch of the life and character of Alexander the Great, or Milton, or Washington. 6 to 8·30 P.M.: French, comprising a passage from Fénelon's 'Télémaque,' (books 1–10) for translation into English, with grammatical and general questions; a passage from a French newspaper for translation into English; and some English sentences for translation into French.

Wednesday, 9 to 12: Latin. 2 to 5 P.M.. Arithmetic, Algebra to Simple Equations, and higher Algebra. 6 to 8.30 P.M.:

Dictation of an English sentence, with the analysis of a short English passage from Cowper's 'Task,' book 1 (the Sofa); the parsing of another short passage from the same poem, and a few questions suggested by the First Book of that English poem.

Thursday, 9 to 12: Euclid, books 1, 2, 3, 4, 6; Mensuration. 2 to 5 P.M.: Mechanics and Elementary Mechanism. 6 to 8·30 P.M.: English History.

Friday, 9 to 12: Greek. 2 to 5: Trigonometry, and the Use of Logarithms, with Practical Geometry. 6 to 8·30 P.M.: German, Botany, and Zoology.

Saturday, 9 to 12: Rudiments of Faith and Religion, including questions in the Books of Genesis and Exodus, the Gospel of St. Luke, and the Acts of the Apostles, as well as on the Catechism, the Morning and Evening Services, and the Litany of the Church of England. This section is not compulsory on candidates, whose parents or guardians object to their examination in it, and the places on the lists of certificated students are not affected by success in it. The fact of a candidate having passed in this department will, however, be entered on his certificate, and signified by a mark prefixed to his name in the division lists.

Saturday, 2 to 5 P.M. and 6 to 8·30 P.M.. Drawing.

Monday, 9 to 12: Higher classical paper in Latin and Greek. 2 to 5 P.M.: Elementary Facts in Chemistry. 6 to 8·30 P.M.: Practical Examination in Chemistry.

Tuesday, 9 to 12: Music.

Papers are set on the following eight subjects: Latin, Greek, French, German, Mathematics, Mechanics, Chemistry, and Botany with Zoology; and every candidate is required to offer himself for examination in one of these subjects at least; but no candidate will be examined in more than four of the above-mentioned eight subjects. Drawing and Music are optional.

A similar variety of examinational business would be advantageous in Trinity College, Cambridge, if the arrangements of the College could be extended beyond the training of students merely in Greek, Latin, and Mathematics. Three principal College tutors and twelve assistant College tutors now undertake the department of lectures, besides a host of private tutors, each one of whom has, for the most part, several pupils.

In the first, or freshman's, year, College lectures are delivered on—

>   Euclid, books 1 to 6.
>   A Greek Play, such as the 'Electra' of Sophocles.
>   Algebra.
>   Trigonometry.
>   A Greek prose subject, such as an oration of Æschines.
>   A Latin subject, such as a Book of Tacitus.

Examinations in the lecture-rooms vary the daily course of College tuition, and a general College examination takes place in June on all the subjects treated of in the College lectures of the year. The names of the students are arranged in classes; prizes of books are given to those who are in the first class, and persons who are found not worthy to be placed in any class are liable to be seriously admonished, and may after repeated annual failures, be removed from the College.

College lectures are continued for second and third year men, as follows, but are not so well attended as in the first year:—

>   *Junior Sophs, or Second-year Men.*
>
>   MICHAELMAS TERM.
>
>   Composition in Latin and Greek.
>   Classical subject of previous Examination.
>   Butler's three Sermons and Dr. Whewell's 'Morality,' Book 1.
>   Division A: Conic Sections, Analytical Geometry, and Mechanics.
>   Division B: Geometrical Conics and Elementary Mechanics (First and Second Law of Motion).

Lent Term.

Composition in Latin and Greek.
Plato.
Dr. Whewell's 'Morality.' Book 2.
Classical subject of previous Examination.
Paley's 'Evidences of Christianity.'
Division A: Newton's Principia, sections 1, 2, 3; Differential Calculus.
Division B: Newton, section 1; Differential Calculus.
Division C: Elementary Mechanics; Third Law of Motion, etc.

Easter Term.

Gospel subject of previous Examination.
Ancient History (Dr. Thirlwall, etc.).
Division A: Statics and Dynamics, with Differential Calculus.
Division B: Theory of Equations; Newton, sections 2, 3.

Senior Sophs, or Third-year Men.
Michaelmas Term.

Composition in Latin and Greek.
Classical Subject for Degree.
Division A: Optics and Hydrostatics.
Division B: Optics; Newton, sections 9 and 11.
Division C: Mechanical Euclid.

Lent Term.

Composition in Latin and Greek.
Acts and Epistles for Degree.
Division A: Dynamics of Rigid Bodies.
Division B: Hydrostatics; Dynamics of a Particle.
Division C: Mathematical subjects for Degree.

Easter Term.

Aristotle (Ethics or Politics); Ecclesiastical History.
Classical subject for Degree.
Division A: Geometry of three Dimensions.
Division B: Astronomy.
Division C: Mathematical subjects for Degree.*

---

* Dr. Whewell's Evidence to the Cambridge Royal Commission, p. 208-9.

In the spring of the second year of academical residence at Cambridge, the University previous examination is held, and a similar previous examination takes place during the October or Michaelmas Term of the same year. Success in the previous examination is essential for Candidates desirous to graduate in Arts.

The subjects appointed for the previous examination of the year 1859 were five in number, as follows:—

1. The Gospel of St. Matthew in Greek.
2. Paley's Evidences of Christianity.
3. Homer's Iliad, Books 3 and 4.
4. Cicero, 'De Officiis,' Book 3.
5. Elements of Euclid, Books 1, 2, 3, and Arithmetic.

About eighteen scholars are elected every year on the foundation of Trinity College. The Examination takes place in spring, and the Candidates are students of the College in their second or third year of residence.

Passages of Greek and Latin classical prose and verse are on these occasions set to be translated into English prose. A portion of English prose is given, to be translated into Latin prose, with several stanzas of English poetry to be translated into Latin hexameters and pentameters.

Two mathematical papers are set, including questions in Optics and Astronomy, and papers are given on Grecian and Roman History and Literature, comprising such questions as the following:—

"What was the occasion of Cicero's Philippics? Briefly state the subjects of the first and second. On what particular event, then pending, do the rest hinge? Give the dates of the first and last. How long did they precede Cicero's death?

" What, from internal evidence, is the earliest date to which Horace's Epistle to Augustus can be assigned ?

" What brought the Romans into Spain, and when was it finally subjugated ?

" When was Britain first seriously invaded by the Romans? What was their first colony in it ? How far did Agricola carry his arms north and west ? Enumerate, from Tacitus, its products and most powerful tribes."

Scholars occupy both in the College Hall and Chapel a position superior to that of the ordinary undergraduate students ; the tenure of their scholarships averages about four years for each individual, and the allowance of rooms in College rent free, with daily commons during residence, raises the value of a Trinity Scholarship to about £60 a year.

Foundation scholars had, as the late Dean of Ely judiciously observes, stipends attached to them, as well as the Fellows, in the arrangement of the ancient statutes, " though the scholars have very rarely shared in the distribution of the surplus revenues which have subsequently arisen : but it will generally be found, that they have received very liberal augmentations of income from various allowances, either in the form of commons, rents, or weekly or terminal payments. It is very doubtful, however, whether it would not be more equitable that they should receive their dividends in common with the other members of those foundations,—an arrangement which would appear to be generally more conformable to the spirit of the ancient statutes, and which would associate them more intimately in affection and feeling, as members of one family, with the Colleges to which they belong."*

* Observations of Dr. Peacock, late Dean of Ely, on Cambridge University Statutes, p. 117.

Dr. Peacock, in his observations on Cambridge College Statutes, advocated the payment of liberal allowances to scholars; he was desirous to consider fairly those "interests and claims which time and long usage, and the changes in the habits of life and of society, had created."

Subsequently, as one of the Commissioners under the Cambridge University Act of 1856, the late Dean of Ely zealously essayed to carry out his views respecting the augmentation of the salaries allowed to Trinity College scholars.

But the proposed arrangements under the new Trinity College statutes do not carry out the praiseworthy scheme of the late Dr. Peacock; indeed the allowance to a scholar is not likely to exceed £25 a year from the College income. His rooms, which are free, may be valued at £8 a term, or £24 a year comprising three terms. Commons, during residence, are provided for the scholars at the expense of the College, and a majority of the total number of 72 scholars are usually resident.

The scholars of the various Colleges at Cambridge are expected, in turn, to read grace before and after hall dinner daily in their own College, and also to read the Lessons in the ordinary daily liturgical services of the College chapel.

Chapters are occasionally read to the assembled students, in the week-day services, which possess but little edification, and the youthful reader sometimes becomes unavoidably embarrassed from the description of ancient sins and transgressions, but little adapted to a religious service in any way partaking of the character of family prayers.

No declaration of religious opinion or belief will for

the future be demanded of a scholar of Trinity College; and it is hardly fair, under this clause of the Cambridge University Act, to compel a scholar to take a part in exclusively Church of England services at the College chapel.

Some general form of daily prayer is required for the College, excluding points of controversial doctrine, and such as the students generally may concur in offering up to the Divine Being.

The prayers for the Parliament, already given in this work, p. 99, afford a practical example of a liturgical form which has been acquiesced in by Members of the House of Commons of all denominations.

A short Bill to enable the Crown to exempt the Colleges of either University of Oxford or Cambridge from the operation and penalties of the Act of Uniformity may be expedient, with a view to improved liturgical services in those Colleges.

Under Queen Elizabeth, in 1571, when Mr. Strickland, M.P., proposed in the House of Commons a Bill for the reformation of the Book of Common Prayer, the Treasurer of her Majesty's household recommended that petition be made by that House unto the Queen's Majesty for her license and privity to proceed in the Bill.

After the restoration of the monarchy in 1660, King Charles II. informed a deputation of leading Presbyterian divines, including Mr. Calamy, Dr. Reynolds, and Mr. Baxter, that "he did not intend to call an assembly of the other part, but would bring a few, such as he thought meet; and that if he thought good to advise with a few of each side, for his own satisfaction, none had cause to be offended at it."*

* Matthew Sylvester's Life of Richard Baxter. p. 232.

On the 22nd February, 1662-3, Lord Roberts (Lord Privy Seal) brought a Bill into the House of Lords concerning the king's power in ecclesiastical affairs;* in which was a clause, "to enable the king to dispense, by letters-patent under the Great Seal, with the Act of Uniformity or the penalties in the said law imposed, or any other laws and statutes requiring oaths and subscriptions;" and the Attorney-general was ordered to bring in a list of all those acts and oaths to which the said enacting clause related.

Upon reading this list, it was found that a greater latitude would be given in favour of the Papists than was intended; and therefore the following general words, "or any other laws and statutes requiring oaths and subscriptions," were immediately ordered to be omitted.

As when these words were struck out, the Bill could give relief to none but Protestant dissenters, and would only invest the Crown with a legal power of remitting penalties (an amiable branch of the prerogative from which the subject could have nothing to apprehend), it was supported by the Earl of Manchester (Lord Chamberlain), Lord Ashley, and several other Lords.

On the 13th March, the Earl of Clarendon appeared in the House of Lords and warmly opposed the Bill, which Lord Ashley with as much vigour supported.

Lord Ashley took notice of the fatal consequences of the Act of Uniformity; that by it great numbers of ministers were reduced to beggary; that many Protestants were running into other countries, to the prejudice of trade and the dishonour of the kingdom: that the reformers in King Edward VI.'s reign had acted in a

* Lords' Journals, quoted in Cooke's Life of the Earl of Shaftesbury vol. i. p. 284.

different manner; for they had, likewise and good men, contrived the doctrine and discipline of the Church, so as to enlarge the terms of community; that they had set open the doors, and by gentle means persuaded and invited all they could into the Church, thinking that the enlargement of their body would redound to the honour of their religion.

Lord Ashley, however, and the other advocates of the Bill could not prevail. It was dropped in silence; which was owing to a resolution of the House of Commons, "that it should be presented to his Majesty as the humble advice of that House, that no indulgence be granted to the dissenters from the Act of Uniformity."

Mr. Cooke is of opinion that "the Commons were at that time under the influence of Lord Clarendon."

The dispensation of the Colleges of Oxford and Cambridge, by letters-patent under the Great Seal, from the operation and penalties of the Act of Uniformity of 1662 would be, in modern times, an admirable mode of advancing the cause of academical reform, especially as the lapse of nearly two hundred years has afforded opportunity for the progress of Biblical criticism, the advancement of science, and the increase of general toleration respecting religious differences.

The researches of Mr. William Winstanley Hull, late Fellow of Brasenose College, Oxford, show that "until the beginning of the sixth century, the early Christians were said to have recited their creeds only at Easter and Whitsuntide, the solemn times of Baptism."*

Mr. Hull continues, that, "if the original use of a

---

* Inquiry concerning the Means and Expedience of proposing and making any Changes in the Canons, Articles, or Liturgy of the Church of England, p. 179. Rivingtons: London, 1828.

creed, as a creed, be any authority, Lord Chancellor King and others seem to have proved, that in the early centuries a creed, and consequently admission into the assemblies of Christians, was derived from and corresponded with the secret sign or conventional sentence, and consequent partaking, of the heathen mysteries. Even the expression, 'a form of sound words,' may not mean any creed beyond the declaration of the character and office of the Messiah; and meaning that only, or more than that, might be necessary when spies and persecution were dreaded; and not necessary, when spies, without persecution attendant upon their representations, might enter into the assemblies of Christians, and perhaps be converted. At all events, the Scriptures themselves do not give any other creeds than such as are limited to the declaration of the character and office of the Messiah in a few words. And in the succeeding years, according to Lord Chancellor King (History of the Creed, 258, and Enquiry, part ii. chap. 3), the creeds may be conjectured to have remained such short declarations, varying in various Churches, without any breach of unity."

"There does not appear any sufficient reason," observes Mr. Hull, "for retaining any creed as part of the daily service in church. If any one be retained for Sundays or holidays, or the Communion Service, the Apostles' creed would generally be preferred. And then its phrases and articles might perhaps be reviewed with advantage."*

Compulsory attendance of students of different denominations at the reading of creeds in which all cannot

* Inquiry on Liturgical Changes, by William Winstanley Hull, Barrister-at-Law, p. 182.

conscientiously join, frequently leads to indifference on the part of numerous students, which may in an individual case take the form of attention to some other book, introduced by a dissenting Undergraduate at the time of unwelcome liturgical services. Mr. Hull mentions, that "the Lessons were not even prescribed in some of the early prayer-books (Jones, p. 196); and a choice of Lessons, since taken away, was given the minister at the end of the first book of Homilies" (Strype's Life of Archbishop Parker, i. 167, old paging, 84). *

It has been proposed, remarks Mr. Hull, with reference to the North American Protestant Episcopalian liturgy, that "one general petition should take the place of the first four clauses† in the Litany of the Church of England." If the compulsory attendance of students not Members of the Anglican Church be expected in the chapels of Oxford and Cambridge Colleges, a limitation of the commencement of the Litany to some general invocation to the Supreme Being would certainly be desirable in those institutions.

* Mr. W. Hull on Liturgical Changes, p. 184.   † *Ibid.*, p. 218.

INTENDED

ENCOURAGEMENT OF MODERN STUDIES

IN

ALL SOULS COLLEGE, OXFORD.

Four Professor Fellowships, each endowed with £800 a year from appropriated Fellowships of All Souls College, were recommended by the Oxford University Royal Commissioners to be founded in that College, which would have left sixteen junior Fellowships for the encouragement of students; the Commissioners also advised, that Professor Fellows should have, as a matter of course, votes in College affairs with the rest of the Fellows.*

Such liberal suggestions were not fully carried out in 1857 by the Oxford University Parliamentary Commissioners, under the 17th and 18th Vict. c. 81, but ordinances made by them, with the acquiescence of the College, directed, that the first, third, fifth, seventh, and ninth Fellowships, which should become vacant after the approval of the new College statutes by her Majesty in Council, were not to be filled up, and that the emoluments arising from these five Fellowships were to be applied to the maintenance within the University of a Professor of International Law and Diplomacy, to be called, from the name of the College founder,—" Chicheley's Professor of International Law and Diplomacy."

* Report of the Oxford University Royal Commission, 1852, p. 220.

The election of this Professor was to be vested in the College Visitor, the Archbishop of Canterbury, and the Warden of the College, the Lord High Chancellor of Great Britain, the Judge of the High Court of Admiralty, and her Majesty's Secretary of State for Foreign Affairs for the time being, or the major part of them.

A Professorship of Modern History was in a similar manner proposed to be maintained on the funds accumulating from the suspension of five subsequent alternate Fellowships, which should become vacant, viz. the eleventh, thirteenth, fifteenth, seventeenth, and nineteenth Fellowships.

In May, 1842, there were four resident Bible Clerks on the Foundation of All Souls College. No Undergraduate students unconnected with the endowment resided there at that time, but there was 1 resident Graduate not on the foundation, and 13 resident Graduates partaking of the College pecuniary emoluments.

Of 40 Fellows, 12 were resident and 28 non-resident; 14 were Clergymen of the Church of England, and 26 were laymen. The Warden of the College was a clergyman.

When the Oxford Royal Commissioners of 1850 inquired into the state of the revenues of All Souls College in 1850, the receipts for that year were thus classified:—

Rent of land belonging to:—	
All Souls College	£5,829
Tithes	1,420
Fines upon renewals of leases	1,889
Copyhold fines	269
Interest from Government funds	315
Revenue	£9,622

The Warden of All Souls receives £633 a year from the College, and he has also the rectory of Lockinge, annexed by Act of Parliament, of the value of £300 per annum.

Annual payments of All Souls College were as follows in 1850 :—

Expense of establishment, including commons of Warden and Fellows, and maintenance of Bible clerks	£480
Allowances to Warden and College Officers, Chaplains, Tutor to Bible clerks . . .	553
Rates, Taxes, Insurance, Agents, Collectors, leasehold and ancient rent.	520
Repair of College, farm buildings, draining, etc.	921
Library, purchase and binding of books . .	590
College servants	710
Fuel and Lighting	243
Various expenses, law charges, etc. . . .	157
Advowson fund	650
Fund for building and repairing parsonage houses in the patronage of the College .	115
Subscriptions to schools, churches, and charities	390
	5,329
Divided between the Wardens and Fellows .	4,293
	£9,622

Each Fellowship in All Souls College may be estimated at £150 a year, as the Fellowships to be appropriated for a Professorship may each be commuted at a fixed annual sum of that amount.

No person is to be appointed Warden, who has not attained the degree of Master of Arts, or Doctor of Theology, Civil Law, or Medicine. The election of Warden is in the hands of the Fellows of the College, but a person may be elected who is not, and has not been, a Fellow of the College.

New Fellows are to be elected by the Wardens and Fellows. No Candidate is eligible for a Fellowship who has not passed all the Examinations required by the University of Oxford for the degree of Bachelor of Arts, and has not either been placed in the first class in one at least of the public Examinations of the University, or obtained some prize or scholarship within the University, unattached to any College or Hall, and open to general competition among the Members of the University.

The intellectual qualifications of the Candidates for Fellowships are to be tested by an examination in such subjects recognized in the School of Jurisprudence and Modern History, within the University, as the Warden and Fellows shall determine.

No present or future Fellow is to be required, as a condition of retaining his Fellowship, to take Holy Orders, or, not being in Holy Orders, to study Theology.

If the revenues of the College should increase, so as to afford to each Fellow an average income of more than £300 a year, the Visitor may direct the application of surplus revenues either to the foundation of new Fellowships, or the institution of Scholarships or Exhibitions, or for other College purposes.

Contumacious ceasing to conform to the Liturgy of the Church of England is to be a cause for depriving the Warden of his Wardenship, and any Fellow of his Fellowship.

The Visitor is to have the power to disallow and annul any regulations made by the Warden and Fellows, for the appointment of Chaplains, the daily performance of Divine Service according to the Liturgy of the Church of England, within the College during full Term-time, and for attendance on such liturgical services; but the Archbishop of Canterbury for the time being, who is the Visitor, is not hereafter to have the power of making new statutes.

A Professor of the College may be elected a Fellow by the Wardens and Fellows, and if not elected to a Fellowship, he may still participate in the use of the Chapel, Hall, and Library with the Fellows, and take precedence after the Sub-Warden of the College.

These encouragements to the study of Jurisprudence and Modern History do not appear to be acceptable in All Souls College, and the plans of the Parliamentary Commissioners, which were ratified for that College in 1857, are not as yet acted upon with impartiality, by the College authorities.

Dr. Arnold, in his introductory lectures on Modern History, delivered at Oxford in 1842, thus alludes to the prevailing spirit of that ancient University, which may explain the unwillingness of several Colleges to adopt modern improvements:—

" Here (at Oxford) there is always a tendency to magnify the past; five-and-twenty years ago I can remember that it was the fashion to exalt the seventeenth century at the expense of the eighteenth; now, I believe, many are disposed to depreciate both, and to reserve their admiration for times still more remote and more unlike our own. It is very well that we should not swim with the stream of public opinion; places like this are exceedingly valuable as temples where an older truth is still worshiped, which else might have been forgotten; and some caricature of our proper business must at times be tolerated, for such is the tendency of humanity.

"But still, if we make it our glory to run exactly counter to the general opinions of our age, making distance from them the measure of truth, we shall at once destroy our usefulness and our real respectability.

"And to believe seriously that the movement of the three last centuries has been a degeneracy, that the middle ages were wiser or better or happier than our own, seeing truth more clearly and serving God more faithfully, would be an error so extravagant, that no amount of prejudice could excuse us for entertaining it." *

Roman Catholic Masses repeated for the souls of deceased warriors once constituted the main business of the Warden and Fellows of All Souls College.

At the Reformation, under King Edward VI. Royal Commissioners issued injunctions, in 1549, which were in part based on proposals of Henry VIII.'s Commissioners in 1535, and contained provisions for the establishment of Professors in All Souls College, with an order that no person should be allowed to remain a Fellow of the College for more than twenty years, unless for his merits he had been invited to the public function of a Professor.†

Under the Long Parliament, in 1649, the following direction was prepared by the Parliamentary Committee on the reformation of the Universities:—

"Lest men should degenerate, and make their means their end, and through retirement becomes drones, no

---

* Arnold's Lectures on Modern History, 357.
† Ward's Translation of All Souls College Statutes, p. 199, quoted in the Oxford Royal Commission Report, 1852, p. 220.

men should enjoy his Fellowship beyond Doctor's standing, or one year after his commencement (as a Doctor) unless they be such as are Professors or Public Lecturers." *

Ten years' possession of a Fellowship is calculated to be the average length of Fellowship tenure † in the University of Oxford: not fewer than thirty-five Fellowships would be vacant every year under the improved plans suggested by the Royal Commissioners of 1852, and there are, on an average, about thirteen first classmen annually in the Examinations for the B.A. degree in Classics and Mathematics, so that many Fellowships must be held by parties not very highly distinguished in academical learning.

Sir James Stephen, K.C.B., formerly Professor of Modern History in the University of Cambridge, regarded it as a capital error, to require of the whole body of Cambridge students the prosecution either of Classical or of Mathematical studies.‡ "A young English gentleman," he remarks, "who has reached his twentieth year, with but a slight and superficial knowledge of Greek and Latin and of elementary Mathematics, may in general be pronounced incapable of any considerable attainments in either. Yet in other literary pursuits, such a youth might pass his time with great advantage and perhaps with credit."

Responsions at Oxford in the second year of academical residence correspond with the previous or preliminary

* Recommendations of Oxford Commissioners, and History of University Subscription Tests, by James Heywood, F.R.S., p. 471. Longmans: 1853.

† *Ibid.*, p. 88.

‡ Evidence of the Right Hon. Sir James Stephen, D.C.L., to the Cambridge University Royal Commission, 1850, p. 112.

examination at Cambridge, which Sir James Stephen recommends to be the limit of ordinary academical reading, for students who are not proficients either in Classics or Mathematics.

"I propose," writes the Professor of Modern History, "that at the close of the preliminary examination, those who have passed it should be arranged in two classes,— the class of proficients and the class of non-proficients. To the members of the first class I would assign the exclusive privilege of becoming, as at present, Candidates for Classical and Mathematical Honours at the end of their academical course, and I would exempt them from the necessity of passing any other final examination. On the members of the second class, I would impose the necessity of passing a final examination in at least two sciences, Moral or Physical, of their own selection; exempting them from the obligation, and excluding them from the privileges, of being again examined either in Classics or Mathematics."

Custom, both at Oxford and Cambridge, usually apportions two years of an Undergraduate career to general subjects, and the third year of residence is frequently in main part devoted to professional study, as, for instance, to preparation for special Divinity Examinations, intended for Candidates for Holy Orders in the Church of England.

New Rules of the Council of Legal Education, presided over by Sir Richard Bethell, may also probably influence the pursuits of the third year at Oxford and Cambridge. These rules have been recently prepared for the public Examination of Students of Law in the Inns of Court, which comprise printed questions, accompanied by an oral Examination in the following subjects, intended, as much as possible, to constitute an essential qualification for a call to the English Bar.

1. Constitutional Law and Legal History,—in which the Examiner will expect a competent knowledge of the leading events of English History, and an accurate knowledge of the reigns of the Stuart kings, of Magna Charta, the Confirmatio Chartarum, the Petition of Rights, the Bill of Rights, the Act of Settlement, and the State Trials during the reigns of Charles II. and James II.

2. Equity,—in which the Examiner will expect the Students to be well acquainted with Hayne's 'Outlines of Equity,' Smith's 'Manual of Equity Jurisprudence,' and Hunter's 'Elementary View of the Proceedings in a Suit in Equity,' part i.

3. Common Law,—in which the Examiner will expect the Candidates to answer questions on the ordinary practice and course of pleading in an action at law; on Stephens's 'Commentaries,' Introduction, book i., Of Personal Rights; book ii., part 2, Of Things Personal; Smith's 'Lecture on Contracts,' (by Malcolm,) omitting Lectures 6 and 7; and the Elements of Criminal Law, which may be read from Broom's 'Commentaries,' book iv.

4. Law of Real Property,—in which the Reader proposes to examine in Joshua Williams 'On the Law of Real Property,' 5th edition; Hayes, on the Common Law, Uses, and Trusts; Sales and Purchases by Persons holding Fiduciary Offices; Sugden's 'Vendors and Purchasers,' cap. i. sec. 5, 13th edition; and Dart's 'Vendors and Purchasers,' cap. ii., 3rd edition.

5. Jurisprudence and the Civil Law,—in which the Reader proposes to examine in the Institutes of Justinian, books i. and ii., and Phillimore's 'Principles and Maxims

of Jurisprudence, page 162 to page 200, (from the Maxim, "Domicilium re et facto transfertur," to the Maxim, "Is naturâ debet," etc.)

Independent undergraduates, or commoners, have never been admitted to reside within the walls of All Souls College, and a long established custom still prevails, of the non-resident Fellows visiting the College four times in the year, viz. at Christmas, Easter, Whitsuntide, and November, when College Meetings are held. On these occasions there is not room, in the College buildings,* for the accommodation of all the Fellows; very little space could therefore be set apart for students.

Collegiate power, in improving education, ought rather to be centred in executive committees of each society, including eminent persons who are actually engaged in professorial or collegiate tuition, than in assemblies of the whole body of Fellows, many of whom are non-resident.†

In the case of Downing College, at Cambridge, the want of Scholarships has been assigned as the reason why undergraduates do not go to that College. Undergraduates are attracted by rewards which may be within their own reach more than by the distant possibility of obtaining a fellowship, which is open, as at Downing, to the competition of all graduates, either of Oxford or Cambridge.

Scholarships were not originally needed at All Souls College, to keep up a regular supply of resident unmar-

* All Souls College Evidence, Report of the Oxford Royal Commission, 1852, p. 330.
† Speech of Mr. Liveing, of St. John's College, at Cambridge, October, 1858.

ried Fellows for the constant performance of Roman Catholic requiems in honour of the faithful who had lost their lives in the French wars of the fifteenth century.

French was, in early times, allowed both at Queen's College and Oriel College, Oxford, as a substitute for Latin, in the daily conversation of the students. The French language has now become generally adopted in diplomacy, nor can international negotiations with Continental nations be conducted without the use of that universal means of communication.

In the evidence presented to the Cambridge University Royal Commission in 1852, the Rev. W. M. Gunson, M.A., Fellow and Tutor of Caius College, remarks that "the neglect of modern languages is a great defect in our system, and is beginning to be felt more and more every year; and if the University of Cambridge is to keep up with the general information of the age, it is a defect which must be remedied." Mr. Gunson advises that Modern History should be separated from the Moral Sciences Tripos, and be united with Modern Languages, to form a "Modern Language Tripos."

Scholarships in Modern Languages, at All Souls College, would be a valuable introduction to Jurisprudence and Modern History for the Fellowships in that institution; and the suspension of alternate College Fellowships, as they become vacant, affords an admirable mode of providing funds for a more modern system of collegiate arrangement.

All Souls College Evidence, published by the Oxford Royal Commissioners in 1852, shows* that none of the Fellows of that College, at the present day, are in the

* Evidence of All Souls College, p. 332.

habit of taking pupils, but all the resident members attend with great regularity the usual Church of England services, which are performed twice every day, for at least six months in the year, or perhaps more, as the chapel is not closed during the vacation until after Easter week, and after Christmas day. Regular attendance at chapel "is quite the habit of the place; nothing like compulsion is ever attempted or required."

Competitive examinations for the election of new Fellows were ordained by the Oxford University Parliamentary Commissioners, and agreed to by the College, in subjects recognized by the University School of Jurisprudence and Modern History, but in carrying out this novel scheme, the Fellows of All Souls, who are a numerous body, have assumed to themselves the right of selecting from among the Candidates passed by the Examiners, such persons as they (the Fellows) deem most eligible for vacant Fellowships.

Three of the Fellows have remonstrated against these arrangements, and complained of College elections having twice occurred, in which the result of the Fellowship examination had been insufficiently ascertained and disregarded, besides classical work having been introduced into the examination. An appeal has consequently been made to the Court of Queen's Bench to compel the Visitor, the Archbishop of Canterbury, to hear the case by Counsel, and to determine the several matters in dispute.

On the foundation of the College in 1437, King Henry VI. appointed the first Warden, and benefit would probably accrue from a restoration of the Royal privilege of appointment to the Wardenship, as well from an equivalent being provided out of suspended Fellowships, for the Church living at present annexed to the Headship of All Souls College.

There is a fund belonging to the College for the purchase of advowsons, derived from some lands at Penhow, in Monmouthshire. Seventeen livings are in the gift of All Souls College, which were thus obtained:—

"*New Romney, Kent.*—On the dissolution of alien Priories, it fell into the hands of the Crown, and was granted to the College by letters-patent, 17th of Hen. VI.

"*Upchurch, Kent.*—Belonged to the Abbey of St. Mary, in Normandy: it was granted to the College by Hen. VI., letters-patent, eighteenth year of his reign.

"*Alberbury, Shropshire.*—Granted by letters-patent, 11th of May, 19 Hen. VI.

"*Harrietsham, Kent; Elmley, Kent.*—In the first year of Henry VI., the convent of Leeds, in Kent, conveyed Harrietsham and Elmley to Henry Chicheley, Archbishop of Canterbury, the Founder, in fee, and he granted them to the College.

"*Lewknor, Oxon.*—Belonged to the Abbey of Abingdon, obtained by the Founder, and granted by him to the College.

"*Barking, Essex, and Ilford.*—Granted by Sir William Petre, as executor of William Pouncet, 1557. Ilford now forms a separate Vicarage, with a new church, and also a chapel, called Barkingside, recently erected.

"*Welwyn, Herts.*—Purchased by the College, 13 James I.

"*Lockinge, Berks.*—Purchased by the College, 8 Charles I., now annexed, by Act of Parliament, 1766, to the Wardenship, without institution or induction.

"*Buckland, Surrey.*—Purchased by the College, 14 Car. I.

"*Harpsden, or Harding, Oxon.*—Purchased by the College, 15 Charles I.

"*Weston-Turville, Bucks.*—Purchased by the College, 1690.

"*Barford St. Martin, Wilts.*—Purchased by the College, 5 Geo. I.

"*Chelsfield cum Farnbro', Kent.*—Purchased by the College, 1754.

"*Walton, Cardiff, Gloucestershire.*—Granted to the College by a Mr. Read, 1658.

"*Newton Bromswold, Northampton.*—Exchanged for two small livings in Wales, by virtue of an Act of Parliament, about fifteen years ago." *

Before the Reformation, when the performance of elaborate Roman Catholic services constituted a large portion of the daily duty of parochial clergymen, the training of residence, during a long period of consecutive years, in a college devoted to prayers for the dead, was probably deemed advisable by ecclesiastical authorities, as a preparation for the care of a rural parish.

In our own day, according to the Report of the Oxford University Royal Commissioners, in 1852, "Colleges are not good dispensers of patronage to their own body." It is a "rule of peace in them to offer vacant benefices in succession to the Fellows, according to seniority, without any regard to their qualifications for the office. A very immoral person, if such there were, would be passed over; but the most important livings may be claimed, from generation to generation, by elderly men, who have lingered in the College, for many weary years, in hopes of the particular preferment, which they eventually obtain, till they are fit neither for the post which they have coveted, nor for any other. If benefactors should be willing to give advowsons to Colleges, it might be inexpedient to forbid the acceptance of their bounty; but, in our opinion, the revenues of the Colleges themselves ought not to be applied to the purchase of preferment."†

* All Souls College Evidence to the Oxford University Royal Commission, 1852, p. 331.

† Recommendations of the Oxford University Commissioners, p. 84. Longmans, 1853.

In accordance with these suggestions the Royal Commissioners recommended,—

"That no portion of the funds of Colleges, except those specifically given for that purpose, should be applied to the purchase of advowsons."*

Some of the Colleges, observe the Royal Commissioners, set apart a portion of their revenues for the purpose of purchasing advowsons. This patronage is a means of providing permanently for a large number of Fellows; and it is thought, that a more rapid succession may thus be caused to College Fellowships. "But it is very doubtful," remark the Royal Commissioners, "whether either literature or the Church derive any benefit from the ecclesiastical patronage of Colleges. That a College should be deserted by any of its abler men in their full strength, for a country living, is a great evil, even when they are succeeded by young men of promise. It is doubtful, also, whether, on the whole, the succession is really accelerated." †

Social considerations, in the choice of Fellows, have long constituted a remarkable characteristic of All Souls College, which the Oxford Parliamentary Commissioners have recently endeavoured to modify, by directing in their statutes, that no person shall be entitled to preference, or be ineligible for a Fellowship, by reason of the condition of his parents. The selection of new Fellows, solely on account of merit, in All Souls College, will, however, require a revision of the whole College system, in order to ensure complete impartiality.

Professor Wilson, of Oxford, is of opinion, with refer-

* Recommendations at the close of the Report of the Oxford University Royal Commission, 1852, p. 239.
† Report of the Oxford University Royal Commission, p. 171.

ence to the University generally, "that any attempt to enlarge or improve the studies of the University will prove ineffectual, unless means are taken, at the same time, to provide a judicious superintendence of the examinations." * The aid of professional experience and knowledge was recommended to the Royal Commission by Professor Wilson, to steady the University Examinations, and to raise their tone and character.

More recently, the new movement of the various English Universities, to provide local examinations on academical subjects, has led to the formation of improved Boards, both at Oxford and Cambridge, for the management of examinations conducted simultaneously in different parts of the country.

Dr. Acland, formerly Fellow of All Souls College, Oxford, may be regarded as the founder of the Oxford system of local examinations. The board of Oxford Delegates, who conduct these examinations, includes 21 Members, viz. the Vice-Chancellor and two Proctors, six Members nominated by these three functionaries; six elected by the Council of the University; and six appointed by the Congregation, or general assembly of resident Masters of Arts and other higher Graduates.

At Cambridge, the Syndicate, or Committee, conducting similar local examinations, comprises 13 Members, viz. the Vice-Chancellor, and 12 other Masters of Arts or other higher Graduates, who are elected by the academical Senate. Four of the elected Members retire, in rotation, every year, and the retiring Members are not re-eligible for the year next ensuing the date of their retirement.

* Evidence of Professor Wilson to the Oxford Royal Commission, p. 298.

Junior Candidates are admitted to the Oxford local Examinations, if their age does not exceed fifteen years. Under the Cambridge system, junior Candidates of not more than sixteen years of age are allowed to enter local University Examinations.

Selection with regard to different languages is allowed to junior Candidates by both the ancient English Universities; and the division lists under the Cambridge system, for December, 1858, and, under the Oxford plan, for June, 1859, show the following numbers of junior Candidates, who were successful at the Examination for Languages :—

LOCAL EXAMINATIONS.

	Under Cambridge System.	Under Oxford System.
French	172	228
Latin	146	322
Greek	66	39
German	29	29

Under each system, the comparatively small proportion of Candidates who volunteered the Greek Examination is remarkable, and in the arrangements for the local Examinations under the Society of Arts, Greek does not appear at all, as one of the subjects.

French, Latin, and German papers were worked, in four consecutive Examinations of the Society of Arts, as follows :—

NUMBER OF PAPERS WORKED IN

	1856.	1857.	1858.	1859.
French	17	38	68	87
Latin and Roman History	15	19	12	18
German	7	15	13	14

Such manifest proofs of the popularity of the French

language should be remembered in modern plans for academic reform. Scholarships for the encouragement of the French language may be formed at All Souls College, by the suspension of alternate vacant Fellowships, so as to attract to that institution young men qualified by their acquaintance with French to enter on other studies which may be useful for diplomacy, modern history, or international law.

Classical *vivâ voce* examination, with trials of proficiency in Latin composition, ought not to be continued as a part of the Examinations at All Souls College, of Candidates for Fellowships.

Greek and Latin subjects, when introduced, must necessarily interfere with the business of electing new Fellows for proficiency in "Jurisprudence and Modern History," and render the election more difficult in modern branches of learning, and more liable to be swayed by social considerations.

UNIVERSITY OF LONDON.

DEGREES IN SCIENCE.

NINE subjects are required for Matriculation in the University of London, viz. Greek, Latin, English, English History, Modern Geography, Mathematics, Natural Philosophy, Chemistry, and either French or German.

At the expiration of not less than an academical year after passing the Matriculation Examination, students may be admitted to the first Bachelor of Science Examination, when they will be expected to show a competent knowledge in the fundamental principles of

1. Mathematics.
2. Mechanical and Natural Philosophy.
3. Chemistry.
4. Biology, including Botany and Vegetable Physiology, and Zoology and Animal Physiology.

At the expiration of not less than an academical year from the first Bachelor of Science Examination, candidates may be admitted to the second Bachelor of Science Examination, on the fourth Monday in October, when a competent knowledge will be expected to be shown in

1. Mechanical and Natural Philosophy.
2. Chemistry.
3. Animal Physiology.
4. Geology and Palæontology.
5. Logic and Moral Philosophy.

Two academical years after taking the Bachelor of Science degree, Graduates may be admitted to the Doctor of Science Examination. Each Candidate may select for himself some one of the following branches of knowledge, and he will be expected to show a thorough practical knowledge of the principal subject, and a general acquaintance with the subsidiary subjects specified in the University of London calendar as belonging to the Branch so selected.

Under the head of Physical Science are included the following branches :—

    Branch 1. Mathematics.
           2. Mechanical Science.
           3. Astronomy.
           4. Chemistry (Inorganic).
           5. Chemistry (Organic).
           6. Electricity.
           7. Magnetism.
           8. Physical Optics, Heat, Acoustics.

Under Biological Science are comprised—

    Branch 9. Animal Physiology.
           10. Comparative Anatomy.
           11. Zoology.
           12. Vegetable Physiology.
           13. Systematic Botany.

Under Geological and Palæontological Science are included—

           14. Geology.
           15. Palæontology.

Mental Science comprises

           16. Logic and Moral Philosophy.

Government has established, in Jermyn Street, London, a School of Mines and of Science applied to the Arts, in which excellent lectures are given, and good examinations held, in Chemistry, Physics, Natural History, Practical Palæontology, Mineralogy, Mining, Applied Mechanics, Geology, and Metallurgy. Such instruction may be useful in preparing Candidates for scientific Degrees.

The following questions are specimens of the Examination in Geology* for the Session 1857–58.

Explain the theory of the formation of coral reefs.

Draw a diagram showing the general relation of granite to stratified rocks, and explain it in writing.

Explain the difference between cleavage and stratification, and how cleavage has been produced.

Describe the origin of glaciers, and the signs by which you would detect their previous existence in regions where they have ceased.

Explain the theory of the formation of the coal of the coal measures.

What relation of date do the rocks of the Alps bear to any of the English formations?

Copy the column of British strata, and draw alongside of it lines showing the distribution, in time, of any ten groups, genera, or species of animals.

* Prospectus of the Government School of Mines, 1858-9, p. 26.

APPENDIX.

DIVINITY EXAMINATION PAPERS,

SELECTED FROM THE ANNUAL EXAMINATION AT

MANCHESTER NEW COLLEGE,

UNIVERSITY HALL, GORDON SQUARE, LONDON.

JUNE, 1859.

EXAMINERS.

Rev. Principal J. J. Tayler, B..A.
Rev. Professor James Martineau.
Russell Martineau, Esq., M.A.

INTRODUCTION TO THE OLD TESTAMENT.

1. Mention the three great divisions of the writings of the Old Testament, and enumerate the books contained under each. State how the Apocrypha arose. What was their relation to the earlier books; and what have been the judgments of the different sections of the Church respecting them.

2. What was the notion once prevalent respecting the earliest collection of the books of the Old Testament into an authoritative whole or Canon? What ground is there for such a notion? In what way was the collection most probably formed; and how will this account for the gradations of authority attaching to the several divisions of the books? What was the natural limit to the collection; and how is this indicated by the latest book that occurs in it? When was the

idea of a Canon first distinctly developed, and under what influences?

3. What was the story of Aristeas respecting the origin of the Septuagint version? Who first exposed the real character of this story? Mention the names of some learned men who still defended it. What was the probable date and origin of this version? What evidence is there of its not having been produced originally as one work? Describe the character of the Septuagint Greek. What authority did this version finally acquire, and amongst whom? What led to the loss of its authority among the Jews? What new versions were the consequence? Enumerate and characterize them, and give their respective dates. Mention the Christian fathers who successively revised the text of the Septuagint. What are the principal MSS. of the Septuagint, and the editions founded on them? Can you state anything remarkable concerning the book of Daniel, as it is given in the extant MSS. of the Septuagint?

4. Enumerate the versions of the Old Testament made direct from the Septuagint. Explain the difference between the *Vetus Latina* or *Itala*, and the *Vulgata*; and show by what steps the latter gradually superseded the former. In what light is the Vulgate regarded by Roman Catholics; and when was that character first bestowed upon it?

5. What was the general belief of Protestant divines in the age following the Reformation, respecting the Hebrew text of the Old Testament? Give an outline of the controversy on this subject, with the names of the principal learned men engaged in it, and an account of the views which they respectively held. By whom was the first systematic effort made in early times to verify and fix the Hebrew text? What is the Masora?

6. What are the Targums; and how and why did they arise? Have they come down to us in their original form?

7. What is Frankel's theory of the origin of the Septuagint? Explain the usages of the Synagogue among the Hellenistic Jews, which he thinks may have occasioned such a

version. What were the *Parascha* and the *Haftara?* Point out the analogy to some usages which have been retained in the Christian Church. How does Frankel account for the many changes introduced into the text of the Septuagint, and its frequent deviations from the Hebrew? Explain the words *Midrasch, Halacha, Hagada.*

8. By what general cause does Geiger suppose that the constitution of the Hebrew text has been constantly affected down to the second and third century of the Christian era? How and why was further change then arrested? Point out the analogy to the early history of the text of the New Testament. Give an outline of his view of the internal development of the Jewish commonwealth from the termination of the Exile till the reign of Hadrian—explaining the mutual relations of the Zadokites or Sadducees, the Boothusians and the Pharisees. By which of these parties was a rationalizing influence exerted on the text; and by which was a scrupulous reverence finally restored for the primitive letter? Mention some limitations that still operated to the full development of this latter tendency.

HEBREW.

Psalms.

1. What subdivisions are recognizable in the book of Psalms, and how are they discerned?

2. Mention some smaller groups of Psalms, and explain the criteria by which they may be distinguished from the outlying Psalms.

3. To what age or ages may the Psalms be referred; and what indications have we to guide us in determining this? What age that has been contended for by some critics ought to be decidedly rejected, and why?

4. Name, translate, and explain some of the terms used in the titles or appended notes to the Psalms.

5. Is it possible that there are any Psalms by David extant? Can all the Psalms which are in their titles referred to him,

be by us regarded as his? In what part of the Psalter do his Psalms chiefly occur?

Isaiah.

6. What is known of the life and character of the prophet Isaiah?

7. Give a brief sketch of the history of the nations of Western Asia in the time of Isaiah.

8. Describe the character of Isaiah's moral exhortations, and the picture drawn by him of the social condition of the time.

9. Mention briefly what parts of the book must be referred to later writers than Isaiah; and for what reasons.

10. Investigate the reasons for referring the later chapters of the book to a different writer.

11. Classify the various pieces forming the book of Isaiah so as to exhibit the principle on which the compiler arranged them.

12. Give an account of the history of Cyrus's conquests according to the chief Greek sources, and show which account is supported by intrinsic probability, and by the evidence of the Pseudo-Isaiah.

EVIDENCES OF NATURAL RELIGION.

1. Different modes of conceiving the interdependence of Morals and Religion. Endeavour to find the true limits of their relation. With what range of meaning is the word *Nature* employed in the phrase "*Natural* Religion"? Chief questions included under this phrase.

2. By what step would Reason alone, without Moral perception, pass out beyond Nature? What different interpretations are given to the "Axiom of Causality" in the several schools,—of Brown, Mill, and Comte;—of the ordinary Natural Philosophers;—and of the "Volitional" psychologists. State and examine Brown's appeal to the testimony of *Language* on the subject. Investigate the conditions essential to

satisfy every inquiry after a Cause. What, according to Trendelenburg, is the ultimate controversy of all philosophy?

3. Why have Theists usually objected to the doctrine of an eternal Kosmos? State and appreciate the kind of evidence adduced by them against it. Show that their anxiety on this head is superfluous and artificial.

4. Into what state does the Theistical problem fall, when "Natural Forces" and Rational Thought are allowed to compete for the genesis of the universe? Account for the mutual jealousies of Science and Religion: and for the different effect of the argument from design on different predispositions. Assign to it its true place.

5. On what ground does Comte deny to man the exclusive prerogative of *Religion*? How did Xenophanes rebuke the anthropomorphism of his time? Assign the just limits to these statements: and find the true measure of religion which they suggest.

6. Trace to their seats in our Moral nature our belief in an invisible Judge; and our belief in a Highest and Holiest of all.

7. Sketch the probable history of the spontaneous religion of mankind, and show its constant relation to the feeling of *personality*, individual and corporate.

8. How is it that the intimations given by our intellectual nature, and those given by our moral nature, meet and coalesce in *the same Being*? Source of our faith in his Infinitude, Eternity, Spirituality, and Rule over the natural universe.

9. Form in which the faith in *Providence* is generally held. How may it be defended, even as it is, against the usual criticism? Point out the practical and moral bearings of belief or unbelief on this matter.

10. What traces are there, in the constitution of the world, of an ascending progression, securing the paramount action of the better over the worse?

11. What is meant by the *physical*, and what by the *psychological* investigation of the question of a Future Life? To what extent may they be resolved into one and the same?

Put the question of "Matter and Spirit" into proper form: and appreciate its place in the theory of human life.

12. Compare the relation of structure to faculty in man and in other animals: and estimate the logical consequences of the difference.

13. Point out some of the prospective features in the constitution, both of our moral nature, and of our lot in the world. Whence the popular tendency to believe that all natural evil is a judgment upon moral evil?

HISTORY OF DOCTRINE.

1. Mention some of the standard Histories of Opinion; and compare them, in their plan and method, with corresponding Histories of the Church.

2. Explain and contrast the different conceptions implied in the three phrases, "History of Opinion," "History of Heresies," "History of Christian Doctrine." Point out the seat of Revelation assumed in each case, and the standard for the determination of controversies.

3. Show that Christianity, in being divine, is not necessarily stationary; and, in receiving human modifications, is not necessarily deteriorated. Mode of finding the genesis of a doctrine. How far does this determine its truth?

4. Where first do we find Revelation regarded as implying a Divine education of the human race? and in opposition to what different conception? Show the superiority of the Christian idea.

5. Why would the notion of a comprehensive human religion have seemed chimerical in the age of Socrates? Chief features of contrast in the theatre on which it was actually introduced. Trace the effect of extinguished nationalities on the religious faith of the ancient world.

6. Conditions which precluded at an earlier age such a spiritualization of Judaism as Christ announced. Jewish stories respecting Alexander the Great; and inference from them. Effect of the deportation of Palestinian Hebrews.

7. At what stage in the history of a documentary religion

do sects first arise ? How long does the Jewish sacred literature appear to have remained open ? At what date and from what causes did the Pharisees probably arise ? Describe, account for, and estimate their chief characteristics.

8. Who was Antigonus of Socho? and who his chief disciples ? Incident which has made their names traditionally famous. Enumerate and estimate the chief reported distinctions of the Sadducees.

9. What questions give particular interest to the history of the Essenes ? Authorities on the subject. Discrepancies in the accounts of their abode and occupations. Opinion of Ewald,—of Ritschl.

10. By what three principles does Philo describe the life of the Essenes as regulated ? By what habits and ideas appropriate to each did they exemplify these ? Peculiarities attaching to their worship. Classes into which they were divided.

11. How far does a purely national sympathy appear in Philo's Essay, ' *De Vitâ Contemplativâ* '? How does he designate the class of people whom he there describes ?—their essential principle ;—their locality ; — their round of habit through the week ?

12. What peculiar sanctity does Philo find in the No. 50 ? and what usage of the Therapeutæ does he thus explain ? What are the ideas of which he recognizes a symbolical expression in the chief peculiarities of that usage ?

13. Sum up the evidence of *some* historical connection between Essenes and Therapeutæ. Chief critical authorities in favour of a Palestinian origin. Explain the hypothesis which deduces them from a *sacerdotal* idea. Also, that which deduces them from a *prophetic* idea. Compare and test the adequacy of these.

14. What Gentile affinities are claimed for the Hebrew ascetics by Josephus and Philo ? Who are meant by the Δακῶν τοῖς πολισταῖς λεγομένοις ? And to what sect is the predicate ἱερώτατος θίασος applied ? On what ground has any external contact between the Italian philosophy and Egyptian Judaism been pronounced impossible ? State what

testimony there is on the other side. How far does the picture drawn by Hegesander and others agree in its internal features with the Jewish historians' sketch? or the latter deviate into Apocalyptic conceptions foreign to Gentile thought? Chief critical authorities in favour of the Hellenic order of derivation.

15. When first did the Messianic belief begin to produce a distinct literature? Traces of its variable and indeterminate condition in the later Isaiah, Ezekiel, Malachi: and of a conscious dying out of true prophecy at a later date. Essential difference between the book of Daniel and the older prophets. How far is a known person beyond the statements of the book itself?

16. To what point do all the visions of Daniel lead up? How many of them are there? Through what antecedent steps does he conduct the world to its catastrophe? Identify these with the great historical empires of ancient times. Trace the repetition of the same subject through the diversity of symbols.

17. Gather up the different time-reckonings scattered through the visions of Daniel, including the interpretation given to Jeremiah xxv. 12, and xxix. 10; and show their convergence upon the same terminus.

18. What ideal personages appear in the visions of Daniel? Examine the question whether Messiah is one of them. State in which this book leaves the Messianic picture.

19. What peculiar difficulties attend the critical treatment of Apocalyptic books? What principles must be applied to them in order to determine their age? Give a history of critical opinions respecting the Sibylline oracles from the time of Fabricius to the present day: and state the limits within which the doubt as to the oldest part is now confined.

20. How does it appear that the author is Jewish? What could recommend to a Hebrew writer a literary form so purely Pagan? With what purpose alone would it harmonize? and by what traces do we discover such a purpose in the writer. Whence do we obtain the lines introductory to the whole work?

21. Describe the writer's theory of the world's history; and the mode in which mythology, Jewish scripture, and the chronicles of authentic empires are worked up in it. At what point does the Sibyl herself stand and assume the proper prophetic form? And what is the last distinct representation in her predictions? How does she designate the Roman power? Collect the marks of time; and give the result.

22. In what form, according to the Sibyl, was the crisis of the human drama to come? and by what signs would its approach be announced? What inferences may be drawn from a comparison of its statements with those of the Christian Evangelists, and of Josephus in his account of the Jewish war?

23. Tacitus says:—'Pluribus persuasio inerat antiquis sacerdotum literis contineri eo ipso tempore fore ut valesceret Oriens profectique Judæâ rerum potirentur :"—what vestiges of this belief are found in the Sibylline poems? How has it been applied in explanation of the following lines?—

Καὶ τότ' ἀπ' ἠελίοιο Θεὸς πέμψει βασιλῆα,
Ὃς πᾶσαν γαῖαν παύσει πολέμοιό κακοῖο,
Οὓς μὲν ἄρα κτείνας, οἷς δ' ὅρκια πιστὰ τελέσσας·

In what other terms is this βασιλεύς spoken of? Critical opinions respecting these passages : and apparent result.

24. Chief features of the Sibyl's picture of Messianic times. In what respects does it differ from the representations in the book of Daniel? Account for these differences.

25. What work is cited in the 14th and 15th verses of the Epistle of Jude? How far did other early citations add to our knowledge of its character? Tertullian's opinion of it. Indications that this opinion was not universally held. Source of Archbishop Laurence's edition of the work : and of more recent translations. Define the limits within which the problem of its origin may be regarded as determined; and the range of discrepancy in the judgments of eminent critics respecting it.

26. On what passages in the book of Genesis is the mytho-

logy of the book of Enoch founded? and where else have we traces of a similar use of them? Tell its story of the superhuman races; and how the prophet is brought upon the scene. What appellation is characteristically given to the Angels? What is the speculative interest or underlying theory of the whole?

27. Draw the picture of the world, as exhibited to the prophet in his circuit of it. How is the scenery at its centre described and expounded? Source and effect of the belief here indicated.

28. In what two forms does the book of Enoch present the drama of human history? Describe and expound the second apocalyptic dream; and the succession of seventy shepherds. Compare and contrast with this the tables of the ten weeks.

29. What is the doctrine of the book of Enoch respecting the unseen state, the final retribution, the sins that most surely incur condemnation, and the ulterior lot of the saved and of the lost?

30. State carefully the evidence contributed by the book of Enoch as to the conception of a Personal Messiah; weighing first the expressions in the undisputed portion of the work.

31. In what section of the book of Enoch is the doctrine of a Messiah most developed? Peculiar features and contents of its doctrine. Explain the chief internal grounds of doubt as to the age of this portion. How far does the external evidence countenance the doubt?

ECCLESIASTICAL HISTORY.
Fourth and Fifth Centuries.

1. Give an estimate of the probable motives of Constantine's conversion to Christianity. State the inducements to a removal of the capital, and the effects of it. Describe the general condition of society in Constantinople, in the third century. State the effects of the public provision for the maintenance and entertainment of the lowest classes. What is Gibbon's account of them?

2. Show how the great outlines of a modern University

were anticipated in the learned schools of Constantinople and Athens. How may the influence of the Rhetoricians and Sophists of this period be explained? Mention the most eminent among them. Where did they teach? What was the effect of persecution on their views?

3. Explain the reaction of the reign of Julian. Give a brief outline of his biography, with an estimate of his character and policy, contrasting them with those of Constantine. In what way has the intervention of his reign rendered service to Christianity?

4. What still continued to be the strongholds of heathenism? What is the origin and meaning of the word *paganus*? What was the influence of classical studies? What is Neander's estimate of the moral power of the latest phase of cultivated heathenism? What was the class in the reign of Constantine and his son, most readily convertible to Christianity?

5. Who were the great men towards the close of the fourth century, that were most active in the violent suppression of heathenism? Mention some excesses that accompanied this period of transition. What would have been the true policy towards the expiring religion?

6. State the circumstances of the conversion of the Goths. Who was their great apostle? What service did he render to their future civilization as well as to Christianity?

7. What is known of the life of Patrick? Under what circumstances did he introduce Christianity into Ireland? and what was the result of his labours? By what name was Ireland known in the Middle Ages? and how was it acquired?

8. What were the different opinions respecting the Logos, or Son of God, represented by Origen, by Dionysius of Alexandria and by Dionysius of Rome, that were still under discussion, when Arius entered the field of controversy? In what school had he been reared? What were the two great principles on which he insisted? What was the early wish of Constantine in reference to this dispute? Give a sketch of the origin, progress, and issue of the Nicene controversy. Who were the two men the most directly opposed to each other?

What word was made the turning-point of the question? What was probably the predominant party in the Council? What three parties remained in the Church after the decision? What was the theological system supported respectively by the Emperors Constantine and Valens? How did the policy of the last of these emperors contribute to the ultimate triumph of Nicenism?

9. Explain the origin and progress of the Pelagian controversy. Show how the different characters and early experiences of Augustine and Pelagius may in part have determined the side which they adopted in this controversy. State the chief points of the question at issue between them.

10. What were the views respecting the divine nature in Christ, which were entertained respectively by Apollinaris, by Theodore of Mopsuestia, and by Athanasius, at the opening of the Nestorian controversy. Describe the occasion, development, and issue of this controversy, with the bearing upon it of the first and second Councils of Ephesus and of the Council of Chalcedon. Whose determinations finally settled the question?

11. Mention the four first œcumenical Councils, with the date, occasion, and subject-matter of each, and the name of the emperor by whom they were respectively convened?

12. Give an account of the growth of Monachism in the East and in the West. What circumstances contributed to spread this institution over the world? Who brought it first into the West? In what part of Christendom was it most vehemently resisted?

13. When did the reverence for saints and relics first begin to show itself in the Christian Church? What parallel tendency do we find among the heathens?

14. Describe the general type of construction in the early Christian Churches. What buildings originally suggested their outward form and internal arrangements? What accessory ideas gradually developed and expanded the primitive ground-plan?

INDEX.

Abbreviation of Oxford and Cambridge College Chapel Services, 62, 97, 142, 292.
Accounts of All Souls College, Oxford, 298.
Acland, Dr. Thomas Dyke, founder of Oxford University Local Examinations, 312.
Act for amending the representation of the University of Dublin, 185.
Act of 37 Henry VIII. cap. 4, on which the union of various Colleges at Oxford and Cambridge was based, 69.
Act of Uniformity of 1662, provisions of, respecting Colleges, 136; remarks of Hallam on, 147.
Act of Uniformity of 1662, tests of, for College Heads and Fellows, 192.
Act of Uniformity under Elizabeth, 159.
Additional Training School wanted on a liberal basis, in the North of England, 45.
Advantage of public schoolmen for Indian Civil Service Examinations, 13.
Advowsons, purchase of, undesirable, by Colleges, 311.
All Souls College, church patronage of, 309.
Alphabetical arrangement of high Wranglers recommended, 182.
Arnold, Dr., on Oxford admiration of past times, 301.
Arnold, Matthew, on the British and Foreign School Training System, 244.
Articles, Forty-two, prepared by Archbishop Cranmer, 193; altered into Thirty-nine Articles by Archbishop Parker, 194; reduced in number by Wesley, 195.
Assembly, Westminster, appointed by Parliament to settle the government and Liturgy of the Church of England, 141.
Athanasian Creed, omission of, in American liturgy, 275.
Attachés to British Embassies, examination of, 1.

Bachelorship of Arts, examinations for, in the University of Oxford, 14; Cambridge, 17; London, 22.
Bachelor of Laws in the University of London, 197, 215.
Balliol College, Oxford, 271.
Bill for the reformation of the Book of Common Prayer, 140.
Boards for Local University Examinations (Oxford and Cambridge), 312.
Bohlen, Von, on the Paradisiacal narrative, 232.
British and Foreign Training School, Borough Road, 43.

Cambridge Colleges, improvement of, 248.
Cambridge Parliamentary Commission, changes in, 249.
Cambridge University Local Examination, 218.
Cambridge Local University Examinations, report on, 267.
Certificated Teachers, subjects of examination for, in Church of England Training Schools, 41.
Certificated teachers, numbers of, 46.

INDEX.

Church of England, members of, proportion of, attending religious worship, 274.
Classical composition, art of, in many cases soon forgotten, 12.
Classical influence in Indian Civil Service Examinations, 9.
Clergy, influence of, 237.
Clerkships under the Committee of Council on Education, examination for, 1.
College tuition, 281.
Colleges, not good dispensers of Church patronage, 310.
Commission, Royal, for revision of the Liturgy, in 1689, 152.
Compulsory ordination of College Heads, 250.
Compulsory ordination statutes, remarks on, 71.
Conditions proposed by Cambridge Commissioners on the tenure of Fellowships, 74.
Conditions relating to the compulsory celibacy of Fellows, memorial against, 76.
Conference intended by King Charles II. for advice, 292.
Constructions, legal, of the Court of Chancery, 240.
Convention, American, on liturgical alterations, 153.
Convocation, Liturgy recommended by, in 1661, 146.

Declaration of King Charles II. on Ecclesiastical Affairs, 144.
Degree in Science, memorial for, to the Senate of the University of London, 106.
Differences, denominational, in trust deeds, 238.
Dillwyn, Mr., Bill of, on Endowed Schools, 241.
Directory for public worship in 1645, 142.
Dissenters, scruples of, arrangement proposed to meet, 93.
Dividends, distribution of, in Trinity College, Cambridge, 279.
Divinity examination papers without Articles or Liturgy, 319.

Eardley, Sir Culling, Bart., correspondence of, with the Provost of Oriel College, Oxford, 189.
Ebury, Lord, address of, for a Commission on Liturgical alterations, 157.
Ecclesiastical history, fourth and fifth centuries, 328.
Electors, summary of, for the Universities of Oxford and Cambridge, 170; numbers of, 187.
Elevation of Man towards God taught in early part of Genesis, 233.
Endowed Grammar Schools, education in, directed by subjects of scholarship and fellowship examinations at Oxford and Cambridge, 266.
Entrance examination for Trinity College, Cambridge, 283.
Evidences of Natural Religion, 328.
Examination, Cambridge, Theological, on original sin, 231.
Examinations, Civil Service, 1; Royal Military Academy, Woolwich, 4.
Extension of academical franchise, 246.

Failures for B.A. degree at Oxford, 174.
Fellowship Examinations in Trinity College, Cambridge, 258.
Fellows, Perpetual, without employment, compared to drones, 302.
Free holding of Scholarships in Colleges at Cambridge, memorial in favour of, 65.
French and Latin, preference of, 313.

Geology, questions in, 317.
Grants to students at Training Colleges, 47.
Granville, Earl, address on the University of London, 198.

Heywood, James, composition of, for annual dues, at Trinity College, Cambridge, 186.
Heywood, Samuel, conversation of, with Dr. Hallifax, at Trinity

INDEX.   333

Hall, Cambridge, 94; second conversation of, with Dr. Hallifax, 95.
High pecuniary fees for registration of University Electors, 183.
Hindrances to shorter Chapel Services, 256.
History of Doctrine, 327.
House of Commons, independent Liberal members of, memorial by, for the removal of religious tests at Oxford and Cambridge, 61.
Hull, William Winstanley, on Liturgical reform, 295.

Improvement of Scholarship examinations, 265, 269.
Indian Civil Service, examinations of, 5; candidates for, 8.
Indian Civil Service, successful candidates, 1859, 260.
Inquiry into Universities and Colleges of Oxford and Cambridge, 49.
Isaiah, Hebrew, 322.

Lectures in Trinity College, Cambridge, 287.
Lessons read in Chapel Services, 291.
Letters-patent, proposed, dispensing with the Act of Uniformity, 293.
License, Royal, refused to Convocation for a modification in the representation in the Lower House of Convocation, 155.
Liturgy, English, preparation of, by Royal appointment, 137; recognition of Parliamentary authority in, 138.

Manchester New College divinity questions, 319.
Marks for proficiency in Woolwich Royal Military Academy, 1857, 11; 1859, 263.
Master of Arts degree, at Oxford and Cambridge, merely a form, 167.
Medical Council, 178.
Medicine, Bachelor of, in the University of London, 215.

Memorial in favour of enlargement of system of granting Cambridge degrees, 56.
Memorials relating to Academical improvement, 49.
Military Academy, Royal, division of examination papers into sections for candidates, 4.
Modern languages, neglect of, a great defect in old English academical education, 307.
Modern studies proposed in All Souls College, Oxford, 297.
Moral and Economic Science, degree of Bachelor in, memorial for, 114.

National educational bodies, examinations of, recognized by the Medical Council, 285.
New religious test for Fellows of St. John's College, Oxford, 272.

Offices, ancient academical, Church of England tenure of, 277.
Old Testament, introduction to, 319.
Ordination examinations, subjects of, 224; questions in Old Testament history, 225; questions on early condition of human beings, 231; questions on Trinity Sunday, 227; questions on original sin, 228.
Open secession of a College Fellow from the Church of England, penalties for, 255.
Opposition at Cambridge to early Statutes of Commissioners, 249.
Oxford College improvements, 270.
Oxford University local examinations for junior candidates, 285.
Oxford University, opening of, 273.

Parker, Theodore, on the development of the human race, 235.
Pelagius, ideas of, 229.
Places of education of candidates for Indian Civil Service, 1858, 11; 1859, 260; for Woolwich Royal Military Academy, 1857, 10.
Pollard-Urquhart, Mr., notice of address by, in House of Commons, 252.

INDEX.

Prayers for the Parliament, 99.
Prayers, short, recommended by Dean Peacock for College Chapels, 98.
Private tuition, 282.
Proctors of Cambridge, powers of, memorial respecting, 160.
Profession of faith proposed under Oliver Cromwell, 194.
Protest of four Peers, against laymen being excluded from an Ecclesiastical Commission, 148.
Provincial Academical Examinations, memorials to the Senate of the University of London for, 116.
Psalms, Hebrew, 321.
Pupil Teachers, numbers of, 46.
Pupil Teachers, under the Committee of Council on Education, examination of, 32; religious examination of, 39.

Queen's Scholars, exhibitions for, 38.
Questions on dogmatic divinity for Cambridge ordinary B.A. degree, memorial against, 102.

Religious denominations, numbers of, attending worship, 274.
Religious tests for M.A. degree at Oxford, 168; membership of the Senate at Cambridge, 169.
Remonstrance against best candidates for Fellowships not being chosen in All Souls College, 308.
Repetitions of Greek and Latin verses, 180.
Representation of the University of London in Parliament, memorial in favour of, 205.
Royal Military Academy, Woolwich, competitive examinations of, 2.
Royal Warrant for discontinuance of political services in Book of Common Prayer, 156.

Salaries of civil servants in the North-western Provinces of India, 7.
Scholarship, abrogated declaration of religious belief at Trinity College, Cambridge, 159.
Scholarship examinations at Trinity College, Dublin, 173.
Scholarship examination in Trinity College, Cambridge, 289.
Science, degrees in, University of London, 315.
Scotch Universities, new constitution of, 176.
Selection of prayers, for College Chapels, recommended by the Oxford Royal Commissioners, 97.
St. John's College, resistance of, to Oxford University Parliamentary Commissioners, 126.
St. John's College, Cambridge, new religious test in, proposed for Fellows, 272.
Staff College, subjects of examination in, 5.
Subjects for certificates of proficiency as Teachers in Church of England Training Schools, 41.
Subjects for examination of candidates intending to be called to the Bar, 305.
Subscriptions for Ordination in the Church of England, 223.

Teachers, Church of England certificated, examinations for, 41.
Training Schools, grants to, 40, 48.
Trinity College, Cambridge, early constitution of, 70.
Trinity College, Cambridge, a secularized ecclesiastical foundation, 253.
Trinity College, Cambridge, success of three members of, in Indian Civil Service examination, 262.
Trinity College, Cambridge, Fellowship Oath, 74.
Trinity College, Dublin, conduct of a former Provost of, 73.
Tunbridge Castle School, success of, in Woolwich Military Academy examination, 262.
Twelve years' tenure of a Fellowship recommended, 251.
Two years only of old academical

studies recommended to be compulsory, 303.
University of Cambridge, course in Arts, 17.
University of Dublin, special class for Military Academy, 5.
University of London, course in Arts, 22.
University of London, petition of, 210; number of Fellows and Graduates of, 213; degrees in science of, 214, 315; Bachelor of Medicine in, 215.

University of Oxford, course in Arts, 14.
University representation, 165.
Woolwich Royal Military Academy, subjects of, taken up by candidates in 1857, 3.
Woolwich Royal Military Academy, subjects of examination of, in 1859, 263.
Writs, Parliamentary, not issued to the Universities under the Commonwealth, 166.

www.ingramcontent.com/pod-product-compliance
Lightning Source LLC
Chambersburg PA
CBHW020245240426
43672CB00006B/644